# SMILE AND BE A VILLAIN!

# Smile and be a villain!

NIALL TOIBIN

TOWN HOUSE
DUBLIN

Published in 1995 by
Town House and Country House
Trinity House
Charleston Road
Ranelagh, Dublin 6
Ireland

British Library Cataloguing in Publication Data. A catalogue record for this book is
available from the British Library.

ISBN: 1-86059-007-1

## Acknowledgements

The author and publishers would like to acknowledge the following
photographers and holders of copyright: Des Lacey (cover photo); Dick
Shakespeare (Photos 2, 6); Jas D O'Callaghan (Photo 7); *The Irish Times* (Photo 9, by
Dermot Barry, and Photo 31, by Jimmy McCormack); Richard Dann Photography,
Dublin (Photos 10, 22, 23, 24, 25, 28, 29, 40); Gemini Productions and the Irish
Theatre Archive (Photos 12, 19); *The Irish Echo* (Photo 14); *The Irish Press* (Photo 16);
Allan Hurst, Nottingham (Photo 18); *The Cork Examiner* (Photos 21, 46); M J
O'Flynn, Cork (Photo 26); Max Studio, Dublin (Photo 27); The Royal National
Theatre of Great Britain (Photos 32, 33, 34, 35, 38); Radio Telefís Éireann (Photo 36);
Thames Television (Photo 37); Terry O'Brien Photography, Achill Island (Photo 39);
Pacemaker Press International Ltd, Belfast (Photo 41); Amelia Stein (Photo 45); The
Central Remedial Clinic, Dublin (Photo 47); Photostyle, Dublin (Photo 48).

The author acknowledges the valuable assistance of Brendan Balfe and Gerald
Davis with research and memory jogging, and of Síghle Tóibín with sourcing the
photographs.

Every effort has been made to trace copyright holders. The Publishers would be
grateful to be notified of any corrections that should be incorporated in future
editions.

Typeset by Typeform Repro Ltd
Printed and bound in Great Britain by Mackays of Chatham PLC, Chatham, Kent

To Judy

Niall Toibin was born in Cork in 1929. He has worked in all areas of entertainment, except strip-tease, ballet and the circus, since he started acting for a living, having left the security of the Civil Service.

His career has taken him to every theatre in Ireland as well as to thousands of clubs, pubs, halls, marquees and stadiums in Britain, Canada, the US, Australia, Iceland, Hungary, Holland, Germany, Switzerland, and the USSR that was.

He worked in radio for fourteen years, then moved to the Gate Theatre for the première of Brian Friel's *Lovers*, then to the Abbey Theatre for the first staging of *Borstal Boy*, with which his name has been linked ever since. He has appeared in nine different productions of *Borstal Boy*, including one in the Cork Opera House in 1973, and the latest 1995 one coming twenty-eight years after his début in the part of Brendan Behan.

He has appeared in many other successful shows in Ireland over the years: *Death and Resurrection of Mr Roche, House of Blue Leaves, Tartuffe, Bells of Hell, Mass Appeal, Liam Liar, Desire Under the Elms, The Field, The Hostage, Taking Liberties,* and had three seasons at the National Theatre in London, including *Long Voyage Home* and *The Iceman Cometh,* as well as seasons at Edinburgh, Nottingham and Bath.

His TV work includes *The Irish RM, The Detective, Confessional, Mitch, Bracken, Dempsey, Who Bombed Birmingham, Ballroom of Romance, One of Ourselves, Holy City, The Rockingham Shoot,* and most recently three separate series of *Stay Lucky* with Denis Waterman. His films include *Ryan's Daughter, The Outsider, Far and Away,* as well as others which were not released, and still more which sadly were.

His first Broadway appearance was in *Borstal Boy,* the 1970 Best Play Tony Award Winner. His second was in *Fearless Frank* in 1980, for which he received rave reviews and which promptly vanished without trace. But Niall's preoccupation for many years has been with his one-man show. His first solo show *Confusion* at the Gaiety Theatre in 1971 was hugely successful and was followed by four more at the Gaiety and Shelbourne Hotel. From this evolved the cabaret-style show which he has toured through Ireland, Britain, the US and Australia for many years.

# ONE

We lived between the Mon Lodge and Farna, in the Bishop's Field. The Mon was the Christian Brothers' School, Our Lady's Mount, Gerald Griffin Avenue (late Peacock Lane), in the North Parish. Farna was St Finbar's Diocesan Seminary, Farranferris. The Bishop's Field was the land around the episcopal palace of Daniel, by the Grace of God, Bishop of Cork, our neighbour and landlord, omnipresent and omnipotent. To us, as small kids, he was simply 'the bishop'.

Some afternoons, about three o'clock, he would walk, or rather amble, aged, slow and ramrod-straight, the half-mile or so to the cathedral. On his way back, as he rounded the corner of Hawks's shop, we'd hear the cry 'Here's up the bishop'. Skipping ropes, hurleys, pickies, spinning-tops, dolls, glassy allies, all were abandoned as we scampered to kiss his lordship's ring. And why not? Weren't we the chosen of his flock, the lambs in his own field. What if the lesser breeds beyond the lodges called us 'the pukies'? They were jealous.

He would stand patiently in his long black soutane, white-lidded eyes smiling from beneath the broad-rimmed hat, as we jostled to kneel and kiss the dark purple stone embedded in the gold band. Sometimes he chatted to his snotty-nosed, mud-encrusted faithful. Once he asked two unusually mucky little girls what they were up to. They had been using the mud, or the gutter as we called it, for clay modelling, and had formed a few faintly recognisable figures.

'We're making priests,' one explained.

'We need them all,' he said approvingly. 'Didn't ye make any bishop?'

'We hadn't enough gutter.'

This saintly, suffer-little-children-to-come-unto-me figure was a far cry from the reactions he provoked among our elders. While Cosgraveites and Free Staters in general showed due deference, many republicans spluttered at the mention of his name. They called him 'Danny Cawlan', their contempt and loathing rejecting the more respectful pronunciation of 'Cohalan'. 'Didn't he excommunicate half of the Boys?' How often were we to hear of gallant fighters in Erin's cause who died foaming at the mouth and cursing the Bishop of Cork.

On our road, the bishop personified gloriously the all-pervading clerical influence, the Church Temporal behaving prematurely like the Church Triumphant.

I feel the eminent prelate would have objected to his involvement, had he known of it, in a moral dilemma of my own. At the age of thirteen or so, I told a particularly crusty priest that I had committed a sin against Holy Purity.

'Alone?'

'Yes, Father.'

'And would you like your father and mother to see you at this?'

'No, Father.'

'Or your teachers?'

'No, Father.'

'Or me, your confessor?'

'No, Father.'

I had begun to feel that the invitations to the masturbatory extravaganza had gone far enough.

'Would you like the bishop to see you desecrate the temple of the Holy Ghost in this fashion?'

Put like that, of course I had to admit that I wouldn't. Neither, I felt, would the bishop.

My father was a member of a building society. There were about thirty members who built these houses on land they had bought from the Bishop of Cork. It was part of the bishop's estate — the

Bishop's Field. Later in life I asked someone why our road was called Redemption Road.

'Redemption Road? What kind of a Catholic are you? Sure it's one of the mysteries of the Rosary, the Redemption.'

'The Redemption is not a mystery of any fucking thing,' I said. 'The Assumption is a mystery of the Rosary.'

'Well,' he said, 'Redemption Road is an Assumption by the Corporation that if you live in the Bishop's Field, you'll go to Heaven.'

Redemption Road was a private road, with a gate lodge at each end. The lodgekeeper had to come out and unlock the gate to let you in. Just outside the private gate there was a little laneway called Factory Square. There was no factory and it wasn't square, but it was called Factory Square. The hideous anomaly was that the family who controlled security at the lodge was so poor that the kids were barefoot, as often as not, when they came out to open the gate. But within a year or two that gate was gone. The Redemption was deprivatised and the Bishop's Field became a public road. Much of the ground beneath that area now forms the approach to the Neptune Stadium.

At the further end of the Bishop's Field was Farranferris College, which was the Diocesan Seminary. From there on it was all green fields. When the gate came down, they built a new Corporation estate called Spangle Hill, since renamed Farranree. Some of the people who lived in Spangle Hill, whom we contemptuously called 'The Spanglers', had been rehoused from the centre of Cork city, in what was known in those days as a slum clearance. It would have been one of the early Fianna Fáil housing schemes, and they were bloody good houses too, and still are. They were great schemes, if a bit misplaced geographically. You can go back there now, fifty years later, and it's still a nice place.

It would be wrong to think that we were all constantly depressed and harried, hounded out of ditches by cudgel-wielding clerics. What we lived through was the norm. It didn't bother many at all. Others made the pragmatic compromise of public conformity and private selection, if not outright rejection.

The air was a-tingle at all times with the prospect of damnation. Everything was measured against the Almighty's possible assessment of its merit. Thus a neighbour assured me that going to the Opera House to see *Bamboozalem*, the great Benyon's magic show, was sinful, because Benyon was trying to take the power away from God. Anyone who has played the Cork Opera House would have advised Benyon to postpone the *putsch* till Wednesday night at the earliest — Monday and Tuesday being a dead loss.

Anecdotes abound about the Opera House as a religious arena. During one show, which had incurred clerical denunciation, a Defender of the Faith who rose in the auditorium and shouted 'Where are the good Catholics of Cork tonight?', got the reply, 'They're at devotions, where you should be.'

Devotions were a great source of 'a bit of hack', and loosely covered all religious activity outside of Mass or Confession. We in the choir were specially privileged, of course, but even ordinary latchikos got carried away by some of the many communal services, especially if singing was involved. It was notable how sedate, respectable neighbours could become quite belligerent when backed by the thunder of the cathedral organ:

> We stand for God and for his glory
> The Lord Supreme and God of all!
> Against his foes, we raise his standard!
> Around the cross we hear his call!
> Strengthen our Faith, Redeemer!
>
> *Chorus*
> Guard us when danger is nigh!
> To Thee we pledge our lives and service!
> Strong in a trust that ne'er shall die!
> *(Repeat)*
>
> We stand for God, Jesus our Master
> Has died to save with Love untold!

His law divine, and Truth unchanging
In this our land, their place must hold!

*Chorus*

There were strenuous objections in the forties against the GAA's use of 'Faith of Our Fathers' as a second National Anthem, a *Tánaiste* to the *Taoiseach* of 'Amhrán na bhFiann'. One of our teachers, equally devout as a Catholic and a GAA man, to my surprise voiced such views. One didn't expect godlessness from this source. Then he revealed the dark secret. There was a verse to that hymn, never sung in Ireland, containing the lines:

Faith of our fathers, Holy Faith,
We'll keep dear England true to Thee.

'Keep dear *England* true to Thee? And the King of England after feckin' off with a married woman? Come off it!'

The proliferation of exclamation marks is essential in printing such hymns, be it 'We Stand for God', 'The Green Grassy Slopes of the Boyne' or 'Wir Fahren Gegen England'.

Like any other Irish kid of my generation, I believed that we upheld freedom of religion. *They* didn't. *We* did. The quotation I recall most often being drummed into us was Oliver Cromwell's belief in freedom of religion, 'but if freedom of religion means the Mass . . . ' (Exclamation marks). *We* cherished all the children of the nation equally. *We* 'extended the same rights, under God, to our Protestant fellow countrymen' . . . which was tolerant of us, considering that the world and Garrett Reilly knew that while we were at Mass on Sunday, they were in bed with their neighbours' wives reading *The News of the World*.

So it amuses me to dredge from my memory another splendid piece of Christian tolerance which deserves to be rescued from oblivion, because none of my contemporaries seems to recall it — 'A Song for the Pope':

A Song for the Pope, for the Royal Pope
Who rules from sea to sea.
Whose kingdom (or sceptre) never shall fail,
What a Royal King is he, is he!
What a Grand Old King is he!

No warrior hordes has he with their swords,
His rock-built throne to guard!
For against it the Gates of Hell shall war
In vain, as they ever have warred!

Then Hurrah! Hurrah! Hurrah!
Hurrah! Hurrah! Hurrah!
And one cheer more for the Grand Old Pope,
For the Royal Pope — Hurrah!

Benediction, the veneration of the Eucharist, provided one or two highly diverting side-shows. It was always accepted that when John McCormack sang 'Panis Angelicus' at the Eucharistic Congress in Dublin in 1932, he was inspired by the Holy Ghost. There were almost, though not quite, witnesses to the presence of a Heavenly Dove fluttering over his head.

McCormack certainly inspired a million mimics. No Rosary-Prayers-for-Peace-and-Benediction was complete without a piercing, pioneering tenor, soaring above the commonality, a half-beat ahead of them all.

Another great game, a sort of profane variant of 'Snap', was the Divine Praises. At the end of the service the priest would kneel facing the altar, back to the congregation, and intone in plain chant, 'Blessed be God!', to which the people responded in like manner. For the rest of the Praises they chanted in unison with him 'Blessed be His Holy Name', 'Blessed be Jesus Christ, True God and True Man'.

So far so good. Now enter Dinny Daly. Dinny's devotion was genuine and vociferous. His competitive instinct was equally so. He was an oul' fella with a booming bass voice that could wipe Father Jurry's reedy tenor off the map, along with all other comers.

6

As the Praises got longer, Dinny's voice got stronger and the will to win took over, so by the time we got to 'Blessed be the Mother of God, Mary most Holy', Dinny pipped everybody to the post. The deep reverberations of his last note were punctuated by the ineffectual piping of the priest's.

We in turn took on Dinny. Now this was not a headlong dash for the tape. The objective was to sneak in ahead of him. It would have been useless, for instance, on the final Praise, 'Blessed be God in his Angels and Saints', to have finished while Dinny was only on 'Angels'. Ideally we should just be on the final 's' of Saints as Dinny hit the first 's'.

It may not have been very holy, but it was a great bit of 'hack'.

Ours was an Irish-speaking family, which may be no big deal to someone who has not been reared through Irish in an English-speaking city, noted for its capacity for mockery. I will not dwell on the mortifying embarrassment of being an 'Ireeshian'. I mention the language aspect because if there is anything more restrictive than being in a minority, it is being in a minority that subscribes enthusiastically to all the aspirations and hypocrisies of the majority; because everybody was in favour of the language — it was cowtowed to in every election speech. *A chairde Gael . . .*

Which made it all the more painful when one's father was dismissed as a 'fuckin' old madman' because he spoke Irish. And this by a member of an impeccably republican family.

I remember radio programmes at that time that to me sounded perfectly normal, because I was in an Irish-speaking household, but which to anyone else must have been baffling mumbo-jumbo. Mícheál Ó Maoláin (*as Árainn* — from Aran, as he proudly called himself) was a friend of Jim Larkin, and presumably some kind of socialist. But his children's programme began and ended with this verse:

> *Gael mise agus mise im 'Ghael*
> *Is ní thuigim gur náir dom é.*
> *Ní chasfainn mo chúl le fearaibh an tsaoil*
> *Is ní fearr d'fhear cách ná mé.*

I am a Gael, and a Gael is what I am
And I don't see that that's any shame.
I wouldn't turn tail to the men of the world
And no man is better than I.

I regarded this as a perfectly normal sentiment, because it was the creed in which I was reared, and it was reinforced by the Christian Brothers' School (as distinct from the Christian Brothers' College, which managed to accommodate a very different ethos within its own version of Catholicism). There was, looking back, a heaviness around the place, an inordinate exercise of authority which often crossed the border between discipline and derangement. For instance, when my brother Tomás decided to learn Russian, being already proficient in French, Spanish and German, he got hold of the grammar easily enough, but the only Russian text he could find on sale was a Russian Orthodox Bible. So strict was the family observance of the rule of the diocese, that my father insisted Tomás should go to the parish priest and ask for permission to read this Russian Bible — of which he could not yet make out one word — because it didn't carry the *Nihil Obstat* of Daniel, by the grace of God, Bishop of Cork. Not for the first or last time, my brother refused to comply.

An English version might have caused just as much consternation, biblical study being regarded as a peculiarly Protestant perversion, a feeling not entirely dispelled after exposure to the Hot Gospellers of Belfast, Ballymena, or the Bible Belt of the United States.

My father, it must be said, was not an easy man to put up with. Any idealist is a pain in the neck if you don't share his ideals, and my father was an idealist, in spades. I loved my father very much, and especially in his later years I think I understood him. He loved me dearly also, but of course I felt that he didn't understand me. My mother said to me when she was in her eighties, and my father touching ninety, that she prayed he would be taken before she was because 'I can mind him'. She knew no one else would have the patience to minister to his myriad eccentricities.

8

NIALL TOIBIN

I find it very hard to write about my father. There is so much of him in me that I recognise and resent. There is also so much that I have eventually come to acknowledge, and am thankful for. Someone said that before we can forgive others, we must forgive ourselves. But first, you have got to forgive your father. To form a sentence that will encapsulate de Valera, Dolly Parton, George Best or Mícheál MacLiammóir, is no great challenge. But to commit your assessment of your own Da to print? That's heavy.

My father was born John Tobin in 1882 in Passage West, County Cork. His mother was a Murphy from West Cork, his father came from Kill, County Waterford. There was no Gaelic-speaking tradition in the family on either side, that I have been able to trace. Certainly my uncle Bill, his brother, and my aunt May, his sister, spoke no Irish and had no interest in the language. They both held my father in great awe. Bill, it seemed to me, found him a sort of intellectual Colossus, by turn a source of pride and discomfort.

At some time in his youth my father took up the study of Irish, joined the Gaelic League, and became utterly and unalterably committed to the ideal of a Gaelic Ireland. He remained absolutely faithful to this, without deviation or compromise, publicly or privately, throughout his long life, in the teeth of embarrassment, humiliation, mockery and isolation, impervious to the traumatic effects on those around him. He never spoke English to anybody until it became obvious that they could not or would not speak Irish. How often did we as kids cringe, and want to run and hide, while my father in his rich, deep, resonant voice, stood his linguistic ground as shop assistants, railway porters, bus conductors, paper boys, policemen, postmen, nurses, doctors, dentists or beggars at the door, muttered 'What, Sir?' or 'Oh yes, quite', or '*Ta sé* mahogany gaspipe', according to upbringing, status or degree of animosity.

*Fear leanúnach*, a consistent man, was how one of his closest friends, Aodh O'Tuama, described him to me with great admiration. How often I wished that this consistency could be lightened with O'Tuama's conviviality, his liking for a small 'Paddy' or two, his twinkling eyes, and billowing pipe full of Mick McQuaid tobacco.

No. My father's Gaelic integrity shone cold and constant as the

9

Northern star. He drank Yerba Mate and other herbal teas, took cold showers as prescribed in Pfarrer Kneip's book *Meine Wasserkur*, made anti-rheumatic potions from fennel and heliotrope, smoked dried coltsfoot leaves for God knows what reason, had a regimen of dietary fads that enlisted halibut liver oil, cod liver oil and malt, Macroom-roasted oatmeal, Howard's One-Way flour, buttermilk, dandelion coffee, and China tea, which he held to be superior to all others.

He performed *Surya Namaskars*, which were Indian deep-breathing exercises, at the open back-bedroom window, which, given his powerful diapason and the development of his thorax, must have frightened the shit out of the crows in Danny Cohalan's cypress trees beyond the back-garden wall.

He spoke of *Béarla gránna Shasana* — England's hateful language — *Béarla* being really an untranslatable word in this context, with its inbuilt antipathy to the practitioners of that barbarian patois. Any speaking of English in the home merited an immediate clip on the ear. 'Kathleen Ní Houlihan, your way is a thorny way.' My father's devotion to the same Caitlín Ní Uallacháin led him on a lonely way.

I have never met anyone else to whom words like steadfast, undeviating, loyal, reliable, unflinching, thorough-going or devoted, could be applied as a matter of course, especially by those who admired his strength of character while sparing themselves the trouble of learning the language he loved. Equally, he was inflexible, egregious, adamant, didactic, fanatical, bigoted, *leanúnach*.

Pope John XXIII recalled that in Bergamo in Italy, where his father came from, the easiest ways for a man to lose his money were through drink, gambling, women or farming, and that his own father had chosen the most tedious of these. It seems to me that the path of the patriot in Ireland was similarly strewn with joylessness. Some chose what came to be called 'the armed struggle'. Others embraced national salvation through co-operativism — the land for the people, cherishing the children of the nation equally, Gaelic athleticism, Irish dancing, or party politics.

My father backed a horse that will never sight the winning post.

Much has been written of the Irish language 'racket' by those who rightly resent the indefensible imposition of compulsory Irish even on people whose aspirations to literacy never went beyond the Football Association league tables. But exploitation of the Irish language spawned no Al Capones. To commit oneself from the age of seventeen to a life of Gaelic puritanism, and to stick with it for seventy-four years, is a curious form of banditry.

My Da loved plants, flowers, trees. He was a very knowledgeable botanist and wrote two nature books in Irish, *Blátha an Bhóithrín*, about wayside flowers, and *Troscán na mBanta*, about meadowland flora. His father was a landscape gardener, and that is where that passion came from. Quite simply, he would have learned all about plants from his father.

One of the dearest memories I have is of my father when he was very old and physically feeble, though still mentally alert. When I went to Cork to visit him, I would sometimes propose going for a drive. He would deliberate about this, and eventually it would come down to one of two routes. The first was to go out the Carrigrohane straight road, towards Inniscara, and back through Blarney, then in through Blackpool, and home. The other was longer, and depended on his feeling up to it: we would drive down around Cork harbour and visit Monkstown and Passage West, and all around that area, and make sure to take in Blackrock and Ballintemple. These were the scenes of his boyhood.

One very old friend he visited on these outings was a playwright, John Bernard McCarthy, who used to complain about amateur companies not coughing up when they produced his plays. He and Da discussed politics and literature, and both disapproved of most Irish writing. James Plunkett's *Strumpet City*, I recall, was denounced out of hand, though neither had read it, the title alone betraying its unacceptable theme. I had not the heart, nor, I regret to say, the loyalty to Jim Plunkett Kelly to correct their error.

On the first such trip he was anxious to locate a certain convent, so I found it, and we drove in around the grounds.

'Do you want to go in and say a prayer?'

'No, no, I just wanted to have a look.'

And we would visit, maybe, a big house, and he would say, 'Pull up the drive there.'

'Why do you want to go into these places?' I asked, and it almost cracked my heart when he announced with great pride, 'My father laid out these gardens, and when I was a little boy I worked here, helping him.' That would have been eighty years before, so we are talking about having laid out these gardens in, perhaps, 1888.

And he would look about as if recalling that those, there, must have been the bushes that he put there, and that there had been rose beds over there, near the fence, and so on. As a kid I had loved to work in our own garden with him. He had green fingers and great knowledge. He poured out natural history, garden lore, horticultural expertise, as we heeled in cabbage plants, crushed caterpillars, shielded strawberries from frost with straw or cardboard, slaked lime or spread horsedung, picked and savoured tomatoes ripened in the outdoors against Danny Cohalan's concrete wall.

This was when we were really close, when I loved him and understood him best. These are gentle memories, and more precious to me because he didn't get through to many people. He probably did to me more than to anybody else, except my mother. He died in 1971, when I was running in a one-man show in the Gaiety in Dublin. I played that night, and then went down to the funeral after the show, and came back the following day to resume the show, which some people might have found callous, but I am sure he would have thought that it was quite right, that you must do your duty, and then do your job.

He had very little interest in the theatre as a professional thing, and when I became an actor he probably thought that this was youthful nonsense, and that I would get over it. Years later, when I got out a sheet of paper and showed him, by adding up, how much I had got for this, that and the other thing, and that I had made more money in that particular year than an assistant secretary in the Department of Education, he conceded that maybe I had done the right thing. But he still thought it wrong that I didn't have a pension, just as Kathleen Behan once told me how worried she was that Dominic hadn't a proper job.

My father then became interested in what show people earned generally, because he decided that I was part of showbusiness, which was something he never understood much about. Up the road from where we lived in Cork, one of his neighbours was Brendan O'Brien of the Dixies, or maybe it was Joe Mac, I'm not sure. He read that the Dixies had signed a two-million-pound contract. I'm sure this story was invented by Joe Mac, but my father read it when he was in his mid eighties. He pointed out to me that they had secured their future by signing this contract. Why didn't I sign a two-million-pound contract?

During my fourteen years in the Radio Éireann Players, my father was only too familiar with my work, as he listened avidly to the radio. In a way, he experienced the outside world vicariously, through radio. Perhaps it compensated for the self-imposed seclusion of his monoglot existence. He never saw me on the stage as far as I can gather, because he was housebound by the time I had begun to visit Cork professionally.

I do know that he was disconcerted by my being in the first production of *Borstal Boy*, because he did not like Brendan Behan. He regarded him as a blasphemer, a pornographer and a Communist. Most people did, of course, including Brendan. He was a bit distressed that I was going to play Behan, but he read the reviews and was impressed. What completely mollified him was a letter he had from a very old Gaelic League friend of his who had been to the play and took the trouble to tell him that it was very moving, that its overall effect was highly moral and uplifting, and that he thought that I had been very good in it and that my father should be proud of me. Praise coming from this source made a huge difference.

Dependence on others for news like this emphasises his appallingly lonely life — of his own choosing initially, if you like, but worse because he lived to be so old. To be tied down physically and bedridden in his last years, and yet to be mentally alert and surrounded by people so much younger, and so totally out of sympathy with what he had stood for, and with only maybe one person in a hundred who had the faintest notion of what he was talking about, or any sympathy therewith, is something that doesn't bear too much thinking about, because you feel you ought to have done more. But of course we don't do it, because we never realise exactly what a situation is — at least, not until it's too late.

The odd thing, and it has struck me from time to time, is that the Gaelic League, in its extension from its purely linguistic interest, embraced a notion of a Gaelic code of morals, harking back to *An Rud Dúchais*, 'the native thing'. It amuses me because *An Rud Dúchais* could almost be a direct translation of *Cosa Nostra*. 'The native thing', and what they called *An Meon Gaelach*, 'the Gaelic mentality', were mirrored by what Maggie Thatcher used to call 'Victorian values' — the idea that a person who worked hard and kept the shop properly was good and moral, and that the poor were by and large poor through their own fault, and that drunkenness was to be avoided, drinking itself being bad anyway.

The only time my father smoked was when some firm in Wexford — was it Sweetmans? — brought out an Irish cigarette, and he felt it his duty to smoke this because it was an Irish cigarette. He didn't persist with it very long, and it was very likely foul stuff, but it showed that something intrinsically bad could be sanctified because of its Irishness; and this was a very confused way of thinking.

But they had this set of Victorian values, and for that reason they had to backtrack on lots of things. If you were reading a poem by Eoghan Rua O'Súileabháin for instance, in which he was obviously referring to the deflowering of virgins while in a drunken condition, that would have to be censored. That did not gel with *An Meon Gaelach*. There was a song 'Do Bhíos-sa Lá l bPort Láirge'. It had the lines:

> *Bhí lán a tí de mhnaibh ann*
> *Agus mise ag ól a sláinte.*

Which translated means:

> There was the full of the house of women there
> And I was drinking their health.

A euphemism, to be sure.

When I went to the Gaeltacht for the first time, that verse was banned during the *Céilí* in Ballingeary. The same week, the first atom bomb was dropped — one of those nonsensical mental links one automatically mentions, to the puzzlement of all.

Before I leave the subject of the Irish language, I would like to clarify my own attitude, to the extent that I have one. Many sections of the press seem to harbour the suspicion that if you scratch an Irish speaker, or someone who uses the Gaelic version of their name, you will find a Provo, that there is something in the Irish language that makes everybody want to fire guns and kill the neighbours and blow up everything on wheels. But if this were true then everybody in the Gaeltacht would have joined the IRA, wouldn't they? Not quite. It seems to apply only to those who deliberately learn and choose to use Irish.

I could go through all the people I grew up with who spoke Irish, the family circle, friends, people to whom I would speak Irish still, if I met them, and there are only two people that I know who could be called Provo-minded. One of them was a teacher, and I know he was influential in getting some kids to go along with that line of action, shall we say, because the Provos did not come into existence until much later than the time I am talking about.

As for the language in schools, my own view is pretty simple, if not simplistic: you can bring a horse to the water, but you can't make him drink. To persist in teaching Irish to people who do not want to learn it, just doesn't make any sense to me. I do think that teaching Irish is a very good thing. I think that the Irish language should be helped to survive. I speak Irish. I love Irish. But I think it's purely a matter of personal choice. It has to be. It is pretty obvious today that imposing anything on students, be it sexual responsibility or saying the Rosary, gets you the bum's rush in double-quick time. So, foisting Irish on those who don't want to learn it or to speak it, is a dissipation of resources, time and energy. Any teaching activity should serve the purpose of actually mastering the subject. In the case of Irish, I don't think that sort of knowledge has been imparted to many. But on the other hand I do know people whose lives have been enormously enriched, who came from a background of no

Gaelic influence whatsoever, but picked up Irish at school, cottoned on to it and mastered it, and intellectually and in every other way bloomed as a result. In most cases the motivation was powered by love of the language.

There can be few things more depressing to someone passionate about the language than street-name signs. Drumcondra Road in Dublin has recently had a new plate put up opposite Richmond Road, which reads 'Bóthar Drom Courach', instead of 'Bóthar Drom Conrach'. Molesworth Street, directly facing the gate of our National Assembly, was given the Irish version 'Sráid Tigh Laighean' at some stage; it has for years worn an identity tag which says, 'Sráid Tigh Laibhean.' Who cares?

The question of my surname has been a greater irritation only than that of my first name. After well over half a century of argument, abuse and discussion with every second person I am introduced to, I have abandoned the struggle to get people to say my name the way I want it. I now respond with docility to variations of my name that once caused me apoplexy. Nile Tobeen, Neil Tobin, Nile Tobine, Nicholas Tobine, Nyall O'Toban, and perm any three out of eighty other versions.

I should have mentioned about my father, that when he was a travelling teacher for the Gaelic League, he was summonsed once for having no light on his bike, or something like that, and he gave his name to the RIC constable as Seán Tóibín. He was summonsed in the name of John Tobin, because as can happen to this very day, if you give your correct name, or at least the name by which you are generally called, some Government officer decides that you have no right to use that name, so he changes it. This happens all the time, even still. Anyway, my father decided — he couldn't have been more than twenty years of age at the time — that the best way to get around this was to change his name by deed poll to Seán Tóibín. And he was able to produce this document and say, 'Up yours, Jack, that is my legal name' (or whatever the equivalent type of insult was in his day). This was a form of passive resistance, peaceful protest.

Some other very odd anomalies emerged from the Gaelic hermitage. My father used to talk to me in his old age about things, quite out of the blue. I once attended a lecture by Fenner Brockway, socialist MP for Eton and Slough, and I mentioned that Brockway had helped to get de Valera out of Lincoln jail. My father said, 'Oh yes, I used to write to Fenner Brockway.' And I thought, 'This man is really gone now. The mind is on the blink.' 'Yes,' he said, 'Brockway and — who was the other fellow? Oh yes, Oswald Mosley. I had a correspondence with both of them. They were Labour MPs.'

Mosley afterwards started the British Fascist Movement. At the time of the burning of Cork, and various Black and Tan outrages, which due to censorship were not reported, my father got descriptions from local accounts of what had happened on the various occasions, when it hadn't made the papers, and sent this information to Mosley and Brockway so that it could be the basis of questions in the House. And I think there were one or two questions. I never went to the bother of looking it up, but it takes a hell of a stretch of the imagination for a man of my father's age to invent such an unlikely alliance between the arch traitor to socialism, Mosley, and the gentle Brockway, who remained the staunchest of all left-wing MPs. I was reminded of this a couple of years ago when I used to walk through Red Lion Square in Bloomsbury to rehearsal rooms at the October Gallery. There is in the square a very good statue of Lord Brockway.

My mother was born in Kerry. She came from Beaufort, near Killarney, and she was a very humorous woman. She was well-spoken, and had wonderful handwriting, even when she was very old. We all liked to get a letter from her because the handwriting was so good, it gave the impression that this letter had been specially and very carefully written for you. It's a lost thing, because typewritten letters can never mean as much, and she wrote very faithfully and very frequently to all her children, and to all her friends. She never really took to the telephone.

She saw humour in most things and she laughed a lot. Hers was a tough life in some ways. I don't mean in matters of material comfort, because we mostly, in her own words, enjoyed 'an ample sufficiency'. But it must have been a great strain for her to be married to my father, because she didn't carry his ideas to anything like the same extremes. And besides, she was very friendly. She spoke English to everybody and kept life on a sane footing while my father indulged his right to be what he was. That's not to say that this doesn't happen in other marriages, it's just that my father's Gaelicism was a more obvious eccentricity than going down to the pub and getting locked every night, which a lot of other men did, and their wives had to put up with that little peculiarity.

At an early age she went to Liverpool and was trained as a telegraph operator, and I remember asking her what Liverpool was like. She said, 'Oh I don't know', because she stayed in some hostel which was run by nuns for the time that she was learning to do the work. She came back to Ireland and worked in various telegraph offices. I know that one was in Knocklong, County Limerick, because she told me about some guy for whom she used to telegraph bets. He seemed a pretty lucky punter, and then suddenly he stopped coming in, and they found that he had some little stunt whereby he could beat the clock and, by the same token, the bookies. My mother and her friends never fully understood the way it worked, and as my mother said, no one in Knocklong was going to tell you.

Later she worked in the GPO in Cork, in a similar capacity. During the War of Independence she and another girl, Nell Donoghue from Mayo, had contacts with 'the lads' (as it was common to call them, and is not any more). On a couple of occasions they were persuaded to intercept telegraph messages which came through for transmission to the military in Cork. They were flushed down the toilet. That was her contribution to the war effort. Apart from that, she never mentioned anything about that period, and I don't know what else her involvement was, if any.

She was a wonderful hostess and a great conversationalist, and you would never be bored if you were sitting at home of an afternoon with my mother in the house. The chat was great. She was full of information, in the sense of lore. She was very well informed. She was very kindly as well, but she also had a motto which is probably the quintessence of 'Kerryness': she would purse her lips occasionally and say, 'Don't let anybody know your business. Be nice to them, but don't let them know your business.' And she stuck to that. People would try to pump her for information about something that happened in the neighbourhood, and she would smile, and I would know by the way the lips were set, that they would get nothing more. *Omerta.*

My mother was one of nine sisters, only five of whom survived beyond infanthood. Her only brother worked the family farm, and she had joined the Civil Service. She had another sister in London, one in Hartford, Connecticut, and two more in Kerry.

My father's one brother and one sister had no family, so that any fairly close relations that I have would be on my mother's side. If your nationality were to be decided by the preponderance of your cousins, then I would be a Kerryman. Mam was Siobhán Ní Shúileabháin — from the time she met my father, anyway. She was Hannah O'Sullivan on the school roll, but Han Sullivan to everybody around Culmagort, between Beaufort and the Gap of Dunloe. Sullivan and O'Sullivan were interchangeable versions, as were Shea and O'Shea in the case of other relations.

Her nephew John Shea, from Hartford, delighted my mother with the story about a Castleisland woman who went to join her married son in Hartford, Connecticut. She coped with long lonely days by ferreting out funerals of Kerry people. Her luck was in when she saw a name she recognised in the 'Deaths' column in the paper, because in brackets it said 'late Castleisland'. Off she went to the funeral home, unfamiliar terrain to her. She blundered into the first parlour, where some lonely Greek exile was laid out under the bored gaze of a black-suited attendant. The poor woman burst into tears, and the Kerry mourners, on their way past to the correct parlour, heard her keening bitterly: 'Oh Mosheen, if twas back in Castleisland you were, it's more than one little maneen you'd have guarding your casket.' From then on, Greeks in Hartford were known among the Irish as 'Castleislandmen'.

It amused her to recall, as a story against my father, the great Gaelic scholar, that when they met at a Gaelic League function, he chatted her up, if that is not a blasphemous description of the staid and starchily proper approach he would have adopted.

'Which O'Sullivans?' he asked.

Our family are the Sullivan *Féile*, to distinguish us from the various other Sullivans.'

'*Féile?*' he said, 'The generous Sullivans? *Croí na féile*, the heart of hospitality. That's a wonderful name.'

'No,' she corrected him, '*Abha na Féile*, the River Feale, as in *Mainistir na Féile* [Abbeyfeale], where my grandfather had a farm before they were evicted.'

This was probably the only time she corrected him on any matter pertaining to the language. Her own Irish was fluent and down to earth, not always strictly grammatical, and Da's ear registered any minor transgression, even when he was engrossed in study, and he would growl an almost involuntary correction.

Once during a severe illness she woke during the night as the vomit threatened to erupt. '*An árthach, a Sheáin,*' she called. Still half asleep as he approached with the chamber pot, he said, '*An t-árthach, a ghrá.*' 'If I'd had the strength,' she swore, 'I'd have made sure to overshoot the pot and let him have the lot.'

Why her grandfather was evicted from Abbeyfeale, I never found out, but they came to Killarney because they were promised a farm from the O'Mahonys of Cuileannagh House. I said, 'Well, whose farm did he get?' To which she answered, 'It wasn't anybody's that was evicted. It was vacant. The O'Mahonys were very good landlords. They evicted nobody.'

So the family came down from Abbeyfeale, and to distinguish them from the locals they were called Sullivan *Féiles*. Even in that name there's a little local history.

There were seven of us, four boys and three girls. My eldest brother, Tomás, was for many years a teacher, then worked in the Translation Office in the Dáil. He is now a highly regarded poet in the Irish language. My second brother, Declan, was the rake of the family — a mild rake. He started off in one of the agricultural colleges doing agronomy or something, but he left that and joined the Forestry Service. Then he was a merchant seaman for a few years, and later he worked for the British Forestry Commission, and spent the rest of his life in Wales. He is buried in a little village called Goistre, not far from Pontrhydyfen, where Richard Burton is buried.

Like Burton, he was very fond of the jar, and very fond of a song. He was lovable, funny, and very much his own man.

My eldest sister, Siobhán, was a nurse. She died at the age of thirty-six, shortly after giving birth to her only child. My sister Phil Higgisson, who lives in Cork, is a good landscape painter. My other sister lives in Windsor in England. She has been there for well over forty years. She emigrated when she was very young, and wisely changed her name from Gobnait to Debbie. She married Liam Lynch, from Portarlington.

Colm, my younger brother, was in the US army, and retired with the rank of colonel. Having worked in Britain as an anaesthetist, he emigrated further afield to Philadelphia, became an anaesthesiologist, and joined the army as a paramedic in the early fifties. He served in Germany and France, and missed the Vietnam war by inches. Since he left the army he has worked for the Veterans' Administration Hospital in Richmond, Virginia.

But what of my parents' effect on my own personality? I am taking it as given that I'm a humorous person. Otherwise, I have been extremely successful in conning the public for over thirty years. I got this humorous slant on life, this quirky way of looking at things, from my mother. She didn't accept anything really at face value. She tended to locate the odd and the peculiar, and you would find her often suppressing a giggle.

First and foremost of course, as an outsider, and a countrywoman at that, she had to contend with the Cork accent. In a foreword to *Cork, City by the Lee*, a guide issued to visitors by Cork Corporation, I wrote:

> But surely Cork's abiding glory is its speech. It is the despair of teachers, the standby of comedians, the delight of linguists, and the bafflement of tourists. Such words as accent, dialect, patois, argot, vernacular, are pallid inadequacies. Cork speech slides and skips and raps and soars and patters. It swoops and crows and gurgles. It splatters and chatters and chants and cheers. It climbs and vaults and loops the loop. It scampers and dawdles, idles and chugs, chuckles and trills.

In speed, pace, pitch and range, tone, inflection, tint and timbre, it pushes vocal achievement towards the limit of all tolerance, and sometimes beyond. On top of all that, we sing. Very well, usually.

She herself retained her Kerry lilt, but loved every cadence and song of the Cork accent. She revelled in the banter and abuse of the shawlies in the market stalls, on the marsh, 'de flat of de city'. The Coal Quay was her delight, and well-spoken though she was, she called it 'the Coalkay', as did real Corkonians. On the opposite bank of the river, in front of St Mary's Dominican church, was the Sand Quay, pronounced 'Sankay'. 'I'll see you a Sunda' after twelve mass in the Sankay' would be a discreet invitation to go for a pint. She was very aware of how people said things, and I suppose the combination of that and my father's obsession with precision of language, Irish or English, made me very aware of how people say things, rather than what they say.

I'm quite obsessive about that. Every time I hear an oddity of speech, an incongruity of description, it not only registers, but it stays there, and will come back twenty years, forty years later. For instance, recently during the fiftieth celebrations of the Normandy landings, there was a lady on the radio who had spent her youth as a nurse in England, staying in a hostel in Highgate Hill. 'The only thing I remember about D-Day was the hymn-singing coming from the Church of Ireland across the street,' she said. Obviously there is no Church of Ireland on Highgate Hill. Nobody corrected her. Nobody spotted it.

But I would have spotted that in Croke Park. A word that is wrong, a fact that is wrong, will jump at me and remain in my mind. Equally, so will some particularly felicitous phrase or colourful oath. For instance, in 1954, in Moore Street in Dublin, I was drinking with two English acquaintances who were Trinity students. One said something which caused a slight, pale, intoxicated man at the corner of the counter to snort in disgust.

'Am I to understand from your conversation that you are attending university?' he asked, disbelief mounting with each syllable.

'Yes,' said the chap proudly, 'Trinity actually.'

The pale man slumped with relief. 'Good,' he said, 'ignorance is a delicate flower. It will flourish untrammelled in Trinity College.' And Myles na gCopaleen (for it was he) turned again to his drink. (Myles na gCopaleen, humorously corrected to 'na Gopaleen' as a sneer at the reformed spelling, an Litriú Caighdeánach, was Brian O'Nolan, Brian Ó Nualláin, otherwise Flann O'Brien, author, playwright, columnist, one of Ireland's greatest exploiters of the wealth of the English language, and even more so of the Gaelic tongue.)

I have often had to contain myself when asked where my much-publicised impatience (meaning bad temper) comes from. That I'm afraid is my own contribution to my character. After all, we don't inherit everything. If everything were inherited, everybody would be like Adam and Eve. And of course we all are. We still make the same mistakes.

But you can't blame heredity for everything. If you absolve a man of a criminal tendency because it was 'kind father' for him, as they used to say, then you must in conscience and in turn absolve his grandfather, and so on, back to Adam, who would blame God for making him the way he was. You would wind up forgiving everyone for everything, which is what you're supposed to do anyway. So much for my idea of logic.

I do confess to a very dour streak, and a pretty lousy temper — probably partly attributable to the classic Irish 'wakeness'— the bad drop. Sometimes a tantrum is a way of releasing tension, because I work very hard. Many people would not accept this contention, of course; but to stand up alone in front of a thousand people for two and a half hours, and keep them laughing, is not easy, it takes a lot out of you. People have after all paid money to come to your show, and if at the end they applaud, it's not because they like your blue eyes. It's because you've given them value for money, because you have provided entertainment. In turn, because the pleasure you've given them is immediate, you feel you should get your acclaim, right here and now. Applause from posterity is for the painter, or the author whose work may survive while he awaits immortality. That's fine, but 'it ain't showbusiness'. It can be enraging, having left the stage in a glow of satisfaction, to enter the backstage bar, only to have some smart ass come up to tell you he didn't think much of it. It's eight to five he hasn't even been at the show.

Worse still is the fulsome compliment of the habitual freeloader. A certain parliamentary obscurity said to me in the Opera House in Cork, 'How can you do a one-man show like that? It is just wonderful. And what a privilege to be here.' Now the show that night was a tribute to the late Donal Crosbie, and all I had done was to MC the concert, and I had just a ten-minute spot in the middle of it. She could at least have had the manners to find out what she was supposed to have been looking at.

Another characteristic of mine, and I don't know where it comes from, is that I usually reject the obvious proposition, and I do this automatically. This is why I keep having arguments with people, and put myself in a position where I am vigorously defending something I don't even believe in, because my first stance was 'I don't agree with you'. I may find after ten minutes that I actually do agree with whoever it is, but I can't admit it. I have to keep arguing against him; and anyway, we're probably both wrong. I suppose it's more fun to oppose. The people who conform and agree get the best jobs, but they don't get the best laughs by any means.

# TWO

O verall I had a very happy childhood. When the war broke out, I was almost ten. I remember very little about the time before. I was afraid of the dark when I was small, I know, and there always had to be a night-light in the room.

I made my First Communion in the Green, otherwise known as St Vincent's Convent. The first nun I can recall was Sister Hubert. Sister Hubert was from the North. Was she ever! When Douglas Hyde was made President, Sister Hubert was teaching us.

'We have a President,' she told us. 'Is there any boy in the class named Douglas?'

There was nobody in the class named Douglas. There was nobody in the North Parish named Douglas. I don't know whether she thought that somebody could have been called after the President that morning and then have arrived at the age of seven in our class the same day, but she said, 'Ah well, sure we have a place in Cork called Douglas.' And that was a consolation to her.

Of course Sister Hubert was never called Sister Hubert, but 'Stubert'. She taught me my first lesson in Geography, quite unwittingly. She was a fervent nationalist, as all nuns were, and all Northern nuns to the power of infinity, and after we had finished the prayers in the morning, she would tack on her own trimmings in this raucous voice, this, to my sensitive Munster ears, appalling Northern accent.

'And now', she would quack, 'we will say a prayer for Ireland. Saint Patrick give us back Derry, Antrim, Down, Armagh, Tyrone,

Fermanagh, in the name of the Father, the Son and the Holy Ghost. Amen.'

And from chanting that every morning, I knew the Six Counties anyway. During every performance of *Borstal Boy* I've thought of Stubert and her Northern voice whenever the Lancashire detective challenges Brendan to name the Six Counties.

Now Sister Hubert was very strident, but she used to give us jobs to do, and we used to go to the school to help out, doing stuff for the missions. One job was framing holy pictures in cellophane and passe-partout — a black leather-like tape. I don't know what the missions or the missionaries did with these artefacts. They probably ate them. We also used to collect silver paper for the Black Babies. I could never figure out why.

Sister Hubert was great fun. There was always something happening. She was a huge woman, and her voice filled the school, and she'd crack you with the ruler as soon as look at you. But didn't they all? At the same time, there was a bit of jollity going around when she was there. She brought in cans of sweets and things. She wasn't entirely a monster — she just sounded like one. Like every other young fellow, I wondered whether she had legs or whether she moved on wheels, because of the voluminous black habit she wore.

Then there was Miss Bailey, not to mention Miss Waters. What a double act! Waters and Bailey, the two mad schoolmarms. It was years later that I discovered that they were what were called 'JAMs', junior assistant mistresses, who would have had no status whatsoever in law or in education, except that they could flake your hand if you held it out properly, and that they could probably spell 'cat'.

I'm sure I'm being very hard on them, but I don't think their qualifications would have been very high. They were mainly there to control a large assembly of brats, and keep them from pissing all over the floor.

Miss Waters was a very small, stout woman, and seemed to me to be at least a hundred years old, because she had hair on her face and a wart on the side of her nose. Yet she was jolly enough, especially when she got annoyed, at which time she would trot out her one and only joke, eternally hilarious: 'Come out you! Come out you! Hold out your hand. I'll give you a hot cake. Oh, I'll give you a hot cake!' And the 'hot cake' meant a flake across the palm. When the humorous mood really got the better of her, she would call it 'a hot caker', which was better from her point of view than a hot cake.

In counterpoint to Miss Waters' guttural contralto, was Miss Bailey's Sundays Well soprano. Every statement was prefaced by a prolonged, trilling 'Oooh!'. 'Oooh, oooh, oooh, you bold boy! Oooh, you brazen thing!' Neither of them ever spoke words of praise. 'Bold boy, brazen thing. Tie your shoelace, wipe your nose.' These formed the basis and essentials of English as taught in St Vincent's Convent.

Only once did I qualify for Miss Bailey's 'Bold boy, brazen thing' award. She was whipping up enthusiasm for the missions, talking about bringing in the 'Black Baby money'. Now the Black Babies were the concern of the home team, the Society of Missions to Africa, the SMA, who were in Ballintemple in Cork. Being local, they were obviously well supported. We also had the Maynooth Mission to China, who distributed the *Far East* magazine, featuring Pudsey Ryan, the ever-youthful schoolboy columnist. The SMA collection box was surmounted by the figure of a black little boy. When you put a penny in the box, his head nodded in gratitude. The second box, for the Missions to China, had a yellow little boy with a pigtail, and when you gave him a penny, he nodded as well. They didn't say 'Tanks massa' or 'Tanks bwana' or 'Tankee muchee', but they might as well have, for the general conception of race was more or less that. It would horrify people these days, but these two figures were referred to as 'Paul U Pee' and 'Sambo'.

'Did anybody bring in a penny for Sambo and Paul U Pee? Oooh! *Bualadh bas.*'

Collecting nuns popped up in odd places over the years. I was passing Larry Murphy's pub in Baggot Street, strange as that may sound, since I was with Brendan Behan, some time about 1954, when a wee nun rattled a box at us.

'What are you collecting for?' Brendan asked warily.

'The night shelter.'

'Oh, fair enough,' he said with a sunny smile, and slipped a note into the slit of the box. 'As long as it's not to convert the poor Africans. Jaysus, haven't they enough to put up with, being black, without having to be fucking Catholics as well!'

And, like Paul U Pee or Sambo, she nodded and smiled in thanks.

To get back to Miss Bailey. I had this guy beside me in class who really must have been evilly inspired.

'Sure, I wouldn't bring in any money for them,' he said. 'The teachers keeps all that for themselves, to buy fags.'

Not to be outdone in sophistication, I said, 'I knows that.'

When Miss Bailey asked him about his contribution, he pointed accusingly at me. 'Miss! Miss, he said the teachers keeps that for themselves, for fags.'

Miss Bailey almost ascended into Heaven, like a hot-air balloon.

'Oooh! Oooh!'

I was put standing in the corner, with my face to the wall. And this fella was laughing his head off. And Miss Waters was obviously itching to lavish 'hot cakers' on me, except that I was outside her jurisdiction.

On my first day in school, since I didn't speak any English, I had no idea what was going on, but my older sister, Gobnait, was in the school, and she was to look after me. When it came to the lunch break, I went to get up, and Sister Hubert told me to sit down. So I sat down, and my sister came in with my glass of milk and my bun, and at that stage I started to cry, because I felt this was wrong. Everybody else was out playing in the yard, and I was being kept in, and this was going to be the same every day. I would never be let out. But Gobnait explained to me that it was just while I was getting used to it.

Anyway, I must have settled in very quickly, and learned English in about half an hour, because I can't remember any other distress at all.

The war started then, and the words that come immediately to my mind from that time are Fords, Dagenham, Yanks, the mailboat.

'Oh, she's over.'

'She's back.'

And shouts of 'Oh, have you been over? Have you seen Charlie?'
— in mockery of 'Cockney' accents acquired in two months.

All this because of a mass exodus of the workforce from Cork to the Ford factory in Dagenham. Others went to Birmingham, or to Luton, to other motorworks, but Dagenham was colonised by Corkonians.

With the pro-German element (and there was quite a considerable pro-German feeling in Cork at the time, although it must be said that it was a variable state of mind), going to Dagenham was the ultimate betrayal of 1916. An older man described to me his own experience (this was in the 1980s). 'I was full of national pride, staunchly neutral. To me, taking the mailboat was worse than taking the soup. But one evening I found myself in a Local Security Force uniform, with a hurley stick sloped on my shoulder, marching up and down Ballycotton strand, ready to repel the Germans. So I said, "Fuck this", and I high-tailed it over to Dagenham.'

Though I was born on the south side, in Friars' Walk, I am a Northsider by adoption, disposition, conviction and upbringing. *Our* north side encompassed Blarneyah, Shandonah, the Fairah, Grawn (an abbreviation of Gurranebraher), Blackpool, Spanglah, the Watercourse, and Gerald Griffin Street. Its architectural glories included the North Chapel (otherwise the Cathedral), the Four-Faced Liar, Murphy's Brewery and the Fever Hospital Steps. Some of the above would appear on the map as Blarney Street, Shandon Street, Fair Hill, Gurranebraher, Spangle Hill.

The North Chapel is St Mary's Cathedral, the Four Faced Liar is St Anne's, Shandon. Naturally there was a fanatically strong GAA tradition, what with Glen Rovers hurlers, and their football cousins, St Nicks — though it must be said that Gaelic football was very much the poor relation in those days.

North End had a compact and devout following for soccer; there was very little rugby to speak of, and tennis and golf were curious affectations of people in the pages of the *Cork Examiner*.

Drag-hunting, though, was really popular, as was bowl-playing. The mention of either sport will light a spark in the eye of any Corkman of my generation, though they were a closed book to the underprivileged of the Pale. My old neighbour Willie Cotter of Cork United, Rochdale and *Cork Examiner* fame, once told a Dublin soccer star in the Vinyard bar after a match, that Cork 'ran a drag with ye'. He had to explain the phrase, but it shows the extent to which obscure activities can colour local speech.

Drag-hunting bore no relation to live coursing. Firstly, the dogs themselves were known as 'bagels', not 'beagles', although they were spelt in the same way. There were several clubs about the city. Two in particular, Griffin United Harriers and the Fair Hill Harriers were within an easy five minutes of our house. These harriers were the 'Boys of Fair Hill' of the songs. There's the well-known one, which sometimes challenges 'The Banks of My Own Lovely Lee' as the city anthem, when the majority of the company happen to be Northsiders. But I much prefer the second 'Boys', beloved of my old friend Tom Twomey, who made Mike Condon's pub in Crosshaven ring with its chorus on many a langerated happy summer's evening:

> On the side of Fair Hill there lived Connie Doyle,
> The grandest oul' sportsman that e'er trod the soil.
> He swore all his life that he'd never give in,
> But he bet all he had on the boys of Fair Hill.
> With me fol-de-ol-addidy, fol-de-ol-addidy,
> Here's up them all, says the boys of Fair Hill.

This would be the same Connie Doyle of 'Doyley's Armoured Car' fame. The Armoured Car was a dog, of course, a beagle. I will spare the blushes of a well-known Dublin ballad singer, who sang that ballad very well on a radio show, but in his intro described The Armoured Car as a greyhound. One might with equal accuracy call Shakespeare 'a scriptwriter'. Even 'Armoured Car' was a nickname for something like 'Lady Jane'.

The 'bagel' is not a pretty sight; nor, if it comes to that, were the men who used to walk the beagles, since with time they developed the same lope, doleful expression and hangdog jowls as their charges.

A 'drag' began before dawn with a couple of sturdy enthusiasts laying down the trail, a process involving dragging hunks of offal tied on the end of ropes several miles across the countryside from a given point to whichever pub was nearest to the designated finish.

NIALL TOIBIN

This work was strictly a hands-and-feet job, since not even a humble bike could be ridden over the walls, ditches, marshes and streams that rendered the terrain suitable.

Several hours after the trail was laid, the various dogs set off to sniff their way out and back, and the day would be suitably brought to a close in Mikey Sull's in Fair Hill, The Black Man, the Fox and Hounds, or maybe Dan Murphy's in Killeens.

Bookmakers attended, as at a regular race meeting. In 1952 I saw a beagle from Liscarroll, a rank outsider, tumble from 200:1 to 4:1 on the head of a five-shilling bet placed with Sammy Charnicker — an indication that rumours of huge gambling transactions were a bit wide of the mark. *A dollar on a dog of doubtful provenance?* 'Who the hell is he? Scrub the board, Miah!'

Bowl-playing looked as if it was due for the knacker's yard a few short years ago, when the need for improved roads to carry heavier traffic caused upgrading of the very boreens and narrow twisting byways ideal for this sport. The general idea is that two contestants each propel a twenty-eight-ounce iron bowl a prescribed distance. Whoever gets home in the fewest throws, wins. The severe lopping of hedgerows also disfigured the traditional courses. Ironically, the increased demand for motorways has freed some of the former highways, and as the hedgerows reclaimed their ground, we have bowling courses ready made — just when the successors of legendary champs like Delaney and Carey are bowling down the Pacific Coast Highway or Route 66. Sad.

The drag was very much a part of the colour of our area. The pavements of Gerald Griffin Street, St Mary's Road and Peacock Lane on a summer's day became one vast carpet of dogness, as the stars of the drag, brindled, piebald, brown, black, black-and-white, or black-and-tan, sprawled in the sunshine, befouling the pathways of my childhood.

You had hurling, of course, on every street, from the minute you came home from school. Even before you'd finished your dinner, you had a hand on the hurley, and you were out, running up the road, gobbling back your bread and jam, dead set on getting picked on somebody's team.

31

Although we ate, slept and drank Gaelic games, and were harangued in school, home and from public platform about the manliness of our athletic heritage, we still dabbled in soccer, because, no less in Cork than in any other city or town with narrow streets and limited space, it was the most convenient game to play. Soccer was a hated 'garrison' game; a contagion visited upon the purity of our Gaelic youth by the contaminated spawn of the oppressor, who, just to even the score, also played hurling. The politics of sport was deep stuff. The disputations of medieval prelates contemplating the angelic colonisation of pinheads was in the ha'penny place compared to the Byzantine contortions of a GAA committee in pursuit of grounds for disqualification of a victorious opponent. Apocryphal they may be, but tales were told of teams being stripped of victory because the paper on which the selected players were named was not of Irish manufacture, as required by Association policy. 'British Watermark Deprives Imokilly of Match', the *Southern Star* might solemnly proclaim. Matches could be declared void on the grounds that an English coin was used in the toss.

Hurling was my first and, if the truth be told, my only real love, and I was a pretty good practitioner until the age of seventeen, when I had to wear glasses. As this coincided roughly with my awakening interest in drinking pints of porter, I became a non-combatant as soon as I left home.

Like everyone else on our road, I idolised Jack Lynch, but the hurler I loved most to watch was Alan Lotty of Sarsfields — a centre-back of strangely dark complexion, who had an unhurried grace and authority that is etched on my memory.

When Spangle Hill opened up our quiet private road to the realities of life, one of the enjoyable sideshows was that we had the Friday-night drunks rolling home. Drunkenness was prevalent, obvious and quite casually accepted. People were not that well fed, and a few pints on an empty stomach caused a fellow to slobber all over the place. Today's drinkers are more controlled and can hold their liquor better, but the decline of public slobbering has little to do with less drunkenness.

'Jaysus, I'll beat you to death with me shawl', we would hear a woman threaten, as her husband sang while he pissed against the telegraph pole outside our railings, or got the gawk through our hedge, draping my mother's carnations with a shawl of vomit. My brother Colm and I enjoyed this spectacle from behind the bedroom curtains. It was almost like 'Friday night is music night', because the revellers, no matter how drunk they were, were always singing. As the regular exponent of 'The Good Old Blarney Stone' rounded the turn a hundred yards up the road, the first protracted notes of 'Marguerite' came on the night air round Hawks's Corner, followed by the weekly taking home of 'Kathleen', and the recitation of the benefits that would accrue to Australia, *If we only had ould Ireland over here*. One memorable night a soldier leaned against the pole and was into *You went away and my heart went with you* for the ninth time when my father finally overcame his dignity and went down and told him to move on.

'*Bailigh leat as san.*'

'What Boss?'

'Clear off out of that.'

'Oh, oh yeah, goodnight Boss.'

Singing was by no means synonymous with drunkenness, but was almost inseparable from drink. A persisting myth has it that there was a great tradition of opera. I have heard people who are now in their forties claiming that twenty-five years ago there was an enormous operatic following in the city. Twenty-five years ago there wasn't even an Opera House. It had burned down. There was no touring opera company in Britain, never mind Ireland, and the opera used to come from Britain.

But there was without question a huge repository of operatic knowledge and consciousness (the same was true of Waterford, incidentally), so that when anybody was asked to sing a song, as like as not you got 'The Moon Hath' or 'Goodbye from the White Horse Inn' or 'In Happy Moments Day by Day', and 'The Heart Bowed Down'.

I myself sang in opera when I was a member of the cathedral choir, which was a very big part of my childhood. Professor Aloys Fleischmann, choirmaster and organist, reluctantly agreed to allow his choir to sing offstage as a backing for the chorus in a production of *The Bohemian Girl*, and some other opera, probably *Maritana*. I have never seen *Maritana*, nor do I wish to see it, but I will not forget standing in the wings, with all the rest of these grimy little tykes, singing:

> Bright and buxom lassies, come the fair shall now begin.
> Show your rosy faces and our hearts you soon shall win.
> We come, we come, the fair begins, yea the fair begins.

It must have been bloody awful. But the great thing was that every night we got cakes and sweets and bars of chocolate, while odd members of the cast would give you an ice-cream or a cigarette on their way in. It was highly enjoyable — not for any reasons to do with music.

'Dopra House' had an enthralling atmosphere. It was a curious-looking building, rounded in shape at either end, with semicircular steps leading up to the main entrance, and a massive iron staircase up the outside of the wall that faced the river. This stairs doubled as an entrance to the gallery, and as a fire-escape. Early-doors patrons sat on the stairs having a smoke or 'an oul' hoult' or reading the *Echo*. Going to the Opera House was quite an event. It was a regular thing, but it was exciting, something you looked forward to, and people talked about it all the time. An oul' hoult (old hold), let me explain, was more aggressive than a cuddle, more restrained than foreplay.

One of the reasons that Cork had a very peculiar atmosphere for four or five years was that all normal shipping was gone during the war. Cork above all else was a port, the more obviously so by the fact that you had two branches of the river, the south and north channels, so that you had in effect four sets of quays. Where I as a child had seen boats tied up all along the river, there now was nothing. The river was generally deserted, except for an odd ship from Sweden or some other neutral country — usually Switzerland, the joke had it. British merchant ships came in sometimes. I recall the quietness of the quays, because I used to go to the School of Music on Union Quay on a Saturday afternoon, allegedly to learn the uilleann pipes.

I learned precious little about music, since it was my father's idea anyhow, but the quays yielded up an occasional educational nugget.

There was a ship tied up outside the School of Music for the entire duration of the war, which was called *The John Joyce*, a pleasure boat which used to go down around the harbour in peacetime. It spent the war rotting away in the 'sleepy lagoon' whose colour recalled a phrase from another Joyce, since it was 'snot-green', and very likely 'scrotum-tightening' to boot. It smelt like shit, which is what it was anyway, and was patronised by seagulls and mullet.

One particular Saturday is very clear in my mind. After an abortive music lesson, as I left the school I saw that a ship had docked well below the City Hall. I strolled down in that direction. A sailor was leaning over the rail, smoking and joking in some foreign tongue with two very pretty girls who stood on the quay.

'God,' I thought, looking at one of them, 'she's a beauty. But she's really plastered the lipstick on.'

The tar was joined by a mate, and they came ashore — but not for long. In short order all four headed back aboard, the girls giggling, and by now smoking like furnaces too. I must have been dimly aware that the girls were two 'flahs', if not fledging whores. If they were relying on Saturday afternoon sailors, they served a prolonged and poorly-paid apprenticeship.

The picture I am trying to paint is of the Saturday afternoons on the quaysides, with grass growing between the cobblestones, because the quays were not being used. On the other hand there must have been some grain coming in, because there were always pigeons picking up corn on the quayside. There was a very lazy, sleepy, screen-Mexican air about the place in the good weather. But it's a lovely warm feeling of that era, that time in my life. The fact that an awful lot of the people were away was very sad, but they were sending money home from Dagenham.

One encounter with another couple of sailors has always puzzled me in retrospect. They stopped me in Parnell Place, a few hundred yards from the scene I've described above, and one addressed me in German: '*Wo kann man fukki-fukki erhalten?*' I had been studying German at home (I was about thirteen at this time), and I understood what he said, and the meaning of *'fukki-fukki'*, which was a new one on me, was rendered crystal clear by the accompanying gesture, a clenched fist and pumping forearm. *'Oh ja,'* I said confidently, *'Drüber in dieser Kneipe'*, and I indicated a pub, which I think was called The Cosmopolitan, as a source of supply for the service he sought.

I should like to have witnessed what happened when he went in, but I was under age and could not follow. Anyway, my academic curiosity had already taken over. How did he know I spoke German? Had he met some helpful Corkman somewhere east of Suez who had assured him that in the happy event of his ever arriving in Cork in a state of arousal, the first adolescent he met would steer him in the direction of relief? In fluent German, of course.

At this remove, what mystifies me is why he spoke German at all. He certainly was not German himself, and if he was a neutral Swede, surely he knew we spoke English. It continues to puzzle me.

All this brings us inevitably, and drearily, to neutrality. Nicholas Monserrat, in his book *The Cruel Sea*, has a description of the *Compass Rose* heading back to the south of England after a rough engagement in the Western Approaches. He talks of sailing past 'the smug Irish coast'. It was a wounding jibe, but quite understandable.

Irish neutrality was inevitable, and also questionable. When more citizens of the Free State were wearing British uniforms abroad than were wearing Irish ones at home, and when anybody from the south of Ireland who wished could work in the munitions factories in England, then the neutrality was technical, if not academic.

Recently, with the fiftieth anniversary of D-Day, latter-day know-alls, in their droves, saw only the shame of our inaction in the face of the Nazi horrors. It is certainly no cause for pride; necessity rarely is. The thing to remember about that time is that it was only sixteen years after our own civil war, and as for going into the war on the side of Britain (not on the side of the Allies — you were going in on the side of Britain against Germany, that was the perception), that proposition was just out of the question. It would have split the nation wide open and caused another civil war that would have made the earlier shemozzle a picnic.

As for emotional neutrality: I remember a lot of pro-German and anti-Jewish feeling. There was one fellow in school who distributed the German Embassy newsletter, which was full of anti-Jewish propaganda. I wouldn't have known what anti-Semitism meant, but I would laugh at the Jews, the same as most others. I can certainly not recall ever being ticked off for looking down on the Hymies. There was a general feeling about, when we were twelve or thirteen, that Hitler was a great man.

At the same time, one read Rockfist Rogan in *The Champion* and bought all the English comics; and of course you had the *Our Boys*, which was filling you full of Irish nationalism. So you praised the German treatment of the Jews as retribution for the Crucifixion, squaring the graphically detailed accounts of the rape of nuns and the murder of priests by the Germans' Japanese allies, with the assertion that the Germans knew nothing about these things You concentrated gleefully on the report that the Japs had marched into Singapore behind a piper playing 'The Boys of Kilmichael'. 'Oh, that's gospel truth, boy', you were assured. And you read the public-school stories of R A H Goodyear and Gunby Hadath, not to mention *The Magnet*. You listened to the sneering nasal drawl of William Joyce on German radio: 'Germany calling, on Bremen, Holland, Hamboorsh and Cologne', as well as devouring *An Nuacht*, read, *as Gaeilge*, by Edward Roderick Dietze. Who remembers him, apart from myself?

The war ended, as far as Cork was concerned, well before VE Day, when the American Liberty ships and the British mine-sweeping flotilla swept up the harbour to fill the Arcadia ballroom with boppers and jazzers and jitterbuggers. Of that whole scene, more anon.

# THREE

Pride in having been born in one place rather than another strikes me as the ultimate silliness, as well as being the seed of all racism. It is a human failing to be overcome, not a virtue to be proclaimed.

Most Cork people would take a divergent view, so let me say here and now that I'm not proud of being a Corkman, nor ashamed either, just grateful.

Anyway, Cork people as a community are largely indifferent to what others think of them. They regard their city as being self-sufficient, more interesting. What happens in the outside world doesn't concern them too much. Their version of this would be that the outside world, bigoted and biased, ignores Cork because of envy.

A man who had been appointed to Fóir Teoranta, a state organisation to help lame-duck industries, and who was himself a native of Cavan, couldn't say enough in praise of Cork after his first visit there on official business. 'Jesus,' he said to me, 'if everyone in Ireland had the same attitude to local produce as Cork people have, we would have no problems. I couldn't buy a Jameson down there. Go into a pub, and I could have a Paddy, and that was it.' The first product proffered was always a local one, and he found that very impressive. That might not be the case today, because factories have closed down and the distilleries have amalgamated; but there was in Cork a tendency to believe that what you have, what you produce, and what your own people do, beats the opposition hands down; it's our own, and what's wrong with that?

This commitment of attitude can be infuriating when you meet a Cork person who has been exiled, unreconstructed, to the rest of the world. In my own case, the irritation springs from the implication that my talent, abilities, success, good fortune, fame and popularity, and any other favours I enjoy, spring solely from my Cork origin. For instance, after a sell-out show, complete with standing ovation (in Ballybofey, let us say, to take the flight of fancy to the limit), I am accosted in the lilting tones of the Lee by a crestfallen John the Baptist, hoarse from crying in the wilderness: 'I told them. I've a pain in my face from telling them how good you are. Because believe me, boy, you are the best. There's no denying that. And mind you now, you did very well, considering. But half your humour went clean over their head.'

'I distinctly heard laughter on several occasions,' I reply, with uncharacteristic, if frosty politeness.

'Granted. Of course, that goes without saying. Like, they got the obvious things. But, come here, for your stuff, you need the Cork background.'

And I think, 'Save me from this. I don't want to listen to this.'

At the same time I know that this guy would lay down his life for me, simply because I am a Corkman, and that possibly the only reason he came to the show is that I am a Corkman, and if it were anyone else's show, he wouldn't be seen dead at it; because no matter how good an artist he might be, he wasn't a Corkman. And it's a thing I'm slightly ashamed of, and secretly glad of.

Cork, possibly to a greater extent than any other town or city in Ireland, leaves its mark on its sons and daughters. Ask the rest of the world.

I cannot ever imagine my early teens in Cork without politics. The politics of my home was one thing, of course, the high-minded, idealistic vision of a Gaelic, free, Catholic Ireland. The reality of the streets was something utterly other. The ringing phrases of Pearse's oration at the grave of O'Donovan Rossa, which I knew by heart from the Brian O'Higgins songbook, were trotted out *ad nauseam* by Fianna Fáil speakers, and even more frequently by their more extreme, dissident, junior offshoots, in *Aiséiri*.

'Splendid and holy causes are served by men who are themselves splendid and holy' is a proposition which on reflection I would dismiss as patently untrue, from the Crusades onwards. But at that time it seemed self-evident that the splendid and holy would rally to causes that were equally splendid and holy; and surely any cause espoused by de Valera, the embodiment of Clarence Mangan's prophecy that 'Spanish ale shall give you hope, my dark Rosaleen', just had to be splendid and holy. Well, maybe. Doubtless up in Dublin, where the elect and exalted prepared the way for the eventual assumption into Heaven of the entire Gaelic nation, the splendid and holy were two a penny, and probably in the fullness of time they would flock to the flag in Cork too.

In the meantime the Cause had to make do with the likes of Gucksie Joyce, who played the cymbals with the Blackpool brass and reed band. Brown-eyed, squat, flat-capped and jovial, he was unquestionably splendid. Holy? Hardly, least of all in his own estimation.

The Blackpool band's rehearsal rooms on the Waterah were in the bed of the valley below the sanctified heights of Redemption Road. Muffled sounds would float up the hill on practice nights; but when the boys emerged from the bandroom into the open air, the sounding brass and booming drums sent the blood surging, and off I would hare, to 'follee the band'. Their signature tune, or the one they always seemed to strike up first, was 'The Liberty Bell', a seductive, sweeping swell of sound, punctuated by a playful 'Rat-ta-ta-ta-ta . . . one, two, three, four . . . ta-ra-ra-ra-ra'.

While I was still at school, there were two general elections — in 1943 and 1944, I think. In the first, de Valera barely scraped home, but within six months he made his famous midnight trip to the Park, got the aged President Hyde to dissolve the Dáil, called a snap election and got his majority.

Douglas Hyde was in a wheelchair by this time. An irreverent classmate of mine, whose father was a British navy officer, had a theory that the President was dead, but had been stuffed, and was manipulated like a puppet by de Valera.

The first election was held in fine summer weather, and provided splendid free entertainment. Public meetings were not just held in public, but by the public. This was the period that really awakened my interest in politics. The full-blooded abuse, the stock heckles, the irrelevant shouts of 'Up the Mollies! Up John Bull!', and the bitter slogans about 1922, and Dirty Dick, and the Seventy-seven, could swing the mood of a meeting from laughter to loathing. An odd flag was burned, an occasional eye blackened.

Splendid and holy me arse! This was election time. I probably only saw the triumphal arrival of de Valera into Cork at election time, twice; yet the effect was such that it seems, still, to have been at least an annual jamboree. Allowing for my fevered youthful imagination, the hyperbole inseparable from all political razzmatazz, I am convinced that the stage-managing of this event owed a lot to the Nuremburg rallies — the build-up was masterly. The whipper-in, cheer-leader and chief rabble-rouser was a man called Seán O'Luasa, who had a speaking voice superbly suited to his task of blaring out with a splendid and holy conviction, that the duty, privilege and calling of all true patriots on this evening was to make the welkin ring for de Valera.

The staging station was Dublin Hill. Here the bands formed up: the Blackpool, the Butterah, the Barrackah, the Greenmount, the Carrigaline Pipe Band. There were one or two fife-and-drum groups as well. The notable exceptions were the Number Two Army Band, which presumably was deemed neutral, and the Cork Volunteer Pipe Band, which would have been hotly hostile, being committed to the republican prisoners.

The final rally took place on a specially erected platform in Patrick Street, and the route from there to Dublin Hill, out through Leitrim Street and Blackpool, was lined with bonfires, set to be lit at the appropriate time. The telegraph poles carried loudspeakers relaying the progress of the march, and supported banners and streamers across the street, paying tribute to the Mighty One at whose feet the city was to prostrate itself. O'Luasa's voice boomed out along the route, between verses of 'Soldiers of the Legion of the Rearguard' sung by Gus Healy.

I recall standing by Blackpool bridge, deeply moved by all this, and reading the slogans that stretched from window to window over Thomas Davis Street: '*Céad míle fáilte, Dev*! Cork welcomes the Chief! Foursquare behind Dev! De Valera for Cork! Cork for Dev!', and other equally inspired, splendid and holy sentiments. One slightly fuddled old woman, vaguely aware that something was astir, popped her head out of her tenement window. The profusion of bunting and pennants must have convinced her that the annual Corpus Christi procession had been re-routed through the sinful streets of Blackpool. She added her own contribution, hanging out the standard custard-and-raspberry-coloured representation of the breast of Our Saviour, bearing the fortuitously sardonic comment on the aforementioned slogans: 'O Sacred Heart of Jesus, I place my trust in Thee.'

Christ rode into Jerusalem in triumph on the back of an ass. Not so Dev into Cork; not even on the back of Gucksie Joyce's donkey. He sat in an open landau and had an equestrian guard of honour. The equestrian portion was formed by the entire delivery team of horses belonging to Sutton's coals (whose managing director, F J Daly, was the Fianna Fáil candidate, and later TD). Of the riders I know nothing. They were a mixed bunch, and managed to stay aboard their mounts, if not exactly astride. They smelt of porter, and didn't look notably splendid or holy.

The parade moved into town, the crowd by now whipped up to something short of fever pitch, but many notches above apathy. The principal speaker, apart from Dev, was Seán McEntee, probably the only rival to James Dillon as a public orator — equally witty, though much less pompous.

In this first election, one candidate, for Fine Gael, was Willie Dwyer — the one and only. He was the black sheep of the illustrious House of Dwyer, the textile and shoe company. He had gone out on his own, started manufacturing, made a deal with Wolsey, and opened the Sunbeam Wolsey factory at Millfield, Blackpool. Sunbeam not only made money for Dwyer, but provided huge employment for the north side, and became in a very short time as integral a part of Cork life, speech and folklore as Shandon steeple. 'The Blackpool girls are fine and tall, up against the Sunbeam wall' became the new verse of an old song.

But no more. It is another heart-scald of this last decade, that the Sunbeam has followed Fords, Dunlops and Haulbowline into the gloom and obscurity that has enveloped the vibrant, cheerful Cork in which I grew up — a city tingling with self-confidence and faith in its future.

Willy Dwyer was anathema to my father's Gaelic mind. He was brash, successful, bibulous and flirtatious, at least by reputation. He was a maverick — a renegade to the Merchant Prince tradition, lavish and libidinous in his recreations, 'a tarry boy', in the local phrase. He had become a wealthy man, and was regularly alleged to have had affairs with lady workers, and others, and put countless lovers in the family way. I imagine he relished his reputation hugely. It brings to mind a Daniel O'Connell meeting: 'Daniel O'Connell,' said the speaker, 'our Liberator, is the father of the Irish nation.' 'Well,' said a heckler, 'he's the father of a hell of a lot of them, anyway.'

Dwyer was unashamedly pro-British, and made anti-Nazi and anti-neutrality speeches from the platform, which caused serious embarrassment for his running-mate, the party leader, W D Cosgrave. However, Willy Cosgrave held his breath, and his seat.

Willy Dwyer got 'flaaed' in local parlance, or 'sustained a disastrous setback', as the Cork Examiner probably put it. But before the second election he put up the money to build a new church in Blackpool — the Church of St Nicholas, better known to this day as 'the fire escape'. He ran as an independent, and headed the poll.

His behaviour appalled his opponents. The victory celebrations included free crubeens and porter at selected pubs, for all and sundry. During the campaign he had distributed free boots to the poor. The Irish Press ran a tut-tutting editorial about his condescension to his less well-off fellows, who didn't give a hoot, took the boots, and got 'langers' on Willie.

McEntee was roped in to do a knife job on Dwyer at the final rally, first time round, and did so magnificently. 'Where did Mr Dwyer hie in 1916?' he asked rhetorically. Then, in reproof, to a non-existent heckler he added, 'No, I didn't say where did he hide, though of course I accept your denial of a charge I never made.' He dwelt on Willie's loyalty to the King, made much play on Willie's Churchillian delivery, and hinted at comparisons between the moral standards of Dwyer and Henry VIII. Then he quoted from Shakespeare's *Henry VIII* (and I have looked up the speech again, as I did fifty years ago, in admiration and glee), Act 3, Scene 2, the end of Wolsey's speech to his servant Cromwell. An emotive harping on the name Cromwell served to reinforce the perception of Dwyer as an arm of the British stranglehold:

> Oh Cromwell, oh Cromwell, had I but served my God
> with half the zeal I served my king,
> He would not in mine age have left me naked to mine
> enemies.

He explained that he was quoting from Cardinal Wolsey's speech in *Henry VIII*, and he suggested that this should instead be given to Cromwell, because, he said, it ought to read:

> Oh Wolsey, oh Wolsey, if you had served your *land* with
> half the zeal with which you served the king,
> He would not in your age have left you naked to your
> enemies.

Whereupon the rabblement, devotees of Shakespeare to a man, and knowing their *Julius Caesar*, hooted and clapped their chopt hands, and threw up their sweaty nightcaps — or at least conceded that the silver-tongued Seán had won that round.

I have never come across an account that did justice to the local elections in Cork at the war's end. I suppose it would have been in 1945 that the students of University College Cork, showing the same contempt for elected leaders that is now regretted widely as a recent phenomenon, nominated one Jeremiah Healy as a candidate for Cork Corporation. Healy was a harmless and decent eccentric, somewhat odorous from casual hygiene and foul-smelling tobacco, which billowed from a crooked pipe as he strode purposefully nowhere in particular, a rust-coloured tweed overcoat flailing in the draught set up by the vigour of his stride. His nickname was

Klondike — God knows why. It's unlikely that he had taken part in the Klondike Gold Rush — at least with any degree of success — and his high forehead, framed by tufted black hair and heavy horn-rimmed specs, diminished any element of the ruggedness of the pioneer.

At a ceremony conducted on the back of a lorry during Rag Week, the students conferred on him the degree of Doctor at Law, and launched his manifesto. He was a one-issue man, possibly vying with Oliver J Flanagan for the title of the first such. Flanagan's platform was Monetary Reform, which he explained later to a puzzled constituent: 'You see, the first time I went up, I canvassed on my bike. This time I have a car. That's monetary reform.'

Healy was less mercenary. He campaigned for Ladies' Public Toilets. It was not an ideal that had sprung from an inner understanding, but one that was foisted on him by the students, who pointed out to him that ladies short-taken in public could 1) use a public-house toilet, which was undesirable from a temperance viewpoint, 2) go to the Ladies in the Savoy cinema, thereby putting an undue onus on Private Enterprise to rectify the shameful negligence of the Municipality, or 3), piss in the street, which was not a serious option. Dr Healy, as he became universally known, ceased to be a joke when he was elected, and he became an effective councillor, to whose memory the first Ladies' Public Toilet in Cork's history stands in tribute, on Lavitt's Quay.

At the next election, as tradition decrees, there was a split, if not a multiple splintering. The lunatic fringe now nominated not only the doctor, whom the ballot paper described as 'Jeremiah Healy, gentleman', but Jerry Bruton, a popular ballad-singer with a wonderful glint in his eye and an extensive repertoire of two ballads. The first was:

> We'll all down the Marina, it's a beautiful place for a hike.
> You can sit on the seat there, and rest your old feet there,
> Or walk to Blackrock if you like.
> We'll all go down the Marina, where we'll meet many
> friends that we know.

> There's no need for fuss, over missing the bus,
> Because down the Marina we'll go.

He sang this at the GAA matches down at the Park, and drank his porter contentedly with the takings. Untroubled by public affairs for years, in a burst of inspiration he produced a new song when Shannon Airport was a fledgling, and still known as Rineanna, the local name for the site. It was pronounced 'Rine-anna', but Jerry took poetic licence in his piece:

> All aboard, we're off to Rinny-anna,
> All aboard for the dear old Emerald Isle.
> I'll introduce you to your Auntie Hannah
> And she'll greet you with a great big Irish smile.

Irving Berlin must have heaved a sigh of relief when the lust for power lured his Irish rival into the wasp's nest of politics. Jerry was more traditional than Dr Healy, in that he had a policy; although he had no policy until he opened his mouth. He delivered a memorable homily on public housing to a fairly uncomprehending assembly of American servicemen, British minesweeper personnel, and sailors from the Liberty ships, all of whom roamed the streets in pursuit of sinful occasions, and wound up as the spectators of democracy in action.

After a blast of 'Down the Marina' Jerry attacked Philip Monahan, the city manager, who hailed from Dundalk, but since he was from north of Mallow, qualified in Jerry's mind as a Dublinman. 'Pill Moynihan', he roared in his hoarse, ballad-singer's voice, 'is supposed to be doing a great job with housing. *Sibbosed* to be. Importing Japanese cement. Japanese cement for Irish houses. Don't he know they're at war? Of course, he's a Dubliner. He knows more than us. Do he think they'll send quality stuff to build houses for the poor people of Cork? They will, John! They're sending over shit. Why can't they use quarry limestone and sandstone from Cork? Look at Shandon steeple. Half limestone, half sandstone — it never fell on top of nobody yet! But Pill Moynihan goes around blowing his own trumpet, like *Little Boy Blue come blow your horn.* Well, I make no false promises. I won't be blowing me horn. I can't — I haven't had a horn for twenty-five years.'

'All aboard. we're off to Rinny-anna. . .'

# FOUR

The teachers who influenced me most — or at least, to whom I liked to listen — were Brother Byrne, Dan Moore and 'Gutty' Callinan, who of course would have appeared on the school prospectus, if there was one, as An Bráthair H S O'Broin, Dónall Ó Mordha and Pádraig Ó Callanáin.

Callinan was a dour-faced, scowling, growling presence, who could impart more knowledge about English or Irish in an hour than many more sunnily-disposed mentors in a whole term.

Dan Moore was mild-mannered and literary, sarcastic but not hurtfully so, and liked to digress from the subject from time to time.

An Bráthair O'Broin was nicknamed H2S O'Broin, because he taught Chemistry as well as English, Irish, Latin, History and Geography, not to mention Singing, Christian Doctrine, and sundry other subjects as required. He also produced the school plays. Brother Byrne was a splendid teacher. His Irish was good, although it was spoken with a slightly suburban Dublin *blas*. For instance, he would call me 'Thobeen'. He had a violent temper, and would pick on somebody and belt them unjustly, which was not untypical of the Order, but it would evaporate, and I doubt if it ever did anybody any real harm.

Brother Byrne had a keen mind, and a wide range of interests, and it was very easy to get him off the subject. You would ask him a question, and he would say, 'I know exactly what you're at, boy, you're bored with the subject under discussion, but I will answer it, in the faint hope that you may understand *that* part of what I say, even if it's totally irrelevant to what we should be doing here.' And he would willingly go off at a tangent, and maybe enthral the whole class for half an hour; and in that way he pointed you to areas of literature that were not on the syllabus, and he did it accidentally, but 'with malice aforethought', if you like.

He also used to go into long rambling discussions about religion, and he would talk about the Trinity, and the reality of the True Presence of the Body and Blood of Our Lord Jesus Christ in the Blessed Sacrament. 'You know, I have a friend who is a Protestant, a very devout lady, and we were discussing this, and she said, "And you really believe that the body of Christ is verily in the Eucharist? How awful!" And I said "I do." And of course she meant "awful" in the sense of awe-inspiring. And she said, "You know, if I could believe that, I could never stray from the path of virtue." ' The Protestant lady used to figure very prominently, and you could always toss in a question that would inspire a reference to the Protestant lady, with whom he had long walks; and everybody wondered if he was having an affair with her, or, as it was put, 'Would you say Bert is flaain' the Protestant lady?' He was a wonderful teacher of Catholic gurriers, whatever about Protestant ladies.

I did a play in the Damer Hall, Gael-Linn's theatre on Stephen's Green, in the sixties, a good play by Seán O'Driscoll called *Tycoon*, in which I was playing a businessman who seduces his secretary, and it contained what was for the time, and for the Damer Hall, a fairly torrid love scene. One night I was told there was somebody to see me, and I went out to meet him. It was Brother Byrne, by now aged, white, frail, but those humorous blue eyes were dancing with amusement. He told all and sundry that he was responsible for my first appearance on the stage, which indeed he was, as the Bloody Child in the school version of *Macbeth*, which he had produced. And he recounted how I had cried at the dress rehearsal because I hadn't had my tea and was starving. 'You've come a long way since then. There were things on that stage tonight that you certainly didn't learn from me, or anyone else in the North Monastery.' And he chuckled, 'But you learned it very well, wherever you learned it!'

I don't mean this as a slight on the Christian Brothers in general, because I have a very high regard for them, with all their faults, but he was an extremely cultured person, in a sense that most of them were not. For instance, his interest in hurling, and all that sort of stuff, would have been minimal. He would welcome the school's winning the Harty Cup, but he would hardly shed a tear if they didn't. It was far more important that you should do your Latin verbs, or that you should appreciate the implicit barb in his little joke that the Gaelic for 'Ciceronianism' was 'Athair-peadarachas'. He loved to quote this, because Munster Irish speakers made a religion of the prose style of An tAthair Peadar O'Laoghaire, author of *Séadna*, regarded as a classic Irish novel, for reasons which have remained obscure to me.

Of all school subjects, Mathematics, in all its torturing manifestations, was of no interest to me — a complete blank. A very long-suffering and kindly man called Seán Moore, known as Pal, a brother of Dan, who was a brilliant mathematician and science teacher, told me very early in the science class, 'Look, you're only wasting your own time and mine. If you ever propose to listen to what I'm saying, that's fine, but if you don't, I'm not going to worry. There are too many other people here to be looked after.' And that was a gentleman's agreement.

To this day I know nothing about physics, except that metals expand faster than glass, so that if the metal cap on the marmalade jar is stuck, and you heat it with a lighted match, or in hot water, then you can remove it, because of the inevitable operation of the above law of physics.

So, in effect because of Brother Byrne, I gravitated towards the theatre. He produced a lot of plays, and the star of most was Eddie Golden, who was a teacher in the school and with whom I later worked when he joined the Abbey company. It was a source of great amusement to myself and Eddie that he would recall 'I taught you, you little shit'. He taught me at a time when two classes would share a room, which could lead to a bit of strain between teachers.

There was one teacher who was generally thought to have influenced lads to join the IRA, or embrace that way of thinking. He took to teaching songs like 'Oró, Sé do Bheatha Abhaile', anthems of 1916, and so forth, even though he was not a singing teacher and couldn't sing for nuts, and this was not part of the syllabus. His class and Eddie Golden's class were in the same room, and Golden got fed up with the singing. The Christian Brothers' magazine, *Our Boys*, used to produce a supplement called *An Gael Óg*, which carried translations of popular songs of the day. 'Deep in the Heart of Texas' was the song one week, at the height of a singularly virulent outbreak of fervour on the part of the other teacher. Eddie produced *Our Boys*, and distributed it, and said, 'Now.' And he led his class singing 'Deep in the Heart of Texas' *(Anseo i gCeartlár Texas)* non-stop for the entire morning. So that put an end to 'Oró, Sé do Bheatha Abhaile' for quite a while.

Eddie had a very engaging way of getting your attention. Teaching history, he startled all by coming into class announcing, 'Henry VIII was a bastard. Queen Elizabeth was a bastard. Mary Tudor was a bastard. In fact the whole Tudor dynasty was a litter of bastards.' And of course everybody listened.

His knowledge of Latin was, I'd say, only a couple of pages ahead of our own, but he made it very interesting. In his way he was memorable, but he hated the school. When I met him later, after he had quit and become an actor, he had been with Mícheál MacLiammóir and Hilton Edwards on tour to America. He loved playing intellectual games and making fun during rehearsals. He was very different from his brother Geoff, who was a great companion in other ways. Anyway, Eddie was the link between school and manhood. He was also part of the phenomenon known as 'The Loft', a miniature theatre founded by the famous Father O'Flynn, who was a great friend of our family, but with whom I had nothing to do in the theatrical sense, nor, on reflection, would I have wanted to.

Father O'Flynn was a Shakespearian scholar, by common consent. How seriously that claim can be taken, I don't know. Remembering that I left Cork at seventeen and a half and I would have spoken to the man five or six times, and that would have been in our own house, when he would have been talking to my father about Irish poetry, or *sean-nós* singing, because they had a common interest in folk music. Father O'Flynn was very colourful. He was extremely popular and seemed to have his finger on the pulse of the plain people of the North Parish. Like his namesake in the song, he went in for rough-and-ready social work, 'soothing the crazy ones, coaxing the aisy ones, lifting the lazy ones, on with the stick.' He went and pulled drunks out of pubs, and so forth.

But an acquaintance of mine almost exploded one night at a party when somebody was eulogising Father O'Flynn. 'That bastard,' he said, 'my father worked hard all his life, and on a Sunday he used to go down and have two pints before his dinner. And that was almost the only drink he ever took, on a Sunday morning. And Father O'Flynn walked into the pub and threw him out. "Get home to your wife and children, you drunkard," he said. And then of course he got into his car and drove off to the family mansion, to his big sirloin steak.'

The family had a chain of butchers' shops, and so there was 'old money' there. But for all that Father O'Flynn was a mighty effective preacher, and he really was a very humorous man. He was also quite a good stage comedian, though to some extent his effect must have owed something to his collar.

The Loft was about three doors away from where the Firkin Crane Gallery is now, near the old Butter Exchange, which is now a kind of museum. The Loft was over Tommy Linehan's sweet factory. It was the home of the Cork Shakespearian Society. Aloys Fleischmann was the cathedral choirmaster, and was almost a caricature. In the early forties there was a Hungarian actor with big jowls, S Z Zakall, known as 'Cuddles', a wonderful old comic character. Aloys Fleischmann was very like him. He was known as 'Bert' to the choirboys, or sometimes 'Bertozzi'. He wore a round celluloid collar which gleamed, and a thin black string tie or bow. His clerical grey suit had a double-breasted waistcoat with pearl buttons on it, and he had a pince-nez which he stuck in the top pocket when he wasn't using it, and he was balding. He never went fully bald, but kept strands of thin hair which were always flying away. He was round-faced, very pale, and he puckered up his eyes to read the music.

He had a bouncy way of walking. He was a very distinctive public figure; you could spot him a mile off. He also wore fawn-coloured spats, winter or summer. This completed his uniform. I never saw him wear anything else. He would be there, enthusing to a bunch of unruly ragamuffins, which most of the choir were, not excluding myself. Most of the kids in the choir were from families in the immediate vicinity of the cathedral.

The music was entrancing. These days I regret, when I go to the Easter ceremonies, that you don't get the Victoria and Palestrina Masses, and the Passion and all that. I can still sing, under provocation, '*Nonn morior, non morior, sed vivam et narrabo opera domini*' or '*Si hunc dimittis non es amicus Caesari*'. It was drummed into me, and it was so dramatic, so stirring, because you had sopranos and altos and tenors and bassi; you had 'the angels', as he called them, the women's choir, which couldn't fit into the space around the organ, in the choir stalls, but sang in the small gallery on the far side of the church. And he would flick his cupped hand up over the top of the partition, to bring their voices in. It was wonderful stuff.

He was also very charitable — he gave away a lot of money, and I know that he helped out people in the choir. To my own knowledge there were a few lads whose fathers weren't working, or were in England, whom he also helped.

His rages were legendary. He became completely apoplectic and unintelligible, and he became more and more German as he went on. He also used to mix up consonants, and say 'poy' instead of 'boy' when he got annoyed. He would hit a note on the harmonium, and somebody whose voice was breaking would let out a squawk. 'Oh, a hen could sing better than you, Sir! Get out! Get out, your voice is breaking.' One of his famous remarks was, when he heard a hoarse boy, 'Since when in the choir we have a crow?'

He was a much-loved figure, but not by Father O'Flynn. Father O'Flynn's style of singing Gregorian chant, or opening up the Credo, was a little unorthodox. It was more *sean-nós* than plain chant, and Fleischmann would be there at the organ, throwing his eyes up to Heaven, and waiting for this caterwauling to stop.

Before the Mass, he would look out through the choir stall grille, to identify the celebrants. He would say, 'When Father Fulham is singing the Mass, we will take the note from Father Fulham. When Father O'Flynn is singing the Mass, we will take the note from the organ.' This was a regular thing, and it was accepted — not by Father O'Flynn, of course. I enjoyed being in the choir immensely. I loved the old-fashioned church music. Apart from any religious content or motivation at all, just to listen to it gives me a tremendous feeling of calm and peace; and the sung Masses, the full High Masses, were so operatic, so dramatic. And the Holy Week stuff, done with all the stops out, is scintillating theatre, whatever else. No wonder the churches were full.

# FIVE

In 1946 I got eighty-eighth place in Ireland in the Civil Service clerical officers' exam, and I was called, and shortly after Christmas I headed off. I started work in January 1947, and was obviously fated not to be a civil servant.

I did my medical exam and all that stuff, and I was handed a 'thing' by the man in Upper O'Connell Street, and I was told to go to the Department of Supplies in Kildare Street and report to a man called Barrett. I went to Mr Barrett's room, where maybe ten or twelve people were working at various desks. Mr Barrett looked up — I suppose he was a man in his mid-thirties — and he said, 'Who are you?' And I told him. 'Jesus,' he said, 'I'm not due any staff here. I never heard of you. If you want to sit down, sit down, but there's no work here for you.' And he looked around, and he said, 'Anybody know we're getting an extra fella? No, no, no, you'd better go back up to Establishment.' So I went back to Establishment, and they said, 'Well, hang on.' Then they told me to come back after lunch. So I came back after lunch and I was sent to a man called Mr O'Reilly, and I handed in this docket of identification and appointment, and his first and only comment was, 'That whoor Connors.' And he shook his head, and put the thing away. 'Okay boy, sit down over there.' And I sat down, and I started working. 'That whoor Connors' had launched me on my brief career in the public service.

What we did in that section was to issue food licences for the export of parcels to our exiled brothers and sisters in England, because they were still very severely rationed over there — the war was only over about a year and a half. The food situation in England was appalling and there was a big influx of tourists who came here simply to eat steak and go back again. Red meat, bacon and eggs were plentiful, tea was no longer rationed, though butter was still pretty scarce, for some strange reason. I was certainly not there for more than a few months when I was transferred to the Census of Population section.

The 1946 census returns were being tabulated and coded. This would have been the first time that anything approaching computerisation had been done in an Irish Civil Service office. You had a ledger with all these folios and census forms, and you coded each answer in pen. This went on to a punch operator, who transferred the codes onto a card into the form of punched holes, and these cards could be fed into a machine which sorted them according to whatever data was wanted.

There was only one sorting machine, at which people used to queue up with their cards. Powers Samas was the firm that manufactured this machine, which had a minder called Bill Hughes, who was so English most people didn't know what he was talking about half the time. He would stand by, and if anything went wrong he would dismantle this machine. What most often went wrong was that it overheated and the lubricating oil burned, and the stink of this stuff was enough to empty the office. Some of us discovered how to make it overheat, by pressing too long on the pedal, and everybody went out to the pub while Hughes was repairing the machine. That of course was a very early version of computerisation. I knew very little about it, and had very little interest in it, because at this stage I had joined the Keating Branch of the Gaelic League in Parnell Square, which had a busy Drama Society.

Any description of my brief but heroic public service must have a mention of two people who provided me with inspiration and merriment. One was a man called Vaughan Dempsey, who spoke with a very distinct Australian accent. He had been recruited into the Irish Civil Service many years before, when he had worked for Seán T O'Kelly in Paris, at the time when they were lobbying the League of Nations, or the Peace Conference. He had been seconded to the staff of the legation in Paris, and subsequently came to Ireland, and was now head of the Aliens section in the Industry Ministry, and near or over retirement age when I was transferred to that section.

He was a law unto himself, in that he came into the office when it suited him, and left when it suited him. I'm not suggesting he didn't work. He did indeed; he worked very hard, but he could arrive in at eleven o'clock and leave at seven in the evening, if it suited him, and the following day he might arrive in at eight in the morning, and leave at four. And because of his history, it was accepted that, well, he was different. He was very pleasant. He would sometimes call me over to his desk to discuss something, and would launch into a long reminiscence about Paris or Australia, or whatever. He had a low opinion of politicians, quoting always a French proverb, *Il faut soigner sa réputation mieux que sa conduite,* which, loosely translated, means 'One's reputation is more important than one's behaviour'. (That's about the only bit of French I ever really heard during my entire time in the Civil Service.) His main preoccupation was growing apples, some of which he would bring into the office, and I became quite an expert on Cox's Orange Pippins and other varieties. He was a lovely fellow — not unduly worried about anything in life.

This was a very pleasant sojourn, but it only lasted about six months. It wasn't that I disgraced myself, it was just a matter of routine shifting around, and I found myself sent across to the other side of St Stephen's Green, to the Department of External Affairs. I spent my first few months in the Accounts section, inevitably, because, be it Sod's Law or Murphy's Law, the Civil Service invariably stuck people like me, who couldn't count up to ten, into positions where numeracy was essential. I managed to avoid major disasters, but after six months, because of my knowledge of Irish, I was shifted to the Cultural Relations division.

This division served the needs and the dictates of the Cultural Relations Committee, the brainchild of Seán MacBride, Minister for External Affairs. MacBride gets a bad press these days, and didn't get much better then. His attempts to broaden the cultural horizon were derided. At election meetings he was subjected to such witticisms as 'Go back to Paris' or 'Speak English'. External Affairs was a tiny department up to MacBride's time. One felt it was really not much more than the downtown branch of de Valera's personal library. It began to expand quite rapidly, until, by 1952 or so, it was as frantically busy as Ringsend Public Library.

Maurice Curtin, who worked with me there, was the second man I have to mention. He had been recruited into the Civil Service as a temporary clerk in the London Embassy, although the reason he was in London was that he had been dismissed from his job as a teacher back in Ireland during the 1930s because he was a member of *Saor Éire*, 'the Red IRA', as it was called. He had been trained as a teacher in a state college, and because he did not spend the requisite number of years teaching, the Government decided that it had the right, if he ever went into another Government appointment, of recouping themselves for his training expenses by taking money off his salary every week. While he was a temporary clerk, it didn't occur to him, or it didn't occur to them in the Embassy; but when he was transferred back to Dublin they started to help themselves to their reimbursements. He was now a married man with four children. He suffered this, though not exactly in silence.

He ran the photographic section, and he did a lot of work which was above and beyond the call of duty. He arranged exhibitions of photographs and paintings and architectural drawings, and God knows what else, and these exhibitions were sent to far-flung places to advertise the cultural advancement of the Irish people. In putting these together he would make contacts with people outside in a totally non-Civil Service kind of way. He managed to get things moving and cut through a lot of bureaucracy. He became indispensable.

In due time he made a submission in which he contended that he should for years have been on some special allowance for work beyond his rank, and indeed outside the normal run of clerical activities. Through some freakish collapse of bureaucratic obduracy, the Department of Finance agreed to his submission. It was also ruled that back money for two or three years should be paid, so there was quite a handsome lump sum involved. And when this arrived in due course, Maurice went down to the pub with myself and a few others, and we had several pints. Then he said, 'Well lads, I'll be seeing ye some time. I'm off to Canada tomorrow.' And he sailed west to Canada and never came back. I met him in Toronto subsequently, although he spent most of his years teaching on an Indian reservation on Prince Edward Island. The good guys win, sometimes.

Seán MacBride was supposed to have been of a very aristocratic demeanour, but in the department he was hail-fellow-well-met with everybody. He would remember the name of anybody he came in contact with. This Cultural Relations office was a great favourite of his, it was his baby, his brainchild, and he would look in from time to time, unannounced, to see how things were coming along. He had a very distinctive Parisian accent (at least, I'm assured it was Parisian; it was French, anyway, so far as I could make out), and I used to impersonate him — everybody impersonated him. Just for a laugh, you would read out memos in the minister's accent. Seán Gaynor, who had a career later on as ambassador, was then a third secretary. His was the room across the corridor from ours, and occasionally he would pop in and almost automatically do his 'Seán MacBride' bit, and you became used to this. One Saturday morning I was up on a ladder filing away photographs, with my back to the door, when it opened, and I heard footsteps coming in, and the voice said, 'Niall, I wonder if it would be possible to . . .', and before he'd finished, I said, 'Seán, will you fuck off, I'm very busy, I'll see you later.' And I turned to see Seán MacBride leaving the room, accompanied by an American journalist. There was never a word about it. The minister did come back later on. He didn't say, 'Why did you tell me to fuck off?' He never batted an eyelid.

This reminds me of an incident involving another minister, the redoubtable James Dillon.

A friend of mine called O'Riordan, who was working in the Department of Agriculture at the time of Dillon's appointment in the first inter-party Government, was having romantic problems. It happened that he'd made a date with some girl in the office and had stood her up. Next morning when she met him, signing the

Attendance Book, she said, 'You are a hound, a dirty dog.' By way of humorous placation he got down on all fours and began barking, just as the regal figure of James Dillon strolled across the lobby. Dillon glanced at this tableau and sailed on. About two years later, O'Riordan was acting private secretary to Dillon, when Deputy Tom Walsh, a former Minister for Agriculture, was savaging Dillon in the Dáil for the deterioration in the performance of the Department of Agriculture. 'May I point out,' roared Dillon, 'that when I took over my department, some of the staff were going around on all fours, barking' — to the total mystification of everybody but his own acting private secretary.

Now during my time in the Accounts section, before I went to the happy paradise of the photographic section, I was in charge of the accounts for the Irish legation in a country which like Ireland had been neutral in wartime. The Minister Plenipotentiary in this country, like my friend of the appleyards, was a man who had entered the Irish Civil Service by non-Civil Service means. He was a count of the Austrian Empire. I don't know where he was born, but he spoke very 'university' English, and he had a white beard and was quite distinguished-looking. I think he was appointed during the war because of his good international connections. He certainly had Austrian, Portuguese, Italian, and presumably British connections, because he had been educated in England. So generally he would have been a useful man to have around. He would have been Irish, of course, broadly speaking, but it would have been 'way back' Irish.

Whenever I was bored, I would open the Public Works file on the count's legation, because he kept up a war with the Office of Public Works about the state of the legation premises, which he said reflected very poorly on our international status. Some of the letters I remember vividly. In one, he complained bitterly:

We don't have any decent chairs in the legation premises. I had occasion to invite the Norwegian chargé d'affaires for drinks the other evening. I can't possibly invite him and his wife to dinner, because we don't have a proper dinner service. (Incidentally, when is this dinner service, promised from eternal years, being delivered?) We don't have the facilities for offering them a full dinner, but they graciously agreed to come for drinks. I ushered them into the lobby. (I must explain that the chargé d'affaires is a rather portly man, probably because he can afford a proper dinner service, and eats better than we do.) In a welcoming mood, I waved him into one of the rather poor chairs that we have, and the chair collapsed beneath his weight. It took an awful lot of very good wine and brandy to assuage his feelings and convince him that this was not an overt act of war on the part of Ireland against the Norwegian people. Can you please extricate me from this kind of embarrassment? It would only take: 1) a decent table cloth, 2) the dinner service requisitioned as of sometime near The Flood, 3) new curtains for the legation windows.

In another letter he also referred to new curtains:

We still haven't received the new curtains, so I have had to remove the curtains from one of the bedrooms and place them in the bathroom. Because of the design of this house, for which I accept no responsibility whatsoever, the bathroom is situated at garden level, and it has come to my attention, in fact, it has become quite notorious, that the milkmaid, and other persons who cross the lawn in the early hours about their lawful occasions, are afforded an uninterrupted view of my alabaster limbs as I rise from my morning foam. I have no personal objection to affording them such pleasure as this may occasion, but in these circumstances diplomatic immunity is a sparse cover . . .

He would go on in this vein for ever, about any subject. They were wonderful letters. I don't think I'm in breach of the Official Secrets Act, because it's well over thirty years ago.

The count had to handle an enquiry once into why Irish seed potatoes, which had been exported to his host country in huge quantities, were suddenly unpopular, and were no longer wanted. He discovered that other seed potatoes, from Cyprus or Morocco or somewhere, were being allowed in because the price was cheaper. 'How did they know how to undercut?' A question to be answered. And it turned out to be because of a piece of espionage by an official of lowly status, whom we shall call 'Benito', who had had a look at one of the files on behalf of the Arabs or somebody, and given them the lowdown on the price situation. This was a major espionage scandal; on the file it was, anyway. I think poor old Benito was fired, or at least fined a week's wages — I don't remember which. But at the time, to read this was pure Heaven. The count was the ideal man to describe this kind of thing, because he obviously didn't give two hoots about the price of seed potatoes, anywhere, at any time. His reports were rare and unexpected delights; treasure trove, really.

It was up to me to formulate the replies to some of these letters, but to my shame they conformed to the regulations. I could hardly match the mood of his pieces, since the replies would have to be signed by some senior officer. But I used to read these letters out occasionally during coffee break, and they were very well received by all and sundry.

It must be said that all this time I was acting in amateur plays with Compántas Amharclainne na Gaeilge, a bilingual theatre company which used to do shows in the Olympia, and with anyone else I could find, because I was now determined to become an actor. The way things cross and intertwine is very strange. I auditioned for the Radio Éireann Players, and my boss at this time in External Affairs was Brian Durnin, who himself had been one of the original Radio Éireann announcers — a famous name, a very fine man, wonderful voice, lovely delivery, a bit self-important, but a really nice guy. And he looked after me in that job, because now and again he would say, 'Come on, why do you drink pints? Could you not have two half pints at lunch, instead of four pints?' A gentle soul, and no way would a bad report ever go up about you. You'd be ticked off gently like that.

He was my boss when I did that audition and got my place in the Rep. The establishment officer in Radio Éireann rang Durnin and said,

'We're taking one of your fellas away. He's got a job in the Rep.' So Brian sent for me, and said very solemnly, 'Well, it was bound to happen. You can't stay here. You'll have to go. And I can't see that anybody is going to be too sorry. You're going down to the GPO on transfer.' 'What section?' I said. He said, 'The Radio Éireann Repertory Company. You've got the job. Congratulations.' And we went out and had a few jars. Let's be honest, he had cause to celebrate also. This was July 1953.

I wasn't going to be appointed for about four weeks, and I had to work out that four weeks, and of course what I did, with that gratitude for which all young people are noted, was to lock all the files that I had on my desk, or in the drawers, into a press, and throw the key up onto the top of the press, and that was that. I read the paper for three weeks. I met Durnin about three months afterwards, in the Tower Bar in Henry Street, the watering hole of Radio Éireann at that time, and I said, 'Hello Brian', and he said, 'Hello Niall, how are you?', and I said, 'I'm fine, and how are you?', and he said, 'I'm OK, now that we've found the key of the press.' That was the only comment he ever made.

# SIX

I had joined the Keating Branch of the Gaelic League, in Parnell Square, mainly because a cousin of mine, Mícheál Ó Murchú, a trainee teacher, was a member of it, and it was somewhere to go when you had very little money, and I hadn't really started drinking seriously. So it was as good a way of passing the time as anything else. They had drama classes, and they used to do the odd *Feis* play, and I became very interested.

One of the members was Neasa Ní Annracháin, whose folks were family friends, because her father and mine had been in the Gaelic League together as travelling teachers. Her brother, Kieron Moore, had just hit the headlines as a big international star. You had Mícheál MacLiammóir at the height of his powers, Cyril Cusack, Seán McClory, who had been in the Abbey Theatre and was from Galway, a Gaelic speaker. He had got a big contract in Hollywood, and Siobhán McKenna was coming into prominence. That meant that anybody who was making headlines in the theatre in Ireland either spoke Irish or even performed in Irish, or was very much for the Gaelic language.

Cyril certainly was, and remained so. He would always speak Irish to me, as an opener — he would practise the *Gaeilge* before he lapsed into the *Béarla*, so that it seemed to me that there was some affinity between the ability to speak Irish fluently, and the ability to act. Remember that I was only seventeen.

I met Tomás MacAnna, who had been appointed assistant director at the Abbey (he was about twenty-three, very young anyway). He was preparing for the Abbey pantomime and asked me if I would be interested in trying to write some scripts. I wrote some and he liked them. Why he approached me, I forget. I certainly wasn't standing at the base of Nelson's Pillar with a placard round my neck saying 'Gaelic scripts for sale'.

Anyway, we became good friends, and I got a part in the panto. Then I auditioned for the Abbey School of Acting, and I was rejected. I was flabbergasted. I thought my genius would have been obvious to all, even without an audition. It was a Board consisting of Ernest Blythe, Tomás MacAnna and Ria Mooney. I think Ernest Blythe just decided that I was a young pup — an arrogant little twerp, and possibly thought that on general principle I should be rejected first time anyway, which is not a bad principle, though I would not have agreed with that at the time.

I was rejected, and at the panto party I had started to take a few jars, and I got very drunk after probably three whiskies, and I told Blythe that he was an old ballocks. That blighted my prospects in the Abbey for quite a few years, I can tell you. He was not a man who forgot these things very easily, although later on I got on very well with him, and though this sounds ridiculous, I had a few very good laughs with Ernest Blythe. There are not many people who would make that claim and expect to be believed.

For instance, there was a story that was common about Blythe. Ria Mooney, who was into spiritualism, was preparing a production of *The Dreaming of the Bones* by W B Yeats, and she wanted an elaborate set, which would have cost half the annual grant to construct.

Blythe was horrified, and said, 'Out of the question, no, no, no.'

Ria said, 'Well, I can't go on with the production, because Willie told me that's the set he wants.'

'Willie?'

'Yeats! He spoke to me last night.' (He was dead at this time of course.) 'He said that it was essential to the production.'

And Blythe said, 'Well, I don't doubt what you say, Miss Mooney, but you are overlooking one important factor. Yeats was a lousy producer.'

Many years later, after some show in the theatre, I was invited to meet the President after the show, and Ernest Blythe, who was then retired, came in. He was in a jovial mood. He was drinking whiskey as well, which was a very different picture of him from the one I would have remembered. I asked him if he could confirm the Ria story. He made me tell the story in full, and he laughed, and then said, 'It's not true, but since it portrays me in a humorous light, I don't mind you putting it about.'

In the sixties I returned to the Abbey panto, which was the story of Setanta, in which the young Donal McCann, in a sort of saffron frilly kilt, played Setanta. This was at the time that MacLiammóir was doing his *Importance of Being Oscar*. I was playing Culann, the owner of the dog that Setanta slew. There was a scene in which Cúchulainn was revealed on a plinth in the classic pose, holding up his hurley, and wearing this kilt-like thing that resembled a mini-skirt. One night I was standing quite near the plinth, so I ran my hand up McCann's leg, and said '*Fáilte romhat, Bosie*' in my MacLiammóir accent, because I was playing Culann as a take-off of Mícheál in *Oscar*.

This gag was very successful, so we decided to keep it in. Then Blythe sent for me one day and he asked me, '*Cé hé Bosie?*' (Who is Bosie?) I explained that it was a reference to the *Oscar* performance, which he had not seen, and that it was a homosexual term of endearment. He laughed heartily and said, 'Cut it.' But it stayed in, despite what he wanted, because he had more or less given up attending every night, though at one time he did attend every night and heard every word.

The politics of the Abbey is something I wouldn't even dream of entering into. But I like the story of Blythe finally resigning from the Board. On his last day as chairman, a photographer came from the *Irish Press* to take his photograph before the meeting. In the lobby, the photographer said, 'I understand this is your last Board meeting.'

'Yes,' Blythe answered, 'can we get on with this. I'm busy.'

The photographer said, 'Well, my idea is, I'll be standing out on the street, and as you open the door, I'll photograph you coming out.'

Blythe thought for a minute and then said, 'I have a much better idea. You stand in the lobby, and you can photograph me coming in.'

And that was the picture, in every sense, because a couple of years later he was still on the Board. Maybe not the chairman of the Board, but he was still running the place.

The Compántas theatre company, which flourished in the forties and fifties, was founded by a group which included Liam O'Ceallaigh, who was married to Caitlín Ní Chatháin, a fine actress from Dingle. Liam was a very unexpected sort of talent, because he was the most Dublin person you ever met in your life, but he had superb Irish. He was a senior civil servant, and looked the quintessential senior civil servant. Yet he produced the most hilarious sketches, and did so consistently.

Most of these were written for Seamus Kavanagh, a truly gifted comedian, with a round, seemingly luminous face, a forehead which stretched to the back of his neck, a growling, glorious Dublin voice, coated to the resonance of mahogany by long years of John Jameson Ten, and full strength, unfiltered Sweet Afton. He suffered heroic hangovers, and it was during the curing process that he was at his most hilarious.

Kavanagh had a big influence on me. He was the first true-blue Dub — a genuine inner city man, from way back — that I'd met, who spoke racy, fluent, impeccable Irish, having spent a lot of his younger leisure days on Inishmore.

His facial expression on stage scarcely changed at all, but the eyes registered incomprehension, or resignation, to huge effect. He taught in Whitefriars Street school, and was still a teacher when I met him. Like many a gifted performer, he was a 'semi-pro', which was a term of abuse by which professionals described those they regarded, usually quite rightly, as taking work from those dependent on acting. In the case of Gaelic-speaking semi-pros, this attitude was only partly justified. There was a demand, especially in radio, for actors in 'the first language', so called; and there weren't many of them who would be full-time pros.

Kavanagh was a strong Union man by conviction. He told with great relish of a film in which he had to drive a car, with John Mills as passenger. After a hair-raising hurtle downhill, Seamus emerged, shaken, but relieved to have gotten the shot over, seeing as he was in his usual delicate state of health before the first administration of Jameson.

'Going again,' called the first assistant, 'back the car up please.'

'Let the stunt man back it up,' said Seamus, the sweat seeping from his every pore. And the stuntman, or props, or someone, backed up the car.

'I must say, I admire your professional attitude,' said John Mills, 'lots of our chaps wouldn't dare take a stand like that. You're absolutely right.'

'Little did he know that I couldn't drive a bloody nail, never mind a Morris Cowley. We freewheeled down, but reversing up was way beyond me.'

Pro or semi-pro, he was a great comedian. He opened my eyes to a whole area of Dublin that I would not have been familiar with. He was a loving chronicler of the Dublin working class, his fund of local lore enriched even more by long years of teaching in the boys' school. He loved to play with words, off the cuff. I remember him laughing hysterically once at somebody's description of the distressful consequences of a sexual encounter. Not only did the victim have the problem that infection set in, but detumescence did not occur for some days, or so the victim said. 'I see,' said Kavanagh, 'bloody painful. Festering home with your thong in the air.'

His drinking was legendary. Once he was a delegate to the European Broadcasting Union conference held in Dublin, and due to present himself at the Royal Marine Hotel in Dún Laoghaire at the unearthly hour of 10.30 a.m. The monstrous effects of the previous evening's reception craved a restorative ball o' malt, not a dry seminar on the allocation of wavelengths.

As he entered the stately vestibule, things brightened. A waiter threaded his way through to him, a tray of clinking glasses held aloft.

'Drink, Sir?'

Seamus nodded assent with due dignity, and helped himself to a largish Jameson. He was soon in animated chat with Sir Ivone

Kirkpatrick of ITV, and things were passing off very civil indeed. The conference was taking on a decidedly jolly aspect when another dinner-jacketed figure approached.

'Are you gentlemen with the bride's party or the groom's?' he asked.

'Both, if necessary, I presume,' replied Kavanagh.

But the pair of delegates headed for the conference hall, considerably lighter of heart.

In those days even reasonably-well-paid people found it hard from time to time to scrape up the entrance fee for the first drink of the day. Money had a knack of going underground, and had to be coaxed back into circulation, and only responded to complex conventions and ritualistic negotiation. A cheque of dubious provenance, and even less promising future, would appear as out of thin air on the bar counter of Madigan's of Earl Street, or the Tower Bar in Henry Street, or Jerry Dwyer's of Moore Street. The manager or foreman would approach this intrusion on the polished marble, or smoke-stained mahogany, with cautious curiosity. The presenter would ignore its presence entirely. When the man in charge finally picked it up, he held it to the light, offering it up with all his other misfortunes.

'Is this all right?' he asks.

'It will be,' comes the reassuring answer.

'When?'

Eyes roll, lips are pursed, shoulders shrug.

'Well, it better be. This is not a handball alley.'

After much tooth-sucking, neck-scratching and ear-tugging, the cheque is placed on the cash register. The ring of the till-bell releases the bated breath. A spurious assurance fills the air, the curate fills the glasses. The session has begun. The gargle will flow. Repeatedly, for the rest of the day, somewhere, somehow, and by someone, rounds will be bought.

Kavanagh's close friend and drinking mate, Dominic O'Riordan, worked for the Post Office as a poet, although they had presumably hired him in a different capacity. He was widely read, disputatious and witty, and given to Thomistic meanderings in his cups.

One Sunday morning Seamus carried out a reconnaissance upstairs in the Tower Bar. Several acquaintances, any of whom might be good for a few bob, could one catch him alone, were drinking together, but awkwardly juxtaposed. The problem was to split the reds. Seamus retreated to consider, and met Dominic at the street door. They quickly established that between them they had the price of one half-pint of Guinness.

'Here,' said Kavanagh, handing over his alcoholic's mite. 'Now, here's the plan. You go up, call for a glass at the counter, and then bore the ballocks off them with Thomas Aquinas. That'll flush them out, one by one, and I can nab them on the stairs on the way down.'

When Maurice Gorham, who had come from the BBC as director of Radio Éireann, was retiring, Seamus as head of children's programmes, a position he then held, spoke his appreciation at the formal farewell.

'Maurice was so helpful. Anything we asked for we got. He just could not say no.'

'Oh, but I always did say no,' Gorham protested, 'but Seamus believes that when you woo authority, "No" means "Yes".'

Kavanagh grew up in Aungier Street, a stone's throw from where Jacob's biscuit factory used to be. Whether he followed Jacob's soccer team or not, he certainly admired their goal-keeper's pride. He told of a match with St James's Gate, during which the Jacob's goalie was deemed to have fouled an advancing forward in the box. Although no transgression had occurred, a totally unjust penalty was awarded. Even the Gate players, who were awarded the penalty, appealed to the referee, but he brushed them, and all protests and appeals, aside, in classic fashion, and pointed to the spot. The marksman placed the ball, ambled slowly back, and to show his disagreement with the referee's decision, tapped the ball forward; and as it rolled slowly towards the goal, the keeper said, 'Fuck you', leant against the post, and let it into the net. 'I'll take your sympathy, but not your charity.'

One of Kavanagh's great friends was Con Lehane, who also used to act with the Compántas. I got to know Con well over many years, through theatre and politics and drink. When he ran for the Dáil, I helped out in the election campaigns — not that you'd notice — but it was good fun.

The first time I met Brendan Behan was at a fundraiser for Con Lehane's election, held in number 9 Stamer Street, off the South Circular Road, a house owned by a lady from Westmeath called Ma Martin, whose son Eamonn and I were great pals. I subsequently was a lodger in Martins. It was there that I met and fell in love with Judy Kenny. We married four years later and have been together since.

Ma Martin was ostentatiously pious. She encouraged the recital of The Most Holy Rosary in the evenings after tea, and some of the girls, who formed the great majority of the boarders, found this a welcome diversion on wet evenings when money was scarce.

Across the street from Martins was the house occupied by Harry Kernoff RHA. Ma Martin had commissioned Kernoff to paint portraits of her two granddaughters, on the never-never. When the payments developed a tendency to sporadicity, Harry would knock at the door and ask for his instalments. The paintings having lost both novelty and some of their resemblance to their now older subjects, Mrs Martin found Mr Kernoff's attentions irritating and insolent. She placed her spectacular plaster Virgin in the front-room window, angled to face Kernoff's house. Then she tacked on to the trimmings on the Rosary, a plea for the conversion of the Jews, adding, 'And we think especially of our dear neighbour, Mr Kernoff.' She also prayed for the conversion of Russia, which her son Eamonn, a devout communist, found hilarious.

In the fifties, Lehane stood in the Clann Na Poblachta interest, with two other candidates, Joe Barron and Jack Brady. Con got a complaint from the rector in Donore Avenue (Church of Ireland) to say that the grounds of the church had been desecrated — election posters put up on the church noticeboards, and scriptural quotations interfered with. 'It's appalling,' he said. 'I'd like you to come down and see it.' Con said, naturally, that this was probably the work of Fianna Fáil people, to discredit him. But he called to the church, and there were the two boards: the first now read, 'When the Lord calleth, vote Clann na Poblachta', and the second, 'For the Jesus saith, Vote, Barron, Brady and Lehane.'

When I was in my first panto at the Abbey, I was asked to join the Catholic Stage Guild. I did so because I thought it would keep me in touch with theatre people and further my chances of becoming a pro. The chaplain was Father Cormac O'Daly, a Capuchin, a saintly and innocent man. Whether the Guild was his brainchild or not, he was its most public embodiment. He was prominent in one of the most eccentric campaigns ever conducted to combat godlessness in the film industry.

The Guild decided that the Oscars, called after somebody's Jewish Uncle Oscar, were in some way tainted by their association with, among others, promoters of the Red Menace. So they instituted their own awards for people in show business generally. I forget, if I or anybody ever knew, what the criteria were by which merit was gauged.

Father Cormac went to Hollywood, and his photo appeared in the *Catholic Standard* with Bing Crosby and other prominent Papists. Whether Bing got an award I don't recall, but surely he must have, and if so, it had to be for Father O'Malley in *Going My Way*, or *The Bells of St Mary's*. Ingrid Bergman and Barry Fitzgerald also appeared in one or both of these, but they were Protestants playing Catholics — a nun and a priest at that.

In time, Father Cormac came to be The Catholic Stage Guild.

The Guild awards were called 'Bridgets' or 'Patricks' or 'Finbars', I can't quite remember which. I don't think they went as far as recruiting St Genesius, the patron saint of actors. One award went to Seán Barlowe, stage carpenter at the Abbey, for forty years' service, possibly because St Joseph was a carpenter.

The Guild organised an annual one-day retreat for people in the business, at the Mount Anville Convent on Holy Thursdays. These were intensely spiritual occasions, and were also great fun. There is nothing quite so mirth-provoking as to emerge from Confession, shriven and forgiven, and to watch a distinguished gallery of whoremasters, drunks, liars and gamblers rapt in prayer. Truly contrite, and with a firm purpose of amendment, to be sure, but hilarious nevertheless.

There was a Stage Guild Prayerbook, which had a stomach-churning, sentimental preface directed at Thespian sinners, in pseudo-theatrical parlance, the only phrase of which that sticks in my mind as well as in my craw was about going to meet 'The Great Stage Manager'. Oh yes, I couldn't swear that the words 'in the sky' did not follow, but surely they were implied.

Cecil Sheridan, superb musichall man, master of the parody, a bundle of nerves at the best of times, and all the better a comedian for that, sat alongside myself, Brendan Cauldwell and Noel Lynch one year, at the first lecture of the day. The preacher was Father Leonard Shiel SJ, a highly effective speaker, reminiscent vocally of Raymond Massey. His subject was the Prodigal Son. Either he wasn't told about the fifteen-minute rule for lectures, or he got carried away by his subject, but he went on a bit. Cecil began to nod off, and finally went into a peaceful slumber. As he sank deeper into sleep, he began to snore, first gently, then intrusively. Father Shiel was now forty minutes into his stride. Benny gave Cecil an elbow in the ribs. He jerked awake, slightly confused, then looked at his watch. In his famous stutter he asked, 'Is this still the same s-s-s-sermon?'

'Yes.'

'What's he t-t-t-talking about?'

'The Prodigal Son.'

'Did that little f-f-f-fucker not come home yet?'

Lorcan Bourke, the head of the great theatre family, took a ferocious slagging from all his mates at these occasions. When someone said, 'Surely you didn't tell *all* you did, Lorcan?', he would answer, 'I told *what* I did, not *how* I did it. Oh, he asked me, but I said, "Mind your own bloody business, Father." '

Jimmy O'Dea, the smallest man who ever graced a stage, would put in an appearance for the pre-lunch lectures, stay for lunch and late Mass, and then repair to the Goat Inn, as did most others. Once, as we sat down to lunch, the Reverend Mother, without prior consultation, called on Jimmy to say Grace. The famous raking look took in the assembled penitents, but there was a hint of panic in the eyes. Everyone knew that expression. It was the hunted look of an actor trying to remember a line. 'He can't remember it,' someone whispered. 'Probably never said it,' giggled another.

SMILE AND BE A VILLAIN!

The standard version of the Grace at that time — at least the Catholic one — was 'Bless us, Oh Lord, and these thy gifts, which of thy bounty we are about to receive, through Christ Our Lord, Amen.' Slowly, James Augustus dragged himself to his full height — very slowly, as the distance was not great — but by the time he was erect, the twinkle was back in his eye. 'For what we are about to receive,' he intoned, 'may the Good Lord make us truly thankful.'

This was the usual movie version, not the Catholic one, as everybody knew, except the Reverend Mother, who in a bewildered voice added, 'Through Christ Our Lord.'

'Amen,' said Jimmy. Game, set and match.

Brendan Behan used to call himself a 'daylight atheist'. 'But when I'm sick, or wake up during the night, I'm very religious.' I have been a Catholic all my life — not a very good one, not the worst either.

Siobhán McKenna once told me about a well-known lady of the theatre with whom she was working, who was in love with an extremely attractive, well-built actor who was a devout Catholic, and crazy as a two-bob watch. This actress asked Siobhán about taking instruction. Siobhán was mystified. 'You mean in acting? But sure you're a superb actress.'

'No, instruction in Catholic doctrine.'

Probably only someone with what they call a 'doubting faith' would understand Siobhán's answer.

'Why?' she said, with no trace of elation.

'Because he says we can only marry if I become a Catholic.'

'Oh well,' said Siobhán, 'that's a very big decision. Now don't get me wrong. It's a wonderful religion, a source of great strength and grace, and it's grand for us that were reared to it. But I'd think twice about it if I were you. I mean, you're very good-living as it is, so far as I can see, but it's hard to live up to, you know. We're a bit fettered in some matters. I mean, there are lots of restrictions, and . . .', at which point the actress left.

'What I meant', Siobhán said to me, 'was that if I wasn't already a Catholic, I'd want a hell of a better reason to become one than just to marry him. Of course, I couldn't explain that.' Anyway, they broke it off shortly afterwards.

In much the same way, I feel great sympathy for those who came into the Catholic Church in recent years and now have to think again. It's not quite so bad for those of us who grew up with it. It's rather the difference between being betrayed by a lover and finding out that your own family were no saints, any more than yourself.

# SEVEN

I want to hark back to early 1948, when a very glamorous thing happened to me — well, to my youthful mind it was very glamorous anyway.

When Ronald Reagan as President decided to dig up his ancestors, surprise was expressed, on a talk show, that he had left his first visit so late. I said, 'It's not his first visit, he was here in 1948, and I met him, and he bought me a drink.' This was treated as a joke. Nobody believed me, but it was true.

It happened one morning, in January or February 1948. I was in the Green Room of the old Abbey Theatre, talking to the then stage manager, Seán Mooney, and Walter Macken, who was a member of the company at that time, having finished his stint with An Taibhdhearc in Galway. Somebody came in and said that there were two people wanting to see round the theatre. One of them was Ronald Reagan — or Reegan, as his name was always pronounced in those days, certainly in Ireland. The other was Joan Caulfield.

Now Ronald Reagan, the best day he ever was, was no turn-on for me, but the effect of the name Joan Caulfield was worth a decade or two of the Rosary by way of penance. She was gorgeous on screen, even in monochrome. Live, and in colour, she was shattering — embarrassingly, achingly beautiful, a cruel torment to an acne-ridden adolescent.

The pair were in Dublin for the charity première of some film or other. They had been having a walk around town and came across the world-famous Abbey Theatre. I can remember the conversation between Walter Macken and Ronald Reagan.

Reagan said, 'I notice you wear eye-glasses. Do you have to wear those on stage?'

Wally said, 'No, I take them off.'

'But can you see?'

'Well, not as well as if I had them on. But I have to take them off.'

Reagan said, 'Why don't you wear contact lenses?'

'What are they?' asked Wally. (Contact lenses had only just been invented.)

So Reagan described them. He said, 'I wear them when I have to.'

'Oh, Jeez, that's a great idea. How much would they cost?'

I can't think of the exact figures, but Reagan trotted out some sum — let's say $700.

'What? I wouldn't get that in six months. I couldn't afford that!'

And that was the end of the subject. When Reagan had finished his little tour, he said, 'Can I buy you guys a drink?', and we went over to the Flowing Tide in Abbey Street, and Mr Ronald Reagan bought me a bottle of Guinness, he bought Wally, I think, a gin and tonic, and Seán had a pint. And these historic events were confirmed by Harry Lush, the manager of the Adelphi Cinema, who said, 'Well, I don't know exactly what drink he bought, but I do know that he did go into the Abbey and he had a chat with some of the people there, including Niall Toibin.'

Reagan had a warm, relaxed presence. He was a very pleasant man, that much I remember. Of course, I was only eighteen. To be honest, I was looking more at Joan Caulfield. She didn't come for the drink, she went back to the hotel. It is a matter of no public interest whatsoever, but I'm recording it anyway.

As for Reagan in his latter incarnations, as Governor and President, it was a pity that he didn't join the Abbey company. He remained a great 'pro', as an actor playing the President, but his market-led anti-Welfare double-act with the Mad Woman of Grantham put me off him for good. I still liked him as a personality; he was very warm and very amusing, but he was political poison.

Reagan's belated love affair with Ireland did us no harm, of course. His ability to deliver an immaculately crafted ad lib was admirable. He and Tip O'Neill had a fine Gallagher and Sheen double act going at a St Patrick's Day lunch in the Irish Embassy in

Washington. O'Neill's speech finished with a tribute to Reagan: 'This morning as I shaved I thought about you, Mr President — about your stunning political victories, your hold over Congress, your assured place in history, as well as in the hearts of the American people, because you bask in their love. Your popularity is awesome. I thought of all your wonderful achievements and all I could say was, Don't let it get to you, Tip.'

Rightly or wrongly, I had a sort of Irish affinity with the Democrats, even though they had, as we were informed in our youth, kept Al Smith, the Irish Catholic, out of the White House. One regarded all Republicans as war-mongers and closet Klansmen, and Democrats, quite unjustifiably, as people who believed in the liberty of the person, freedom from want, freedom of conscience, freedom from fear. No black, south of the Mason-Dixon line, would have subscribed to that view, but it was the one we had. We managed to obliterate the awkward contradictions, such as that it was a Democrat who dropped the atom bomb, and a Republican who sent in the troops to enforce desegregation in Little Rock. For all that, Harry Truman was probably more democratic than Ike; certainly he was far more interesting.

During the 1952 presidential campaign, when Adlai Stevenson faced Ike, I went into the Brazen Head Hotel, Ireland's oldest inn, but still a bit of a kip, with Archie O'Sullivan, actor, and Andrew Ignatius Flynn, barrister-at-law and publisher. One could best the licensing laws those days by paying a half crown for bed and breakfast, on the unspoken understanding that one would not go to bed unless involuntarily, because of drink, and that breakfast was something you would never be bothered with anyway.

Having paid our subscription, we registered as residents. Feeling a topical alias appropriate to the occasion, I signed the register as 'Adlai Stevenson'. The Gardaí raided the bar at 2 a.m. The sergeant told a guard to man the register and confirm the bona fides of each resident.

'Name?'

'Arthur O'Sullivan.'

'He's signed in,' intoned the guard.

'Name?'

'Andrew Flynn.'

'He's signed in.'

'Name?'

I paused, then answered brightly, 'Adlai Stevenson.'

'Oh,' sneered the sergeant, 'we have a fucking humorist in the house.'

'He's signed in,' intoned the uncomprehending one.

So there was no prosecution, and, who knows, some future historian may establish from the register of the Brazen Head Inn in Dublin, that Adlai Stevenson was on the piss in Dublin town in 1952 — or whatever date it was.

As for Irish politics, my own family was always straight Fianna Fáil, by which I mean they followed the de Valera line about the primary aims of reviving the language and reuniting the country.

I can't place when my own disenchantment with Dev set in, but it was fairly early. Certainly I can recall him being vilified by a neighbour, 'He's that crooked, if he swallowed a nail he'd shit a corkscrew.' His verbal gymnastics I found a bit hard to take. It seems to me that, like the Mad Hatter, he held that 'a word means what I say it means.'

He was born in Brooklyn, reared in Limerick, and elected in Clare, but overcame all three drawbacks to become a great leader with more devout adherents than Garryowen, Ahane and the Arch-Confraternity combined — and not just in Limerick. In Cork a noted politician earned the title The Great Lover, because of his familiar mantra, his all-embracing policy statement, 'I love my God, I love my country and I love Éamon de Valera.'

Despite his close connection with Bruree — which meant he was only about three and a half miles from being a Corkman — he was never to my recollection called a Limerickman. Those who loved him called him Dev or the Chief. Many others called him 'That lousy Spanish bastard'.

He provoked extreme reactions. Once when his name was spoken in a Moore Street bar, an indignant Dublin lady complained, 'It's a disgrace — drawin' down that man's name in a public house.' I never could make out whether what she resented was the disrespect to Dev or to the pub.

It was a convention that in front of the faithful you never called him a politician. You would be called to order pretty smartly. 'No. The others are politicians. Dev is a statesman.' Nevertheless, he was the only politician to inspire an anthem:

> Up de Valera, he's the champion of the right,
> We will follow him to battle in the Orange Green and White.
> And when we meet the English we will beat them in the fight,
> And we'll crown de Valera King of Ireland.

An odd fate for a republican, to be crowned King. Then you had the official Fianna Fáil anthem, and a great song it was:

> Tone and Emmet guide you
> And though your task be hard
> de Valera leads you
> Soldiers of the Legion of the Rearguard.

In later years Donie Cassidy produced 'Rise and Follow Charlie', which still leaves Dev as the only politico to inspire a song.

He was deeply religious and abstemious. Someone remarked to Seán Moylan, a North Corkman who was a member of the Government, 'Of course the Chief is a walkin' saint, God bless him . . . he goes to Mass and Communion every morning.' And Moylan said, 'tis easy for the bastard, sure he doesn't drink or smoke.' He loved the Irish language but lacked the poetic touch. He once asked for help with a speech in Irish. He wanted a phrase that would be equivalent to 'gilding the lily'. 'And all I can think of is *Ag cimilt bhlonaige le tóin muice.*' Which means 'rubbing lard to a sow's arse'.

His successors have a patchy record with regard to the language. After Lemass, whose occasional attempts at speaking Irish were 'occasional' and 'attempts', Jack Lynch and Charlie Haughey tootled out the odd speech in Irish, but the combined speeches in Irish of Garret, Albert and Bertie, if located, could be swallowed in one gulp by a half-trained spy.

One morning in 1947 I bought a booklet in a newsagents in Blackrock, County Dublin. It was by Benjamin Farrington, whom I've never heard of since, and entitled *Connolly of Ireland*. I assumed it would be a stirring anti-British tract, detailing yet more of the eight-hundred-year saga of outrages and atrocities perpetrated on the persecuted Gael.

But this pamphlet was about socialism. It revealed a side of 1916 that had never been brought to my notice by the Christian Brothers, or anyone else. I had watched Jim Larkin's funeral earlier that year, as Dublin went silent on a day of snow and scything winds, in tribute to Labour's fiery orator. A bus-driver had left his cab to stand ankle-deep in melting slush beside me in O'Connell Street, an expression of inexplicable grief on his face. Larkin cropped up often in the Connolly story. My mind began to make connections. The busman's grief was no longer strange.

From then on, my leanings were leftward. I read Connolly, I began to buy the *Tribune* and the *Daily Herald*, and *Reynold's News* became my Sunday missal. My political mentors were Nye Bevan, Michael Foot, Hugh Delargy, Tom Driberg, Geoffrey Bing. Driberg's exposure as a sexual deviant with exotic tastes, who worked for the KGB while squatting in the Jesuits' house in Farm Street in London, came as a multiple shock to me years later, as did Geoffrey Bing's enthusiastic suppression of civil rights in Nkrumah's Ghana. But that was long years into the future.

I've never fully shaken off my early passion for socialism, nor would I like to lose that hankering after a decent Welfare State, nationalised banks, all of that. 'True to thee, Cynara' in my fashion.

It was a very callow indoctrination — or indoctrination at a very callow time. Nevertheless, it survives, and I've never been persuaded by the free-market bullshit, and all of this Thatcherite nonsense. The proof that Reagan had no brain at all was that he seemed to have been genuinely influenced by Maggie Thatcher; speaking of whom, I would put the proposition that the greatest achievement of any Irish politician in modern times was Garret Fitzgerald's getting Maggie Thatcher to change her mind from 'Out, out, out' to a conciliatory stance. And whatever contempt his detractors may heap on that woolly-headed academic, his luring Magso into the Anglo-Irish Agreement started the first creaks in the log-jam. Charlie's teapot and Albert's simplicity notwithstanding, Garret is entitled to his credit too. Within reason, of course.

All Irish achievements seem to diminish in importance when you spend any time out of Ireland. You are struck, if you have any sensitivity at all, by the total lack of interest that the entire world shows in what we consider the centre of the universe, the fountain of all knowledge and virtue and bravery and learning. Humankind is unmoved by all this codology about Irish monks going out and civilising Europe. The perspective changes, and you feel they don't really give a damn one way or the other.

There was an example of this when President Mary Robinson went to Somalia during the famine; there wasn't a word about her visit in the American or British papers. Some woman in great distress, God love her innocence, called Marian Finucane's radio show about this international indifference, genuinely hurt and surprised that the outside world had not vouchsafed us the admiration that was our due.

Her attitude was typical of even well-educated Irish people who should know better, who feel that we in Ireland have taken moral stands, given the honourable lead, in the United Nations in particular. Whereas the truth is that half the people in the UN couldn't even spell the name of this country. We have to disabuse ourselves of our idea of our own importance. How often have I heard some egregious globetrotter recount how, on being mistaken for an Englishman in France, Spain, Montenegro, Ulan Bator, or wherever, he put the record straight with a reproving 'Non, non, nicht Angleterre, Irlandaisi, viva Irlanda!', or some equally illiterate farrago of half-baked Berlitzish. 'Ah,' the enchanted Croat, Magyar, Basque, cries, 'Si, si. De Valera! Viva Irlanda!' Only Coca Cola evoked as much instant recognition as de Valera.

Seán Lemass was obviously very businesslike, a very practical man. On the other hand, he made a famous statement that Fianna Fáil was 'A slightly constitutional party'. And since Lemass was never known as a joker, I wonder was there an implied threat here that 'If we don't get our way, we can always go back to what we did before'. I heard de Valera described as 'the greatest red herring in Irish history', and I think he was, because everybody went off on the scent of the rather curious ideas that he held, and he seemed totally out of touch with reality.

De Valera certainly had a deep love of the Irish language, and on the one occasion when I had a conversation with him, he spoke to me in Irish. He told me he had often heard me on the radio, and congratulated me on my fine work; but then he was hardly likely to bite me. Radio was a great solace to him, because by this time his sight was very poor. Most of the programmes he mentioned were in Irish.

Seán MacBride was held in deep suspicion, probably because of his foreign manner of speaking, and because in the popular mind his mother was associated in a loose and immoral fashion with W B Yeats. But de Valera managed to turn his Spanish name and mysterious background to his own advantage. He had the mystique of being the verification of the Róisín Dubh, Clarence Mangan, prophecy: 'And Spanish ale shall give you hope, my dark Rosaleen.' One Christian Brother averred that Spanish ale was a poetic description, if not a prophecy, of the advent of de Valera to save us all from whatever it was we were to be saved from. The wine from the Royal Pope, which the poem alluded to as a possible back-up, never showed.

When Jack Lynch retired, the joke went that the greatest thing we had to thank him for was that he had kept Fianna Fáil out of office for twelve years, since he was really a Fine Gael Taoiseach. Fianna Fáil must have thought that he was anyway, because ever since, the Republican Party hagiography lists the succession as 'De Valera, Lemass, Haughey, Reynolds'. In the same fashion, Fine Gael regarded Garret Fitzgerald as really a Labour Taoiseach. Jack has been air-brushed out. I used to get very hot about these things, but I couldn't care less now. I do, I suppose, have an academic, or even sporting interest in Irish elections and politics, just as I have a morbid interest in American and British politics. Politics is a sport, really. Like the electorate, I have become shock-proof from recent events. I can still muster up a scabrous line in vitriolic abuse during private political discussions, but it's only Pavlov's dog pissing in response to political prattle.

# EIGHT

The 'Radio Éireann Rep' was officially the 'Radio Éireann Players'. It was, when I joined, and remained long after I'd left it, hide-bound by regulations dreamed up by the Post Office officials who resented its having been foisted upon them, way back when.

It was the Big Time — oh yes, you became very famous, in a limited kind of way by today's standards. But really it meant an awful lot, and I was very pleased and very proud. I didn't realise when I joined that there were other aspects to the job as well as the Sunday-night play, because that particular event was huge in those days; its only rival was Mícheál O'Hehir's Gaelic football and hurling commentaries, and the Hospitals' Request programmes on Wednesday afternoons.

The play was performed live every Sunday night, and the tension in the studio before it went out was palpable. People shivered with nerves, in a way I've hardly seen in the theatre. The reason was, of course, that you had only one shot at it, and if you made a mistake, that was it. Not that I ever remember any disasters.

One minor mishap, however, one has to record (and I will not name the person involved, except to say that the act was perpetrated, however unwillingly, even unwittingly, by a lady). In a production of *Shadow and Substance*, by Paul Vincent Carroll, the parish priest's housekeeper began a scene with the words 'Oh, Canon!', and then released a thunderous fart, live, on air. It was heard in the Control Room, and everybody went out of control, and the cast corpsed. 'Was it a first? Should we call in the Guinness Book of Records?'

Eamonn Keane, God bless him, who was affectionately known as 'The Joker', and who joined the company on the same day as I did, had a habit of addressing people who failed to see his point, which wasn't always that easy to discern, as 'You blind whore, you'. During a schools' programme, full of hoof-beats, neighing horses and battle-cries, he was playing a messenger who was coming to Hugh O'Donnell with a message. He had to jump off his horse and say, 'Take me to Hugh O'Donnell.' The Effects man, busy with his coconut shells, forgot to stop the galloping sound after Keane had done his own jump noise. This gave the impression that he had jumped off a horse at full speed, while the horse gallopped on, regardless. After a slight pause, Keane said, 'Take me to Hugh O'Donnell, you blind whore, you.' And nobody ever said anything about it — which could mean that nobody was listening, or that nobody cared.

Many years later I met Eamonn on a Good Friday morning, coming out of Donagh O'Dea's betting shop in Rathmines. He was very ill at this time; I knew he had had three heart attacks fairly recently. We had a chat, and then he said he had to be back in the nursing home in Clonskeagh at twelve o'clock. 'Like Cinderella, old boy,' he said, 'I am allowed out, but I have to be back by noon, and I am only allowed out on condition that I do not stray beyond the environs of Ranelagh and Rathmines.' I drove him back, and as he was showing me the hospital, and where he sat and picked his horses in the garden, I asked him did he have many visitors. He laughed. 'I had a visit from Willie Styles, and he told me that "So-and-so" was asking for me. And I said, "Tell him that I am preparing for the end, and for the first time in my life I am over-rehearsed." '

We had known each other in amateur drama in our teens, years before that, having done plays with the Dublin Repertory Company, an amateur company which was an offshoot of the NTG, the National Theatre Guild, a very left-wing group. We had been in *The Petrified Forest*, by Robert Sherwood, a couple of Odets plays, at least two of Paul Vincent Carroll's plays, *The Moonlighter* by George

Fitzmaurice, and other productions. Eamonn had massive talent, an incomparable voice and great passion. Discipline, however, ranked low in his order of priorities. He would make sudden statements of startling irrelevancy, such as telling me on one occasion after a performance that he purported to admire, 'You are a Booth, old boy', leaving me to figure out whether he meant Edwin Booth, or John Wilkes Booth, or for that matter Webster Booth or General Booth of the Salvation Army. And when he wanted to acquaint me gently of the break-up of his marriage, he just said, 'I am with a Lebanese lady now, old boy, a creature of infinite docility and versatility.'

Keane once appeared before Justice McCarthy on a drunk and disorderly charge. The judge was obviously disposed to taking a light-hearted view. When a garda giving evidence said Keane had called him an obscene name, the judge asked what he had called him.

'I'd rather not say, your Honour. I'll write it down.'

'You will tell the court. What you consider an obscene name may strike the court differently. What did he call you?'

'He called me a Clare fucker.'

'I see. And to which portion of this appellation do you take exception?'

You hear a lot of sentimental nonsense about companies, but the Rep really was a recruitment of all the talents. The best radio actor I've ever heard, or anybody else has ever heard, is Tom Studley. That has been said so often, simply because it's true. He had a painstaking, detailed approach. He really studied his text and worked on characterisation and motivation for even the most minor roles — not that he got many of those. And it never became for him an automatic falling into a part, which it did for a lot of us, inevitably, if we were doing up to twelve different programmes a week, which we could be, especially when we were doing them in two languages. For example, you would do a schools' programme on Monday in English, and you'd do the same thing on Thursday in Irish; and the one you did on Tuesday in English, you'd do on Friday in Irish. You could then, having done all that, go in and rehearse the Sunday Night Play, go on to read the Northern Soccer Report on

*Sports Stadium*, and the Cattlemarket Report on *Farmers' Forum*, and advise on trimming golden privet hedges in *Gardening Magazine*, and God knows what else. You would also, sometimes, read a short story or two, and introduce *Céilí House*, or *Women's Magazine*. So things often became fairly automatic.

Among the stars of the Rep were the O'Dea brothers, Joe and Lal (professionally known as Lionel Day). They were brothers of the great Jimmy O'Dea — something of which Joe in particular wasn't too fond of being reminded. Joe was an institution, because he could be pompous, but he was very kind. He was split between two worlds: he had a stationery import business, of which he had made quite a success, so he was proud of that; he was also proud to be an actor, and I think his loyalties were a bit divided between the commercial and the artistic. And then he used to do the Public Address thing in Lansdowne Road. He was in any case known as a rugby referee in his time, so he had a personality outside his Rep persona.

He could be quite humorous in his pomposity. Playing cards once, I said, 'It's old Joe's deal.' 'Less of the old, young man,' he said. 'In many ways you are far older than I will ever be.' 'I suppose', I said, 'you mean in the ways of sin.' 'Well, if the cap fits, old boy . . .'

Joe also produced one of the best put-downs I ever heard. John Stephenson, one of our producers, did not hit it off with Joe, and John in his own way had divided loyalties too, because he had been a printer in his youth — he had worked in Independent Newspapers and in the Stamping Office at Dublin Castle — and he would say, 'Well, I don't care. I can always go back to the printing,' as though that let him off the hook if anything went wrong. But at the same time he dressed like an actor-manager. He wore tails, or a frock-coat I suppose one could call it, and grey trousers with stripes, a celluloid collar and a little thin tie, sometimes a bow-tie. Once Joe, by prior arrangement, missed a rehearsal in order to go to his daughter's wedding. He had done this by simply going to the head of programmes rather than to John. Because of the relationship between them, John's answer would most likely have been, 'No, you can't, that's it.' Furious, John rang Joe at home, and said, 'How dare

*Contd on p.105*

1. My mother, Siobhán Tóibín, née O'Sullivan (1890–1987), 1910

2. My father, Seán Tóibín (1882–1971), 1957

3. Class photograph, North Monastery school, Cork, 1940
That's me in the back row, second from right.

4. Abbey Theatre panto, *Niall agus Carmelita*, 1948

*Left to right, kneeling:* Joan O'Hara, Rita Foran, Bill McCormack, Jack Donnelly, Doreen Madden, Gráinne O'Shannon, Angela Newman. *Left to right, standing, first level:* Niall Toibín, Micheál O'Briain, Kitty Corcoran, Bill Shawn, Alice Dalgarno, Seán Mooney, Phelim Johnson, Máire Ní Dhónaill, Walter Macken, Ray MacAnally (the prince), Peggy Wilson (the princess), Hugh Gunn, Eamon Keating, Maureen Toal, Una Lynch, Íte O'Mahony, Larry Gallagher. *Left to right, standing, second level:* Mick Dunne (the giant), Bill Foley, Ronnie Masterson, Ronnie Walsh. (*Back trio, left to right*) Micheál Ó hAongusa, Jack MacGowran, Eddie Golden.

5. Niall Toibin, *c*1949

This was in a play called *Na hEalaíontóirí* by Gearóid Ó Lochlainn, who had considerable professional experience in the Danish Theatre in his younger days and was later president of Irish Actors' Equity. He gave me great encouragement. The above production would have been in the Oireachtas na Gaeilge Drama Section in the Dagg Hall, Royal Irish Academy of Music, Westland Row.

6. Niall Toibin and Judy Kenny, Rosse's Hotel, Dún Laoghaire, October 1957

7. Niall Toibin as 'Ram' and Siobhán McKenna as 'Sibby', the elderly lovers, during a production of *Daughter from Over the Water* by M J Molloy, Gaiety Theatre, 1964

The line that makes her smile is 'Oh Sibby, you're as nice as an American apple'. This became a catchword of ours over the years, and on a couple of first nights I found my dressing-room table adorned with a big, red, shiny 'American' apple.

8. *The Hostage*, directed by Louis Lentin, Gaiety Theatre, Dublin, July 1964 (three months after Brendan Behan's death)

*Left to right:* Niall Toibin, Marie Kean, David Kelly and Mícheál O'Rourke.

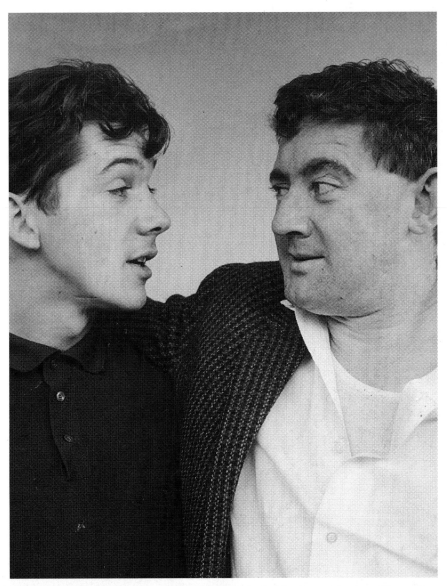

9. Frank Grimes and Niall Toibin at the dress rehearsal of the first production of *Borstal Boy*, Abbey Theatre, 1967

Frank was playing the younger Brendan. Before that, in an Abbey panto, when I played Culann, he played my dog, a spotty Dalmatian, not the noble hound of the Cú Chulainn legend. Apart from *The Outsider*, an excellent movie directed by Tony Luraschi, we did no further work together, but we have remained good if uncommunicating friends. He was superb as young Brendan, totally believable, vibrant, charming, violent and vulnerable. Professionally, he was very courageous, foolishly so perhaps, with an arrogance matching my own. I've always liked him enormously, even when we blew up.

10. Niall Toibin as Brendan Behan, 1967

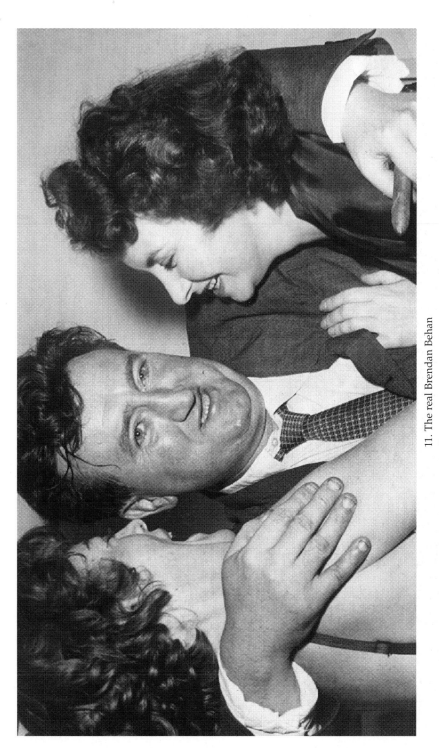

11. The real Brendan Behan

I don't know where this picture came from, nor who the girls are, but it was most likely taken at the Cort Theatre, New York, at the *Hostage* première. I love it because it shows the happy, gregarious Brendan, the Laughing Boy we loved.

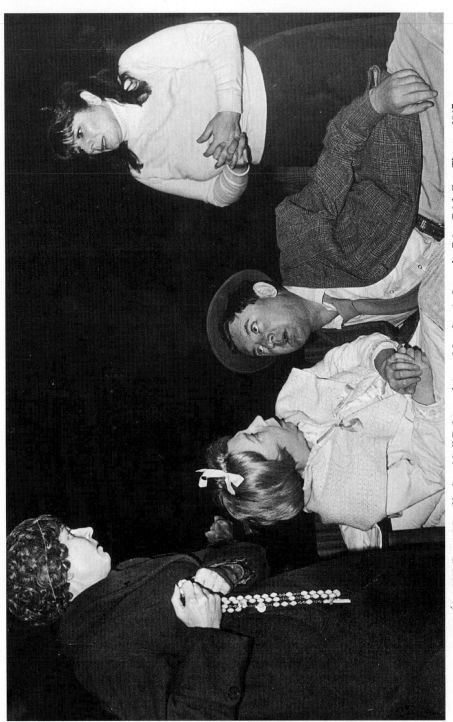

12. Áine Ní Mhuirí, May Cluskey, Niall Toibin and Anna Manahan in *Lovers* by Brian Friel, Gate Theatre, 1967

13. Barry Foster, Emmet Bergin and Niall Toibin in *Ryan's Daughter*, Dingle, Co Kerry, 1969

14. Arriving in New York for *Borstal Boy*, 1970

'You look well pissed,' said Frank Grimes on seeing this.
He probably had a point.

15. Niall Toibin, Ronnie Drew and Breandán Ó Dúill at the Chariot Inn, Ranelagh, *c*1970

God knows what we were singing, but it would be reasonable to assume that the combined intake beforehand would not be far short of a score of pints.

16. Anti-EEC meeting, General Post Office, Dublin, 1971

*Left to right:* Fintan Kennedy, Paddy Donegan, Michael O'Leary, Niall Toibin and Ruairí
Roberts.

you go behind my back, you snake.' And Joe said, with enormous dignity, 'How dare you speak to me like that in my own home.' And he hung up. This sense of propriety sums up Joe wonderfully. I met him in hospital when his memory had gone completely. He hadn't a notion who I was. It was saddening, because he had been so upright, precise, confident, and just plain decent.

Equality of excellence, without uniformity, is not too crawling a description of the Rep's women. The names Peg Monahan, Daphne Carroll, Deirdre O'Meara, Neasa Ní Annracháin, Ginette Waddell, will awaken memories of many enchanted evenings by country firesides in a less complicated world. To my mind, they generally handled the classics, Irish or otherwise, with greater assurance and flair than the men. But I suppose the one who claimed the most attention, because she was very flamboyant and temperamental, was Una Collins. She was blessed with an embarrassment of talent: she was an excellent singer, with a mercurial, elusive beauty, physical and vocal. But she was very emotional, and easily upset — very actressy, in other words. She had a star quality, rare in that cloistered and claustrophobic environment. The powers up the Long Corridor were terrified of her. She was able to storm in and throw a tantrum of electrifying intensity; and having got her way, come out smiling a sweet smile, almost of regret, that such behaviour was necessary to make people see reason.

I spent fourteen years in the Rep in the company of Chris Curran, Frank O'Dwyer, Seamus Forde, Kevin Flood, Des Nealon, Henry Comerford, George Green, Deirdre O'Meara, Maura O'Sullivan, Eamonn Kelly (who had a huge following in his other persona as 'The Seanchaí'), Brendan Cauldwell, Barry Casson, Aidan Grennell, Brendan Ó Dúill. Others came and went: Dennis Brennan, Godfrey Quigley, guests from the Abbey, from England, MacLiammóir, Denis O'Dea, Cyril Cusack, Anew McMaster, Siobhán McKenna. It was exciting, glamorous, amusing, absorbing, instructive — some of the time.

But the everyday reality was a pot-boiling job, acting in a secure and pretty well-paid company, in conditions which were the envy of all pros outside. Radio drama had its golden years, during which it carried out the extremely important function of providing, cheaply and regularly, an astonishing range of material. It was great to be a part of it; but I should have packed it in years earlier.

Apart from the actors, the radio station was crawling with eccentrics, oddballs and mavericks in every discipline of the performing arts.

Seamus Breathnach was a radio director or producer, and while he was not as quotable as Sam Goldwyn, perhaps, he did produce phrases that raised a laugh, mostly of derision, and yet expressed basic good sense. For instance, his most famous saying was, 'Will ye stop acting and get on with the bloody play.' Now, that may seem a peculiar thing to say, but when somebody was camping around, or maybe going over the top, or agonising a bit too much, it did, within the context of a rehearsal, make sense. But repeated outside of those circumstances, it sounds very crass. On one occasion, after we had read some Russian play, he said with a long sigh, 'Well, I suppose it means something to the Russians, but it means nothing to me.' Nor, in all honesty, did it mean very much to the rest of us.

The fact that we laughed at some of these people did not mean that they weren't very able. John Stephenson, for example, was a very experienced producer. He was good. But if you're in a convent, even the Reverend Mother, no matter how holy she is, becomes a bit of an old whore after a while. And there was a certain convent-like atmosphere within the Rep, where you were locked in, in a professional sense.

John had very set and definite ideas as to how plays should be done. When the world-renowned Tyrone Guthrie came to direct the Rep, it was a big deal indeed. John was unimpressed. The play was *Peer Gynt*, or, as Guthrie insisted on calling it, to everybody's discomfort, 'Pair Gunt', this, apparently, being the correct Norwegian pronunciation. John said, 'I have nothing against bringing these fellas in to do productions. Well and good, if we're going to do *Peer Gynt*, but if he wants to do it in Norwegian, that's another matter.' And he dismissed Guthrie and all his works and pomps, while at the same time excelling himself as the Troll King in the same production. No flies on our Jack!

Guthrie was, to the likes of us in the convent, a breath of fresh air, because the first thing he did was to start using four-letter words, something that was unheard of at the time. He also had quite a badly blocked nose, so he sounded like a Protestant minister in a variety sketch. He tended to pin labels on people: he called me 'the fat boy'. I was very fat at the time, from drinking porter and so on, but despite that, and though he remonstrated with me now and again, he was very nice to me socially, which I could not say of everybody. He could be very nasty, and on purpose. He used the word 'fuck' in discussions in front of persons of high authority.

It will show you what things were like in those days, that when he wanted to ring his sister in Monaghan, he had to apply through the producer's office for permission to make a trunk call. At this time he was reckoned to be one of the four best producers in the world — though who prepared these league tables, and by what criteria, no one could have said. Still, he probably did merit the courtesy of a free phone call.

RTE had just opened a new studio, a new 'Drama Suite', as they called it. There were all these squiggles on the wall, plaster figures to baffle sound, or whatever, and the place was luxuriously carpeted by the standards of the time — which meant that there was something on the floor other than varnish.

Yet the first order Guthrie gave was, 'Take up that carpet. Take it away. Take all those screens. Throw them out in the corridor. We need a bright atmosphere. It's set in the mountains, for God's sake. We need voices rebounding off ice, all the hard objects we can, to reflect back sound.' We rehearsed for two weeks, which was a week longer than normal, and the play went out live.

After the transmission there was a hooley, and very, very unusually for RTE at that time, drink was given to actors. This was almost like giving fire water to Indians. We continued the party and got pissed properly in Tim Danaher's flat. Mr Guthrie came along, and we went on until dawn. Now, we had asked Mr Stephenson if perhaps he would postpone his rehearsal on the Monday morning, which he had called for 9.30 a.m. No chance.

We arrived in the following morning, mostly very badly hung

over, and sat around. John came steaming in, in the wake of his pipe, which was always belching forth foul tobacco smoke, because he puffed at it all the time. He came sailing down the corridor, pushed in the door, and glared around. 'Put back them fucking carpets. There's going to be no more arty-farty productions here.' The old hard-line Kremlin was back in power.

Seamus Forde was, I would say, the most colourful of all the actors in the Rep, because he had toured with many companies (though not as many perhaps as he gave you to understand), and he talked about 'the old days', although he wasn't all that much older than most of us. But he did bring this great aura of the travelled actor, the man who had seen it all, and done it all — as indeed he had. He had a wonderful power. His great asset was self-esteem; he was an actor, and he was proud of the fact. He was grateful for it. It was not a matter one should ever apologise for, or be ashamed of. There was tremendous self-respect, a feeling of self-worth about him, even when he was pissed out of his mind. There was this pride in what he did, and most of the time he did it very well indeed.

His O'Casey characters were unmatchable. His Shakespeare was magnificent. He could be very quirky, and a bit narky, but he did have, like a lot of us, not just a battle, but a thirty-years' war with the booze. At a time when he was written off as a complete 'lush', he confounded everybody by suddenly packing it in and staying off it for years. Silver-haired and suave, serene and most elegantly rigged out, he became an adornment to his profession; a remarkable man, but a very hard man to categorise.

Dermot O'Hara, conductor of the light orchestra for years and years, had a caustic tongue which lost him many friends and gained him many fans. He and the other resident conductor were diminutive figures, and they didn't get along too well. When Dermot was introduced to Tibor Paul, the Austrian maestro, a very tall man, when he came to guest conduct the symphony orchestra, Paul found himself towering over O'Hara. Whether from amusement or embarrassment, he let a smile show, but quickly suppressed it. O'Hara, sharp as ever, spotted this, and gazing into the tall Austrian's eyes, said, 'So well you may smile. Wait till you see the other little fecker! You'll break your arse laughing.'

Philip Rooney, the novelist, had an office in the Long Corridor also, and he frequented the Tower Bar and Jerry O'Dwyer's. He was a close friend of Brinsley MacNamara (aka Jack Weldon), the playwright, an awesome figure physically and intellectually, who spoke in an amused, nasal sneer. Despite his forbidding presence, he loved to talk and laugh with younger people, which was not at all in keeping with his reputation. One lunchtime, Phil Rooney launched forth on a story just as Brinsley joined the company. He realised, to his horror, that the story involved Brinsley in a far from complimentary light. So he began to improvise the narration to get out of his pickle. Accomplished writer he may have been, but he managed only to dig himself into a deeper hole; and finally, in total confusion, he excused himself and made for the Gents.

Later that evening I heard Brinsley describe the scene to others: 'I'm very worried about Rooney, you know. He needs to be watched, taken care of. He's drinking his head off. Well, he must be. I met him at lunchtime, and a whole group of us just stood there, listening to this farrago of the most appalling gibberish. Pointless nonsense, totally meaningless. Then he dashed into the toilet and got sick. I wonder what's got into him?'

One ludicrous example of arbitrary allocation of chores in the Rep, comes to my mind. I was visiting a relation of mine in Kerry, Dan Shea, a farmer, who tuned in to Radio Éireann to hear the Cattlemarket Report. It was read by Seamus Forde. Now, any actor worth the name has an automatic pilot which can take charge in time of bewilderment, fatigue, diarrhoea, sore throat or pissedness. I remember Siobhán McKenna, overcome with grief at the death of Jackie MacGowran during our *Juno* in Toronto, playing a whole scene as though it were a soliloquy from *Riders to the Sea*, lapsing, presumably, into what came easiest, when the concentration went. On a more comic note, Forde's equivalent fall-back was a flamboyant, Shakespearian, declamatory style, and because he was pissed, and agriculture was unfamiliar territory, he proceeded to 'iambic pentameterise' such sentences as, 'The toll of brucellosis grows apace', and deliver the same with resonant passion and drama only faintly reminiscent of a fair day in Caherciveen. My cousin's eyes glowed in admiration. 'He don't know what he's talking about,' he said, 'but by God, isn't he well able to give it out.'

During my early Rep days, the Abbey was given over to the comedies of John McCann. They were playing at that time in the Queen's Theatre, and although McCann's plays were not held in high regard critically, they were good popular theatre. Once, when acknowledging an ovation, John McCann modestly said, 'God gives us the talent', only to be greeted with 'You can't blame Jaysus for this', from someone in the auditorium.

The Gate had its own agenda, mainly Shakespeare and Restoration, what the public thought of as 'costume plays'. Consequently, quite a lot of new drama originated on radio, notably due to the diligent encouragement of new talent by Mícheál O'hAodha. Brendan Behan benefited from Mícheál's interest, as did James Plunkett, himself subsequently a radio producer. The original version of Plunkett's *Strumpet City* was a radio play called *Big Jim*. On stage it became *The Risen People*. In book form it was *Strumpet City*, a title to which it returned as a highly successful TV series. Ironically, at a time when feelings were high about employment of semi-pros, Larkin was played in the radio version by Ruairí Roberts, a senior trade union official. Roberts was an accomplished verse speaker, with a deep musical voice, but a rather bland performer. Larkin's enormous voice was of a different order, and his North Country accent a sea's width from the elocuted tones of Roberts. Equity found the casting embarrassing, but presumably okayed it — or maybe they were never asked. Trade unions can be odd fish; after all, American Equity sacked some of their office staff for joining an office workers' union.

O'hAodha also produced a highly prestigious series of plays by Pádraig Fallon, mostly in verse. *Diarmuid and Gráinne* was the first, and there were many others. What their popular appeal was, I don't know, but they were lauded highly by the press. Certainly, each one was treated as a major event. It was poetic stuff, and a bit highbrow, and fulfilled an unspecified cultural mandate. It was sure to get good reviews, but you might meet the fellow in the pub afterwards who would say, 'I don't know what it was about, although I suppose it must be good, because your man in the *Irish Press* says it was terrific.'

That was one of the great things about the Sunday Night Play; you did get reviewed, week in, week out.

Many memorable productions which today would probably bore people, were very popular then, like *Autumn Fire,* and some other T C Murray plays, but there were also some splendid productions of Paul Vincent Carroll (Dennis O'Dea I remember in *Shadow and Substance),* O'Casey, Brinsley MacNamara, George Shiels, Bryan McMahon, M J Molloy, Synge, Yeats, Beckett, O'Connor, O'Faoláin (in adaptations, mostly) and Eugene O'Neill.

Dan O'Herlihy was another distinguished guest. He did Eugene O'Neill's *The Iceman Cometh,* and naturally he played Hickey. P J O'Connor directed. Dan played it in a southern drawl. There's nothing wrong with that, so far as interpretation goes, because he was very good at it; but it's a long, long play, and if you're going to drawl, that makes it longer. I played Rocky the barman. I also played in two subsequent productions on the stage. It is an extraordinary piece of theatre, and easily my favourite play. Seán Cotter directed an unjustly overlooked production of *The Iceman* in the Abbey in the sixties, and it was this which caught my own imagination.

Somebody said that O'Neill was a great playwright, but not a great writer; and I felt, as I took my seat, that nothing could justify the arrogance of this deranged Irish-American piss-artist in inflicting six hours of alcoholic autobiography, not just on the audience, but on the theatre company itself. Yet, as the tidal wave of talk, talk, talk, broke over the footlights, I was swept away by the flood. I hung on every word of self-loathing, delusion, recrimination, mockery, reminiscence. Bill Foley, as Jimmy Tomorrow, would have brought tears from a stone. Philip O'Flynn, as Larry Slade, a part I later played in two productions, was memorable. Vincent Dowling played Hickey, and, unless I am mistaken, he was a very late replacement for someone else. The very feat of memorising all of Hickey's lines, in itself deserves a citation. Vincent was physically, and probably vocally, too light, but he was convincing.

A few years ago I spent an absorbing evening with a New Yorker, Ed Quinn, an *habitué* of The Lion's Head in the Village, who knew O'Neill well. I had the kind of conversation with him about Eugene

O'Neill that I would have had in Jerry Dwyer's in Moore Street, with Paddy Hunt, a tannery worker and self-taught socialist, who knew Seán O'Casey very well. Quinn was a journalist, and not attached to the theatre, but he did know O'Neill, and had drunk with him, knew his hangouts, and so on, and was able to identify for me who Larry Slade was — a guy called Terry Carlin, from the North of Ireland. He was able to put real-life names on the characters, and that was great for me. I'll come back to *The Iceman* later.

Radio Éireann, as I said, was a bit like a convent. The Sunday Play, like Sunday Mass, was compulsory. It came once a week, and the star of the Sunday-night play was a bit like a visiting priest. Then came the age of technology proper. They began recording the plays, and that was all right in its way — it didn't make much of a difference. But when they started to record them piecemeal, almost using film technique of doing 'takes' of scenes, editing the stuff together, the spontaneity went out of it, and an awful lot of the freshness of performance was gone. And that exhilaration, the first-night nerves that you got, all vanished. Once it was being recorded, you didn't feel the same, because you knew you could do it all again.

The greatest lie is that 'the camera cannot lie'. The greatest truth is that 'you cannot fool the mike'. I really believe that the microphone picks up the personality, even when one is totally silent. I don't mean that if you just stand in front of the microphone, you're going to project feeling or meaning to people out there; but once you have established a character, even your silences can be used as effectively as words. And I believe that the silence of one character will vary in intensity and meaning, from the silence of another character. That is obviously a psychic phenomenon. It's not something I can explain or analyse. There is a magnetism that just exists, and you get to recognise it, and use it. It's also easy to be very bad on radio — easier than on stage, because you are relying on the voice, and timing, and radio timing is obviously different from timing in the visual presence of other people. I will go back to my firmly held suspicion that if you examine it too closely, it will go away.

The great debating point about radio plays was whether you were addressing the people of Ireland *en masse*, gathered about their sets, or whether this was a *tête-a-tête* with the individual, unseen listener.

This kind of codswallop could while away hours of leisurely drinking time, and no harm done; but unfortunately it also exercised some minds in the Broadcasting Service when it came to the Irish language.

In English, the phrase 'You have been listening to the News', has no more impact than the phrase, say, 'That was the News'. The listener doesn't wonder whether the personal pronoun is singular or plural. In Irish, however, the singular *tú* and the plural *sibh* represent the versatile 'you' of English. So some nitpicking busybody decides every now and again that *Bhí tú ag éisteacht* is the more desirable usage, since the broadcaster is in a one-to-one relationship with the listener. The first effect of this is to give the uneasy feeling that nobody else is listening to this drivel, but you. So is there a mental proscenium arch when it comes to radio drama? Probably the microphone fulfils the purpose; a mental rather than a vocal projection. In practice, one is playing to one's colleagues, because in real life you do play to the person who is with you. Whether you're looking at them or not, you're playing to them.

Radio acting in Ireland is a dead duck now, though radio itself flourishes as never before, with all this spurious openness and 'access', which simply boils down to cheap programming. Some gobdaw, whom nobody would tolerate for three minutes in a pub, is given the freedom to air half-formed opinions of noxious inanity at the prompting of a host with the linguistic competence to run a coconut-shy.

The Rep, for all its great virtues, lasted too long. When you have a standing pool (no offence) of actors, they inevitably stagnate. After I left the Rep, I had a drink one day with Dan Treston, an urbane and charming man, who was still directing in Radio Éireann. As the Holy Hour drew nigh, he sighed as he finished his glass of beer. 'Back to work,' he said, 'another two hours of old So-and-so's touring Rep, Lord.' It was not meant unkindly. I knew he had great respect and affection for old So-and-so; but it was only to be expected that after twenty odd years of scanning the same faces across the mike, inventiveness would begin to flag.

# NINE

**M**y childhood neighbour, Joe Lynch, left the Rep a couple of years before my arrival. But his energy still reverberated through the studios. Joe was a rumbustious and colourful character, a great showman in his time, and there's no question about that. *Living with Lynch* was a very good comedy series. Though the scripts, by Dermot Doolan and Michael McGarry, were churned out to a formula, they did it very well, and regularly. They maintained a high standard, and Joe had tremendous drive, and was able to carry a show. He was also a rock-and-roll singer, musician, raconteur, footballer, cricketer, golfer, snooker-player . . . . . please fill in the blank spaces. One cannot begrudge him whatever satisfaction he gets out of *Glenroe*, but it would be a pity if he were to be judged on the strength of that soap, by people who never saw him in serious theatre, or in really top-class variety, where he was very, very good.

Of course it can also be a dreadful injustice to somebody to re-show something as an illustration of what he was like, simply because it happens to be the only available piece of tape. One painful example of this comes to mind. When Jimmy O'Dea was getting on and not in good health, he did a series with Dave Kelly in which he played a railway signalman. It was scripted, I think, by Myles na gCopaleen. It wasn't all that funny, and Jimmy was well past the height of his powers, and it came across as lugubrious and rather tired humour; and anybody who saw only that (and that means anybody under the age of fifty-five, probably) would wonder 'Why all the fuss about O'Dea?'

Luckily, there are a couple of sketches with Maureen Potter which were preserved, by some freak of good fortune, and you do get an inkling in those of how electrifying they both could be, and the strength of O'Dea's personality. He was easily my favourite comic stage performer, especially, in fairness, with Potter. I used to go back to the matinees of the Gaiety shows, deliberately, because when Jimmy had a few little scoops in the morning, or maybe was recovering from the night before, he could be in a slightly skittish mood, and he would produce some great 'ad libs'. He had this trick of just coming on and raking the house with his eye; and before he ever said a word, the place was in stitches. And you got no hint of that mischievous quality in that TV thing. It's a pity that a lot of good stuff (including some of my own, if I may be very modest) was destroyed, some of it deliberately no doubt, and that more pedestrian stuff should have survived — also, perhaps, deliberately.

The Gaiety Theatre was the personal pride and joy of Louis Elliman, the head of another great Dublin theatre dynasty. 'Mister Louis' was the undisputed King. Then there were Jack, Maxie, Abie and maybe others. I only met Louis in 1964, to discuss my salary — he negotiated me out of the office in about three minutes at just over half the money I wanted. His wife Hetty had an objection to some line of Jimmy O'Dea's in a panto sketch, and Louis conveyed this to Jimmy along with a suggested substitute line. At the next performance Maureen Potter and Vernon Hayden were surprised when O'Dea trotted out this line neither had heard before. 'That's not your line,' protested Maureen. 'No. It's Hetty Elliman's,' said Jimmy, and flaked ahead with the sketch. No further censorship was attempted.

I had met many visiting stars and directors who came from time to time in radio, but no one ever brightened the scene as much as our own Mícheál MacLiammóir — who of course was not our own at all, as we now know, and perhaps subconsciously suspected even then, so exotic was his whole persona. Invariably, Hilton Edwards directed; and what a devious pair of schemers they made. They had arguments that crackled like lightning around the studio — all phoney, as I discovered accidentally during a rehearsal of *Julius*

*Caesar.* I was lying doggo in Studio 9, doing the *Guardian* crossword behind the screen, when a screaming match began. Mícheál rejected some fiddly direction from Hilton, the decibels mounted, blasting the mike off the air, and Mícheál flounced out and into Studio 9. Hilton rushed from the Control Room, remonstrating and calling his recalcitrant pup to heel. But as soon as the door of the seemingly empty Studio 9 banged shut behind them, Hilton said, 'What's the matter, Micky?' And they went into a muttering huddle, at the end of which Hilton said reassuringly, 'I'll get rid of him. Can't do it now, of course, but he'll be replaced by tomorrow.' (The following day, an unexplained switch of parts took place. Nobody lost his job, but whatever irritation one particular actor caused Micky, was removed.)

After a plausible interval, in which the far from heated Mícheál allegedly cooled down, he re-entered Studio 10. Hilton's voice boomed over the talk-back, as I followed in. 'Michael,' he said (because he always called him Michael, or Micky), 'You will just have to control this foul bad temper of yours. Remember that you are among talented, dedicated professional people, who have come to do their work, not to put up with your childish tantrums. The least you might do, before you inflict yourself on them again, is to apologise for your monstrous behaviour.'

Mícheál ran an exquisitely manicured, be-ringed hand over, but not through, his hairpiece, adopted an attitude of deep contrition, tucking his right knee into his left thigh, and sweeping the studio with the gaze of a sorrowing spaniel, he puckered his lips as though kissing the company *en masse*, fluttering the mascara-ed lashes in mock contrition, wiping non-existent tears from the made-up furrows of his cheeks. 'My dear, dear professional colleagues, please forgive me. I know my behaviour has upset you terribly. *Peccavi. Mea culpa, mea culpa, mea maxima culpa.* And as for you, Hilton, dear, it's not your "Wild Irish boy" you'll be dealing with any longer, but a dedicated artist.' (The 't's of the last four words were softened almost to esses in true Dublin 'Chrissie' fashion.)

I had only a sporadic acquaintance with MacLiammóir. He was witty, quite cruelly so. When someone read from the paper, 'I see that woman who was raped got £50,000', Mícheál mock-innocently asked, 'As well?'

In the late 1940s, O'Connell Street underwent a transformation, with cinema marquees vying with garish ice-cream parlour fronts for attention, as Cafollas, Fortes and Capaldis neon-signed the attractions of the 'Knickerbocker Glory' and the 'Melancholy Baby'. Then in 1952, as a Spring Festival attraction, Dublin Corporation erected the infamous 'Bowl of Light' on its concrete plinth, instantly Dublin-dubbed as 'The Tomb of the Unknown Gurrier', which ran the entire length of O'Connell Bridge. The concrete (or maybe it was bronze — certainly it was 'brewtle') bowl, sprouted plastic shafts, supposedly tongues of flame, but resembling plastic shafts. Mícheál described it as 'Cafolla's revenge for Versailles — the Palace, dear, not the Treaty'.

When someone had the idea of staging a combination of extracts from solo shows by Mícheál MacLiammóir himself, Marie Kean, Siobhán McKenna, Eamonn Morrissey, Anna Manahan and myself, at the Gaiety, for the Equity Benevolent Fund, Mícheál's sight had already failed too badly to allow him to participate, but he sat in the wings and heard all. When I had finished my stint, I came and sat beside him.

'Hello, Mícheál,' I said.

'*Cé tá agam?*' (Who have I?) he said, reaching for me in the dark.

'Niall.'

'Ah, sit here. We Cork boys must stick together.' He put an arm around me. 'My God, how slim you've got,' he said, prodding my ribs. (I had recently lost some weight.) 'Slim, trim and brimful, isn't that what they say? Fit, anyway. What an example you are to all of us! Keeping fit, doing all those manly things, like jogging, playing golf, living on yoghurt, dieting . . .'

'Well,' I said, 'no, not quite. I just gave up the drink.'

'Were ya havin' bother with it?' he said, in a thick brogue, putting on this phony concern.

'Well, I was, a bit.'

And he said, 'But surely, that wasn't all you did to achieve this sylph-like form?'

'No,' I said, 'I take a reasonable amount of exercise. I go to the sauna occasionally, get a massage.'

'Oh, how lovely! We must go to the sauna together, you and I, some day, because it would be so nice to have somebody intelligent to talk to there, instead of being, as I always am now, surrounded by two Christian Brothers and some jockeys.'

I had often tried to puzzle out where Mícheál came from. I'm not claiming credit for being a detective — I never suspected for one minute that he wasn't from Cork — but I did feel that he was trying to conceal his origins. Having read *All for Hecuba* and his descriptions of his childhood, I was trying to identify where in Cork he would have been born; one would expect anybody to name a street, or at least the suburb in which he was born. No area was specifically identified. Places were described: a beautiful house where the back garden ran down to the river, and I was thinking that must have been Sunday's Well. I asked him, 'Did you live in Sunday's Well?' He said, 'No, it wasn't Sunday's Well, it was Blackrock.' As my own father had lived near Blackrock, I couldn't figure out where there were gardens that would run down to the river. I found it a bit puzzling. Anyway, he didn't elaborate.

I was visiting number 4 Harcourt Terrace once, and Mícheál showed me a Gaelic Bible, an antique which had been presented to him years before. It was a Gaelic translation, done in the time of Elizabeth, who wanted to convert the Gaelic-speaking Catholics to Protestantism. The fly-leaf was inscribed 'Mícheál O'Leathlobhair MacLiammóir'.

'Why "O'Leathlobhair", Mícheál?' I asked him.

'Oh, didn't you know? My mother was a Lawlor. She was from Limerick.'

I think he even suggested that she had something to do with Lawlors the candle people — somebody did mention that — but of course this was all nonsense.

I had thought that because he lived in Cork, near the river, his father might have been a British Army officer, or even more likely a naval officer, and that he didn't want this to be known. It wasn't prudent or fashionable for Gaelic speakers to be from such a background. But, as we know now, thanks to the diligent detective work of Mícheál O'hAodha, he was not Irish at all.

There was the concept of baptism by desire, so why not nationality by desire? For surely, when he became an Irishman, he went the whole hog — more Irish than the Irish themselves, and him not even a Norman!

His Irish writing is superb, a great pleasure to read. His spoken Irish was exceptional: impeccable, but extraordinary, a linguistic Niagara, a cataract of compelling, charismatic speech, spellbinding rather than informative. I suppose there's nobody more zealous than the convert. He got inside the *Gaeilge bhinn bhlasta*, drew it over himself like a second skin; no question about that. His mastery of the *Gaeilge* was complete, and his stories about Connemara, and drinking with the old biddies in the pub, late at night, and all these old fairy tales and ghost stories they told him, he could produce with hair-raising accuracy; and he sounded exactly like one of those old Connemara women.

He went to quite extraordinary lengths to establish that he was not blind. He was very vain about his sight, and he couldn't bear to be seen wearing glasses in public. On one occasion, when someone called to see him at Harcourt Terrace, he came out of the bedroom in a dressing-gown, whipped off the glasses, stuck them in the dressing-gown pocket, and promptly fell down the stairs, because he couldn't see where he was going. He could be very sharp, though. When *Telefís Scoile* was on the go, I was reading some poems by Seán O'Ríordáin, in a programme with Mícheál, who had come in to read some of his own poems. But because I was reading the poems, and everybody else had read the poems, he was going to read his poems, even though he knew them all by heart. When the programme started, he was carefully seated, facing the camera. He ostentatiously took these spectacles from his pocket, put them on, and proceeded to read the poems, which he couldn't see. But he went through this elaborate act of reading, just to show that he could see.

I was fooled by this, I must say, until we had a break, and I felt this clutch on my elbow, and he said, in Irish, 'Please guide me to the toilet. Don't let on, just stand up. I'll stand shoulder to shoulder with you. I'll put my arm on your shoulder, and we'll chat as we go out.'

So I led him out, and then back to the studio, all in the prescribed manner; and it pleased him to think that nobody realised that he couldn't see. But of course everybody knew perfectly well that he couldn't see. We spoke in Irish the whole time, as we had spoken to the director all through. I won't mention the director's name, because I think the comment that Mícheál made was a bit unfair. Having spoken only Irish up to then, at the end the director came in and said in English, 'There's your contract, Mícheál. You might as well sign it now.' And Mícheál said acidly, 'Isn't it remarkable how fluent we become in English when we need to talk about something important, like fucking money.' And he did say 'fucking money'. He could be quite foul-mouthed when he wanted to be.

It was generally believed that he wore stage make-up in public. This in inaccurate. He wore street make-up. It was different. Somebody who hadn't ever seen him except at the theatre, and always in make-up, met him in O'Connell Street and said, 'Mícheál, your make-up.'

'What about it?'

'You have your make-up on, in the street.'

'O God, you scared the life out of me. I thought I'd forgotten to put it on.'

It puzzled people, I suppose, that anybody would wear make-up that was blatantly obvious; but of course the whole point was not to wear discreet make-up, not to conceal anything, but to draw attention to it, to flaunt it. He was a homosexual. Maybe it was a statement.

Barbara Leaming's book on Orson Welles recalls how Hilton and Mícheál scandalised provincial American towns by going around, practically with erections, in shorts, in summer. What they did in Ireland was nothing compared to their flagrant carry-on when they were away. Speaking of make-up, Niall Buggy tells about two Dublin women watching Mícheál in a pub.

'D'ye see that man over at the counter? Would you say he's wearing a wig?'

'Wait till I see. Hm . . . Ah yes, he is, he's wearing a wig all right. (Pause.) But no one would ever know.'

He once wore a bald wig over his own wig, to show that he wasn't bald. The mystery is why he ever wore a wig at all, because he was not bald. (I was once assured by Jimmy Burke that his wig was made 'from his own pubickers'.)

When he went blind, and finally took off that wig, presumably because he could no longer put it on straight, he displayed a head of wavy, silver-white hair. He went grey, but he couldn't bear it, so he had the black wig. Anybody else would have dyed the hair. Maybe he did dye it for many years — but why wear one over the other? Why one layer of false bald skin, over a layer of false black hair, over a layer of real white hair, plus, on occasions, a hat?

*Lovers*, by Brian Friel, which premièred in 1967 at the Gate, was directed by Hilton, and after the dress rehearsal, Mícheál came in to me and said, 'I want to correct your make-up. It's not right.' And he began to make up my eyes, holding me in a rather sexy embrace all the time. That sort of thing was par for the course, I suppose, but he did correct my make-up.

Afterwards we were invited for supper at Harcourt Terrace, and at about three o'clock in the morning, Mícheál was telling stories. His technique was hypnotic. He told us about Edward Ball (and this story was authenticated afterwards). Edward Ball, who came from a wealthy family, had killed his mother by chopping off her head with an axe. He worked at the Gate as an assistant stage manager, apprentice stage manager, or something, during Mícheál's time.

'We were doing *Crime and Punishment* at the time, and I was playing Raskilnikov. Every night when we came to the murder scene, as I left the stage, I could see Edward Ball standing in the wings, transfixed. He never missed that scene. Every time the play was done, he came, and made sure that he watched that scene.'

Raskilnikov committed the murder with an axe. Looking back, Mícheál found it very strange to feel that this man was plotting a murder as he watched the play, and that maybe he was gathering ideas for its execution from Mícheál's performance.

That story was told in response to a question about good and evil and sin. He was very interesting on those subjects, and he talked about them a lot. He'd talk for ever on topics such as religion and morality. (James Neylin and Mícheál were leaving the Gate one evening after a late Christmas Eve rehearsal and they had to step over the prostrate forms of drunks on the Parnell Street pavement. Mícheál looked disdainfully. 'See how they celebrate the birth of their Redeemer!' he boomed.)

Anna Manahan had asked him, 'Mícheál, have you ever met anybody who was truly evil?'

He said, 'I only met two people in my life who were fully and completely evil. The first one was this man, Edward Ball.' (And then he told in detail the Ball story.)

'And who was the second?'

'Ian Priestley Mitchell.'

For no reason at all — just to throw in a name. Poor Ian Priestley Mitchell, the elderly presenter of the Irish Hospitals' Trust sponsored programme. He could just as easily have said 'John McCormack'. He had this kind of wickedness. Of my colleague George Greene, in the Rep, Mícheál said, 'He's so sinister-looking.' Which indeed he was. 'He looks like the illegitimate son of de Valera and Mephistopheles.' (Which he did.) George played Tom Foley, the original suburban Dublin, long-suffering husband and father in *The Foley Family*, a very successful radio series over many years. When a TV version was proposed, George said, 'I don't look a bit like Tom Foley. It would never work.' He was right. He looked like a Spanish Dracula.

Mícheál in drag was quite disturbing to watch. He played in panto at the Gaiety when Hilton and he were sharing that theatre with Jimmy O'Dea, for some reason. They had probably been frozen out of the Gate by Lord Longford — I think there was some legal wrangling, or it may have been at a time when renovations were taking place. Mícheál played one of the Ugly Sisters. He was so good that it was repulsive. It wasn't funny, it was chilling, very weird. It was a transvestite thing, really, rather than a funny dame, so deadly accurate that he looked like a seedy old tart. At that time O'Dea wasn't all that keen on the co-operation, the merging of the two companies. Jimmy was fond of his jar and he liked to rehearse in his own way. When Jimmy strolled in from Neary's one day, smelling strongly of liquid lunch, probably Jameson, Hilton said, 'You're late.'

Jimmy shrugged it off. He wasn't used to being spoken to like that, by anybody. Hilton continued acidly, 'I dislike having to work with drunks.' And O'Dea replied, 'Well, I don't like working with perverts.' That stopped that conversation. Nowadays Jimmy would be called 'homophobic', I suppose, but I think he just picked the handiest stick to beat somebody who had challenged him on his own patch. In any case, whatever about Hilton, Mícheál certainly would have taken no exception to that remark. He was no 'gay libber'. He said, in my hearing, 'I hate that word "gay". Why can't they be "queer", like the rest of us?' And that wheel has turned full circle.

He had little sympathy with the mundane problems of little people. When he arrived late for rehearsal in Radio Éireann, he fumed, 'Couldn't get a taxi. They're on strike. Why the hell do they have to go on strike?' Someone said, 'Well, you know, Mícheál, they're very badly paid.' 'Oh, don't tell me about the misfortunes of the exploited workers. Fuck 'em!' When a campaigner for prisoners' rights went to him, to try to get him to sign a petition to save some hunger-strikers, he thought that Mícheál would sign. Mícheál looked at him and said, 'Fuck them, why don't they take a bath?' (They were women prisoners.)

I am not ashamed to say that I speak of Mícheál with awe, as well with admiration, because I would hardly fit into the same category of actor as MacLiammóir. I would be more a naturalistic actor, whatever that means. If it means that my characterisations are grounded in the reality of my personal experience, where possible, then I would go along with that. Mícheál's approach would be much more romantic. I admired him as somebody who could command an audience, just grab them, and make them believe what he was doing, and resort to the most extravagant excesses of speech and gesture, and make it appear acceptable. I have seen him be terrible in parts — naturalistic parts; but I looked up to him as an entertainer, somebody who could beguile you for three or four hours, and make the evening go, and leave you feeling you had been touched by magic.

That was what he did for many, many years, in thousands of situations, with all sorts of people. He was an incomparable entertainer, and therefore, he must have been an actor. The distinction

I would make is that whereas I am a naturalistic actor, I am probably naturalistic, or natural, in my own lifestyle as well — he wasn't. His whole life was an act, on which he superimposed a series of performances. It was inevitable that he would go over the top.

I saw him in a play he wrote, called *The Mountains Look Different*, in about 1949, with an English actress, Sheila Burrell. It was the story of a young country boy from Connemara, played by Mícheál, who is working in London and falls in love with an English girl. They marry, and he brings her home to the cottage in Connemara to meet his father, played by Denis Brennan (who would have been about twenty-five years of age then). Now, for all Mícheál's impeccable Connemara Gaelic, his English-speaking Connemara lad seemed to have picked up a rich Munster accent in London. It certainly wasn't a Connemara accent.

In one scene, on their arrival at the cottage, he puts his arms around Barbara, his new bride. She pushes him gently away — not for the first time, we gather. Face contorted with anguish, he cries, 'Barbara, when will you . . . ?' (He pronounced it Bairbre.) 'Not now.' (At least he didn't have her claim she had a headache.)

Later, there is a stark confrontation between his father and his wife (who actually looked like brother and sister). It turns out that she had been a prostitute, who had had an interlude with the father when he had visited London. He proposes to lay the lady once more, in return for which he will keep quiet about the past. And he produces the imperishable line: 'After all, what's another sin to the likes of you?'

If I recall rightly (and there is ample room for doubt), she says she has VD, and that this is why she can't have intercourse with the son; though whether she contracted it from the father was not very clear. A merry little romp, far too tame and everyday for the present climate, but meant at that time to be a searing indictment, at the very least, of something or other. It was appalling rubbish.

Bartley (surely he must have been called Bartley) murders the father. He has to, or the play can never end, or get to a curtain, anyway. Finally, he is taken away by two policemen, neither noticeably gay. Even I, hardly out of short trousers, could only wonder how such an established and exotic star could have bothered with such banality. Was this the same man who played the crazed character in *The Old Lady Says No*, the actor who thinks he is Robert Emmet, and intones the wonderful line of Denis Johnston's, 'I have heard the angels chanting the beatitudes to the souls in Malabolge, and I have done with you'? So, on a level of plain, workaday acting, he may have disappointed; but as a free spirit, left to his own devisings, he whipped the divil.

He almost invented the one-man show with *The Importance of Being Oscar*. There were other one-man performances before that, certainly, back through theatre history. In the fit-up days, Val Vousden did monologues, recitations and sketches solo. Percy French sang and played the piano, as well as reciting, but it was a one-man show nevertheless. Yet *The Importance of Being Oscar* was the first attempt to celebrate (there is no other word for it) the life, loves and literature of an author, through his writings, through hearsay and through history. It was an unforgettable show. I don't think anybody ever reached such heights in a one-man portrayal after that. He achieved it when he was quite old as well — sixty-odd years of age. He toured it to America, Australia, Britain, and he was adulated everywhere.

He was also fortunate to have lived well ahead of endearing little pranks such as 'Outing'. Homosexuality, while assiduously hidden, was rarely directly referred to. In London he was known, not quite slightingly, as 'the poof with the brogue'.

# TEN

Cyril Cusack was a totally different kettle of fish. Nicknamed 'Squirrel', he was also a weasel, on stage. He was the unofficial underplaying champion of the Western World. Anyone playing opposite Cyril, even in subdued undertones, seemed to be shouting his head off. There was a great rivalry between Cusack and MacLiammóir, who devoted quite a piece of *All for Hecuba* to Cyril. He was fairly lukewarm in his praise of Cusack, to be honest. Cyril was also pretty lukewarm in his praise of others. He had a vicious streak in him, though he had a sly wit. The first time I worked with Cyril was in a radio play, set in the time of the burning of Cork by the Black and Tans. He was playing an informer who used to play billiards with the British soldiers in the barracks.

Chris Curran and I were playing two IRA men who were on to this fellow, and we had a very tense scene in the billiard saloon. During all the rehearsals, Cyril played it real 'cawny', as that type of Cork character would have said, meaning 'canny', acutely aware that he was playing a Cork city man, and that he was playing against two Cork city fellas. He had a very clever way of suggesting an accent, and then muttering, only half using the written dialogue. Then on the live broadcast he cast all that aside and rattled through the lines, speeding up his delivery and driving the plot forward, so that the scene was over before we could get our breath back. And then, with a saintly smile, he gave a hint of a little smirk, as if to say, 'Well, that'll put them in their box, anyway.' This kind of thing went on all the time when he was about.

At the same time he used to make rather elaborate little jokes, flattering jokes. I was with him in a passion play in the pro-cathedral in Dublin. He played Herod, and didn't come on until the second half. I played Caiphas, in the first Act. It was a very popular production, with queues for tickets. One night, in the dressing-rooms upstairs in the pro-cathedral, above the High Altar, after the first Act, Cyril came in, having fought his way through the queues at the box office, and said, 'Ah yes, I think the time has come for me to retire, pack it in, call it a day. I really must retire now.' He would always throw out this kind of vague statement, which would prompt a question like, 'But why?' or, 'Ah, come on, for Heaven's sake.' So somebody, naturally, said, 'But why, Cyril?' 'Well,' he said, 'as I was coming in, there was a queue for tickets for tomorrow night, and one lady turned and she said, "Move out there now and let Mr Toibin in!" I think it's time to retire.'

That was, of course, a complete invention, designed entirely to flatter me and to reassure me that we were pals, just in case he had caused me some offence. He was quite capable of that kind of ingratiation, as well as the most scarifying put-downs.

We were coming from a location on *Far and Away*, a big film made in Dingle, in which I played Tom Cruise's father. Jimmy Devlin (J G Devlin), Cyril and I were sharing a car with two young actors from London. I shouldn't call them English actors, because one of them was actually Richard Harris's nephew, and the other was a lad called Steve O'Donnell, who was a Londoner, but of Irish extraction. Jimmy assumed that they were both English, or at least that they knew very little about the area, and proceeded to tell them how very historic it was. He told them about its great literary tradition, about Robin Flower, whose book *The Great Island* concerned this area, and he spoke of Peig Sayers and Tomás O'Crohan, and so on. When we got out at the hotel, as Jimmy headed for the bar he said, 'I'm sorry, Cyril, I had to explain all the literary heritage to the lads, you know. I hope I didn't bore you all the way back from the location.' 'Not *all* the way,' said Cyril, with a cherubic smile.

Cyril was a totally theatrical being, in every way. Yet he was also a transfiguration into a Gaelic-speaking, outspoken republican. He was also extremely Catholic, and aggressively Holy Roman when he wanted to be, which was an aspect of him that a lot of people objected to, because they felt that he was having it every way. But that's his personal life, and nothing to do with his status as an actor, which is unchallenged. I didn't spend any great time on stage with him, but Bob Quinn made a film called *Poitín*, with Donal McCann, myself and Cyril.

I rarely look at the rushes, or the 'dailies', as the Yanks call them, for two good reasons: I'm rarely invited to, and if I did view them and found something I didn't like in my performance, I'd never have enough clout to ask for them to be re-shot, so there's no point in the exercise, really. But one night McCann and I were looking at the rushes of a scene between one of the local Connemara actors, Tom, and Cyril. They were talking over a bottle of whiskey, the bottle being on the table, and this was the local lad's big scene. McCann and I got hysterical as it went on, because in Take 1 you had Tom, full face on, with just the suggestion of Cyril's presence. Take 2, you had Cyril's shoulder slightly in, and occasionally Cyril's profile would insinuate itself; and by Take 10, Tom was in one corner of the screen, and Cyril's forefinger was dead centre, caressing his eyebrow as he sized up his man. I presume that in the film they used Take 1. The rest was pure archive material — a beautiful lesson on how to upstage someone on camera. None of this was accidental, though it may have been done from sheer habit, and with a sense of fun as well. He just couldn't allow anybody to be there, in the middle.

In the British National Theatre Production of *The Plough and the Stars*, an old friend of Cyril's, Harry Webster, played the barman. The bar counter was upstage, slightly elevated, so that when Harry polished glasses, or wiped the bar in the central position, he towered over the downstage action very distractingly. The Lord had endowed Harry with an endearing eagerness to please, without a concomitant ability to absorb direction; so when Bill Bryden, the director, gently intimated that a less central position and a reduced work-rate would be a help, Harry got flustered. He was an oul' pet, whom no one would knowingly upset, so it took a long time to sort out the optimum correlation of rinsing, and proximity to the principals. Even very good actors can be quite dense about taking direction (some of them genuinely so). Eventually even Harry was happy. At the break, Cyril took Bryden to task.

'That was very naughty of you, Bill, very hurtful, what you did to poor Harry.'

'But all I did was give him a direction.'

'Ah, but that's just it. You see, he's not an actor.'

There was what became a famous incident during the film of *Cry of the Innocent* with Rod Taylor. Rod was burying his wife and child, who had been killed in a sabotage plane crash. Cyril was playing the police inspector investigating the case. At the burial, it was obviously Taylor's big emotional scene, tearful, choking. In mid-scene he stopped. 'Will someone tell Cusack to stop crying! I'm the one crying — he's just fucking watching! He doesn't know these people. Why is he crying?'

In *The Cherry Orchard*, there was a scene where Philip O'Flynn made a long explanatory speech, to which Cyril, who had just arrived in, stood listening, hat in hand (a hat with a round crown on it), and wearing gloves. As Philip delivered the speech, Cyril removed the first glove, one finger at a time, centre stage, standing by a low table. He then similarly removed the second glove, switching the hat to the other hand. Then, he dumped the gloves into the hat. All this was done with such perfection, such finesse, that everybody in the house was looking at the hat and the gloves; yet Cyril was concentrating entirely on the face of the speaker. When it looked as if he had finished with that little pantomime, he put the hat, crown downwards, on the low table, and, apparently accidentally, flicked the brim with his little finger as he retracted his hand. Now, you have this hat, rocking and rolling silently on the table during the speech, and everybody is on tenterhooks, watching. When is the hat going to stop rolling? And poor Philip O'Flynn is fit to be tied. There's nothing he can do. He knows exactly what's going on. Confronted, no doubt Cyril would have made an innocent protest: 'But I have to take off my gloves!'

Why do this? Why steal scenes? Why steal shows? Why steal thunder? It is Thespian kleptomania.

Upstaging by being over-helpful is rare, but I recall one outstanding example of it in the first production by Jim Fitzgerald of *The Death and Resurrection of Mr Roche*, by Tom Kilroy. Derry Power and I had a scene, at the end of which I went upstage and sat on a bed, while Mr Roche took up the scene with Derry. We had been running for several weeks at this time. The actor playing Mr Roche was renowned for his ability to paraphrase, without going to the trouble of learning the original lines. Like getting your retaliation in first, he got the paraphrase in first. He had managed to use the paraphrased version of his part to date.

Whether he had had an attack of conscience, or what, one night he came in, absolutely D L P (Dead Letter Perfect). He must have stayed up all night to learn this scene. He spat out the lines. Derry, who was at least a foot shorter than he, looked up, quite startled. In the middle of Roche's next long speech, he walked upstage to me and said, 'What's this fucker up to? Giving us cues at this stage of the run?' And he went back down and resumed the scene. Learning his lines when the run was nearly over, he upset everyone, because it is unnerving to be thrown cues you haven't heard since the first day of rehearsal.

In Cyril's case there would have been a deliberateness about all this carry-on. I mentioned his knack of throwing out a line that would invite a question. He came into the lounge bar at the Plough, opposite the Abbey, one evening. He just stood there, in the middle of the lounge, and struck a pose. Eventually, when everybody had focussed on him, even the young actors, overcome with curiosity as to what this 'ould fella' was up to now, he said, addressing thin air: 'You know, we'll all have to work much harder.' 'What's all this about?' the pub wonders. 'We really will, we'll have to work much harder.' (He's got their full attention now.) 'Yes, we'll have to work much harder.' By this time, they're all agog — well, if not agog, at least mildly impatient for the payoff. He moves towards the bar. 'In order to make Ireland a fit place for Edna O'Brien to live in.' And that was obviously provoked by something he had heard, which she had said about him, or about Ireland, or about whatever — who knows?

I met him once coming out of the rehearsal rooms in the BBC place in North Acton. He called me: 'I'll give you a lift — I've a car coming for me. They send a car for me, you know, I insist on that.' Cyril was the only one for whom they would send a car, as distinct from ringing for a taxi. So I rode along with him, and he was talking about the profession, and how distressing it was that young people showed no respect. They were full of 'What's the word they use? Aggro, isn't that the word they use? Yes. I suppose they mean aggravation. Hatred, really, it's just hatred; and it's very sad to see young people like that, all through the profession, going through life full of hatred. I couldn't do that, because I've never hated anybody . . . except Siobhán . . . but then, this is a different world.' I took it that the whole point of this soliloquy was that I had recently been working with Siobhán McKenna, and he wanted to point out, none too gently, that I wasn't associating with the right people.

Siobhán was well able to reciprocate, of course. When asked when rehearsals would start for *The Cherry Orchard* (the Abbey production), she said she wasn't quite sure, 'But Cyril is already rehearsing his cough.' She meant his irritating, barely audible clearing of non-existent phlegm, preferably during someone else's intake of breath in the middle of a long speech. But even here, we must leave the last word with Cyril. In that same production of the *The Cherry Orchard*, Madam Knebel, from the Moscow Arts, was directing through an interpreter. Her English was minimal to none. She conveyed that Cyril's performance was unconvincing. 'It lacks truth,' she said. Cyril considered this.

'I know little of the Soviet Union,' he said, 'but you have two great newspapers. *Izvestia* and *Pravda*.'

'That is so.'

'I understand that *Izvestia* means 'information' and *Pravda* means 'truth'.

'Yes.'

'Well, Madam, if you give me more *Izvestia*, I will give you *Pravda*.'

\* \* \* \*

Cyril had a bee in his bonnet about Ireland's lack of an Honours List. Presumably he didn't aspire to be Sir Cyril, but he brought the subject up publicly often enough to suggest that his interest may have reflected a sense of personal deprivation. He needn't have worried. Ireland has its own way of conferring recognition. There was only one Cyril.

It wouldn't have pleased him to think so, but there was also only one Siobhán. They were held in equal affection, all the more so, perhaps, because of their reciprocal animosity.

But on Godfrey Quigley alone did his peers, who held him in high if aghast esteem, confer a title at once formal and casual. They called him 'The Quig'. Words like 'behave' fall far short of adequacy in describing him. Rather, he comported himself with Patrician poise and aplomb. He was arrogant, aristocratic, arresting in appearance and majestic in manner. He was known as a gambler, and had invented many board games. Uninterested in athletic activity, he was intensely competitive, even in his gambling, and would play any game for money. He and I used to play Scrabble till the morning hours during a long season in Scotland. The score carried into the next session, and at a penny a point I was at one stage twenty-eight pounds down, when I played the word 'enrol', which he challenged. The marathon session was at Stirling University, where we were playing *Iceman*. The campus was snowed in. Nevertheless, I trudged across to the Uni Shop and bought a dictionary. I returned in triumph with proof of my academic superiority, which was graciously acknowledged. It was the turning point. I levelled the series as we waited in Glasgow airport lounge, on the way home.

Godfrey revelled in any kind of battle of wits. A great example of his ingenuity was when some English members of a film crew on location in Clare came to him with a difficulty. Filming in remote areas, they were cut off from the bookmaker's. Their spokesman, Knobby Crosse, asked could Quigley help out. Godfrey had already opened an account with the Newmarket-on-Fergus branch of the Alf Hogan gaming empire. As long as he could phone in the bets, everything was all Sir Garnett. At the time, place-betting was not allowed in off-track shops, except as part of an each-way wager. The single bet therefore would be, say, five pounds on the nose. In the case of a horse which the Quig thought good enough to be placed, though not to win, he would bet five pounds each way, his own fiver for a place having a free ride on the back of Knobby Crosse's fiver for a win. Thus, a horse coming in first, second or third at say eight to one, would pay Godfrey two to one. It worked quite often.

He was the master of the grand gesture. Once when we went to a take-away Wimpy bar in Limerick, the Quig, in full flight having been to an evening race meeting, produced a roll of notes that would choke a bullock, and demanded a table for two. It was pointed out that all food was 'to go'. Incensed, he went out and looked at those waiting for take-aways, lined up at the window. 'F . . . you and your soup kitchen,' he bellowed, 'I will feed the poor of Limerick.' And he showered the queue with notes until we managed to manoeuvre him into a cab.

The enduring impression The Quig left was of a crusading aversion to timidity in any area of life, personal professional or recreational. He was a legend but never an institution. 'We are rogues and vagabonds, dear heart,' he would crow in delight, 'and so defined by regal proclamation.' He revelled in this ruffianly classification as if he had coined the phrase himself.

I was only eighteen when I first saw The Quig, an extremely handsome but already bulky presence, standing at the bar of Tommy Lennon's, the Abbey Bar in Abbey Street. He had a cocktail swizzle-stick in his mouth and was stirring a hot whiskey with a cigarette. He was describing to Denis Brennan, and all others within wider than average earshot, his first meeting with Denis Johnston, in Port Said. Naturally, where else? It had to be. Exotic, exciting. Even when I became very pally with him, he retained these qualities. He was never less than unpredictable, sometimes menacing, always fun. When I joined Radio Éireann, he and Brennan and Rodway and Michael O'Herlihy had founded the Globe Theatre, and after a radio rehearsal I recall him turning on me even though I had, perhaps uncharacteristically, said nothing. 'Oh, I know! You have it all in here,' he said, tapping his temple. 'You've intellectualised the whole fucking thing into a pallid, anaemic cerebral exposition. But I . . .', and the whole of Moore Street held its breath, 'I have it in here.' And he thumped his massive thorax with a ham-like fist. 'That's where it counts. In here. And out here.' Followed by a deafening roar illustrative of proper projection.

# ELEVEN

Despite the 'all right on the night' tradition, shows usually succeed, not by luck or fluke, but because everything has been thoroughly rehearsed, and properly done — which can be very gratifying, but not half as interesting as when things go horribly wrong. Get a group of actors in jovial mood, laughing like jackasses, and you can bet your boots they are remembering every gruesome detail of a flop.

Business tycoons remain tight-lipped about their failures; authors buy up remaindered copies of their books, or have them incinerated or recycled. Actors, on the other hand, glory in their humiliations, among themselves at any rate. Daniel O'Connell is reputed to have said that only someone with a heart of stone could read of the death of Little Nell without weeping. Oscar Wilde said that only someone similarly hard-hearted could read the same without laughing.

I have played in two theatrical disasters, which only a man with a heart of stone could speak of without boasting. One, *Crock*, was a home game, played at the Gaiety. *Fearless Frank* was an away fixture, played on the incomparably bumpier Broadway pitch.

*Crock* was an absolutely splendid flop, a really gigantic, spectacular flop. It had seemed such a good idea to take *The Crock of Gold*, by James Stephens, a book that had never, so far as I know, been presented on stage, and turn it into what was loosely described as 'a rock musical'.

I have mixed feelings about rock. Some bad, others worse. Unwanted noise is the greatest pollutant of the atmosphere, at least to unwanted people like those who dislike rock. To me, the adulation of U2 is, like their name, a mystery. Is it an abbreviation of F U2? If so, why so coy? It does carry the implication of a retort (to FU).

Still, live and let live. Deafen and let deafen. Who am I to begrudge credit to U2 or UB 40 or U-me-bollix or any other youthful millionaire hit-squad who assault the Richter Scale with unintelligible lyrics and three million dollars' worth of heavy equipment? Who am I to deny their right to organise musical masturbation on a massive public scale? As long as I can stay out of earshot, if such a place there be, it worries me not at all.

What I find disturbing is that the likes of Garret Fitzgerald and Albert Reynolds, two seemingly balanced persons, former prime ministers, and Richard Burke, when commissioner in Europe, have gloried in attending these sessions, applauding Mick Jagger and Michael Jackson and their likes. I disbelieve their posturing political pretence that they really like this stuff. Even Giscard, or Jacques Chirac, who have indulged in similar grovelling to their intellectual inferiors, haven't been able to carry this nonsense off.

I met another minister, a very likeable man, once, at a fundraising event for the SDLP in the National Stadium in Dublin. He told me, with startling frankness, that while he saw the need for supporting the SDLP, he suspected that had he been catapulted into Northern politics, he would ideologically have had to stand as a unionist.

As we spoke, the Dubliners were finishing up their set, to a huge ovation. The minister said, ruminatively, 'The Dubliners. They're very good, aren't they? But I'm afraid their music has a populist tinge that does not impinge upon my range of sensibilities.' It was not the sort of phrase that one expected in a casual appraisal of 'The Dubs', so it lodged in the astonishment-retrieval zone of my own comprehension, Subsequently, when I saw this same minister photographed at a rock concert, I wondered how that was impinging upon his range of sensibilities.

But to get back to *Crock*. The two lads who had adapted it were of Donegal origin. They were living in Manhattan, and they came back, and they called their musical *Crock*, which was unfortunate, because a 'crock' in New Yorkese, at that time, meant 'a crock of shit', so it was almost a prophecy of what was going to befall their baby.

Why they called it 'a rock musical' puzzled me also, because the music was, well, some of it anyway, very pleasant. Some of the singing was very nice, but the whole concept was ruined by the fact that the singers were all wearing microphones. This was bad enough, but they all had to dance, and the set was constructed to represent a grassy knoll, so that there was a very exaggerated slope to the stage, which meant having to dance on it at an angle of approximately thirty-five degrees. A flat, round stage-weight had been placed on top of the knoll, under plastic grass, in order to keep the beam supporting the knoll in place. But dancing on this platform loosened the weight, which somehow managed to stand up on its edge and roll down the grassy knoll. This thing would have been, I suppose, about two stone in weight, and it crashed into the middle of the orchestra pit. Since this was a rock musical, you couldn't have heard a bomb, so nobody noticed. It almost brained the MD, who indicated that perhaps he wouldn't have minded . . .

That was the most exciting thing that happened in the whole run. But the run wasn't long.

We opened on the Monday night to delighted applause, a huge reception, mostly from relations of the two lads who had adapted it; and they were very pleased, and even we in the cast, who had been less than enthusiastic about it after four weeks of rehearsal, and had come to feel that this really was a 'crock', were fooled by the magnificent ovation it got. Of course, the following day the truth dawned, because the Irish critics, who will always tell you the sad truth, no matter how much pleasure it gives them, did their duty to a man and woman: fearlessly they revealed what a lousy show it was — and they really slammed it. Recriminations broke out, and the only one who was totally unperturbed by all this was Alan Simpson, who had directed it. Simpson had had some superb flops on his hands, and none of them ever bothered him. Nothing ever bothered him, in fact. He was very laid-back and, while sunny disposition would hardly be accurate, he had at the same time a certain sang-froid.

I played the Philosopher, and Marie Kean the Thin Woman of

Inishmagrath. They were wonderful characters in the book, but became diffused and peripheral in the musical adaptation. It doesn't bear thinking about, really. It flopped, anyway, and I met Marie Kean at a funeral a few weeks afterwards, and as we walked behind the coffin, she said, 'We only meet at funerals nowadays — on or off stage.

I wasn't with the adaptors the following day, but they were obviously very crestfallen, and they tended to blame the director, and the cast, and eventually they had to fall back on blaming the audience. But they couldn't really do that, because the audience had been quite enthusiastic. So they just packed their bags and stole away, as all disappointed authors do, presumably.

It is a hurtful, horrifying thing to get a savage notice, even from some semi-literate who wants simply to make a name for himself; and if actors don't have the sympathy they should, for writers who get knocked, it's because the same happens to actors on a very regular basis. They often carry the can for writers' failings. The author of a play in which I played one of the leads, was interviewed by a theatre magazine about the reviews for one of his plays. These reviews were less enthusiastic than he had become used to, and he did concede that the first act had perhaps been a bit over-written, or that certain things had been a bit obscure. 'But,' he added, 'I have seen the play again since I rewrote portions of the first act, and I find it has been improved immensely.' Not one syllable of that first act was cut, rewritten or even talked about after the first night. Not a comma was changed. He also suggested that the first night's lack of sparkle had been due to some of the actors being tired. If they were, it was from mouthing his rubbish for weeks on end.

Reviews used to matter less in Dublin. Word of mouth was what counted. But Dublin has changed, and to some extent for the very same reason that obtains in New York or in London. People accept the papers' verdict, not necessarily as being totally accurate or absolutely true, but they do go so far as to say, 'Well, if the papers think this is a stinker, there is no point in spending two hours getting ready to go into town, paying for parking the car, paying for supper, and spending anything from £80 to £140.' Whereas if the papers say, unequivocally, 'This is a good show', well, then, it's at least worth the risk. It comes down to money in the end. The punters rely on the critic to guide them, as a matter of economics rather than taste.

Which brings me to New York restaurants, and Sardi's, and first nights. The word Sardi's was almost synonymous with first-night parties. *Fearless Frank*, my second favourite flop, was booked into Sardi's — or rather, its first-night party was, though even that is not quite accurate.

But first of all, it had been booked into the Princess Theatre, right under the Castro Convertibles hoarding, one of the world's best-known advertisements, right on Times Square. The Princess had once been a nightclub, and was the scene of Frank Sinatra's first New York appearance, in nineteen forty something. It subsequently served as a cabaret spot, theatre and porn movie house, before being converted to a 500-seat bijou theatre. 'Bijou' translates in this instance as poky and gloomy. And now, defunct.

The play was based on *The Life and Loves* of *Frank Harris*, adapted by Andrew Davies, and superbly so. I had forebodings about this enterprise.

I was playing in *The Iceman Cometh* at the Theatre Royal, Bath, when I had a phone call. 'This is David Black in New York City. I want you to star in my new Broadway production.'

A Breton friend of mine, struggling with idiomatic English, used to say, 'You are putting my leg.' I phrased it differently: 'Stop taking the piss. Who is this?'

'Can you hear me?'

'Yeah, but I don't believe you.'

He gave me the Big Spiel. It was time, he pointed out, to return to Broadway.

'We need your artistry in these United States.'

I rose predictably to the sweet bait of flattery, couched in terms of social responsibility. I owed it, he said, to the playgoers of the Western world, to re-lume their drab lives with my effulgent talent. So, I did the full Molly Bloom again; and ten years almost to the day after my first arrival in Heaven-on-Hudson, I was trudging up the stairs of a rehearsal warehouse on 42nd and 10th, attempting intricate dance routines with well-rounded sex kittens, clad mostly in deodorant. I echoed the cry of a late developer I knew, who took to lust in his declining years. 'Ah, where was all the crumpet when we had the wherewithal.'

Our first big problem had to do with direction. Marvin Hamlisch put it memorably in song, that 'what's too painful to remember, we simply choose to forget'. So I have elected to banish any recollection of the director from my mind. The most beautiful lady in the cast confided in me that she had the problem of banishing him from areas less inaccessible than her mind. This was two nights after we opened, and she was drinking champagne to celebrate his departure.

His first *faux pas* (and it was a clanger that resounded through the green glassy glens of the Great White Way) was when he cut a line from the text, as he felt it would not be understood. 'It's not', he explained, 'that Americans are stupid. They are quite intelligent really. It's just that our sense of humour is too subtle to cross the Atlantic.' Had he pissed on the flag, he could hardly have dropped more rapidly in the polls. From then on, a certain anti-English frigidity prevailed at rehearsals.

Other minor distractions, unimportant in themselves, combined to mitigate against harmony. For instance, the producer simply never spoke to anybody, even to bid them the time of day, without switching on his tape recorder, which was hanging, usually, around his neck.

'Hi Valerie, how are you today?'

'Oh, I'm fine, I guess. Only I lost one of my legwarmers.'

'Hang on. Let me hear that back. Yes, just as I thought. I've lost your legwarmers too. Maybe you could just say that last bit again, a shade louder?'

This guy must have an enormous archive full of my views, solicited by him, on the Vietnam war, Teddy Kennedy, crime in the streets, the trouble in North Ireland (sic), herbal teas, transvestism, the probable incidence of oral sex in Abbeyfeale, and why baseball, not hurling, took the North American continent by storm. He may have scrubbed my unsolicited comments on cretins with tape recorders.

The rehearsal schedule was Sunday to Sunday, with no day off, twelve noon till twelve midnight. It was intense, unflagging, unimaginative drudgery, devoid of light relief. It is a mystery of Mary Celestian impenetrability, why people who actively loathe actors become directors; just as people who cannot abide the theatre become critics.

There was, apart from the beauties, whose presence cheered me up no end, one other ray of light that split the gloom. He was a Cuban refugee who had fled from Castro with his parents, at a tender age, and had a job as stage doorman, general maintenance man and dressing-room cleaner. His stage doorman job was possibly his easiest, since there was no stage door. His name was Pepe, and despite his long residence in New York, he still said, 'Are jew chure?' for 'Are you sure?' Maybe he was just 'puttin' on the brogue' for the tourist.

He called me 'Frank', because I was playing Frank. As I was changing to go home after our fifth preview (there were eight, six nights and two matinees), Pepe lugged his vacuum-cleaner into the dressing-room.

'Hi, Frank. Howya doing, buddy?'

Just then, the stage manager's voice came crackling over the aged Tannoy. 'Your call for tomorrow, Ms Mahaffy, Ms Barron and Ms Meadows, is 11 a.m. to rehearse the dance sequence. Thank you, goodnight.'

Pepe knocked off his machine. 'So what's that about, Frank?'

'What?'

'What the hell they wanna rehois the dance for?'

'To make it better, I guess.'

'But who gives a shit? You're closing on the 26th.'

I looked pityingly at this Latin idiot. 'We haven't opened yet,' I pointed out coldly.

'OK, sure, this is correct. But you're still closing on the 26th. I was in the boss's office this morning, and even with the Hoover going, I can hear every word, and he's telling this guy on the phone, "No problem, you can start rehoisals on the 28th." So, Frank, you gotta close on the 26th.'

This man was a soothsayer. He got it right on the nose. I should have known — for what's happening in The Theatre, you read the critics, but for what is happening in a theatre, ask the stage-doorman, even if there ain't no stage door.

But of course, before we could close, first we had to open.

*Fearless Frank*, as I said, was booked, as per tradition, into Sardi's, and all the usual nonsense was gone through. Television sets were wheeled in, and everybody was waiting for the first edition of the *New York Times*.

As I was making my way into Sardi's, Mr Vincent Sardi was standing at the doorway, and somebody coming in said, 'What's the party tonight? What's the show?' And he said, 'Oh, it's a thing called *Fearless Frank*. It's not going any place.'

So I knew, even before I went up the stairs, that was it. This was going to be a short evening.

The producer arrived in, and it was dreadfully embarrassing, and also very misleading. He produced Frank Rich's review from the *New York Times*.

As he read it out, it seemed to be a positive review. It mainly talked about me, and I got some glowing tributes from Mr Rich, for which I am very grateful, because it's a nice thing to be able to defend Frank Rich when most actors spit at the mention of his name, and you are in a position to say, 'Oh, I don't know. I think he's a very fair man.' But I can also say the same, on the same grounds, for Clive Barnes, who was even more hated in his time, and yet found the good word for me.

As the producer, David Black, read out these extracts, people began to nod, and say, 'Oh, that's good. Hey, that's very good.' What I and other people didn't realise was that he had heavily censored this review. He had drawn lines through all the knocking copy, and only read out the favourable references. He skipped the paragraph that said the director might be more usefully employed directing traffic, and that the music 'trickled over the action like thin gruel'.

Of course, the truth had to come out. Somebody unsportingly switched on a television set, and there was this man telling us what a load of old codswallop and bullshit this was. 'Horrible, dreadful, don't waste your money, don't bother.' And people began to drift away into the night, at eighty miles an hour, clutching coats and umbrellas. I realised, of course, that once that happens, there's no cause to celebrate. The management are not paying for any more drink for you, goodbye. The cat is dead, let's bury it.

So, within twenty minutes there were just a few desultory conversations going on, and Sardi's waiters were packing things away, and that was it.

The Irish consul-general, who had just been appointed that very week — in fact, he was only about two days in New York, having been transferred from Chicago, or Boston, or somewhere — had done me the honour of attending the first night, with his wife; and since he did me the kindness of showing the flag, I in return will grant him diplomatic immunity from identification.

He and his wife were thrilled that they had got tickets for the first night of this play, and they were duly invited to the party afterwards. They had enjoyed the play very much — or said they did, anyway. In fact, quite a few people confessed that they had thought the play was very funny; but they were all Europeans, or at least Irish, which is almost the same thing.

I had warned the consul and his wife that we were not going to get good notices. But I said, 'Please hang on, and you will witness a phenomenon which will stay with you for the rest of your life, because as people realise that the notices are bad, they will begin to melt away like snow.' And lo, he tarried, and witnessed this phenomenon, and was greatly taken by the sight of the people melting away. He reflected that even though this evening had brought joy to nobody, it furnished forth enlightenment on the world that was Broadway — as indeed it did.

There might be friends of the management, friends of the cast, and so on, who would tarry marginally longer, but even they would vanish pretty sharpish too. It's understandable. True friendship would lack the ingenuity to soothe the feelings of somebody who has just been told by the press, by an audience possibly as well, that he's no good, forget it, become a bus conductor or something. Suppose he's your best friend, even. What can you say, apart from smirk when he's not looking at you. The adage that the ultimate joy in the theatre is not just that you should be a hit, but that on the same night your best friend should have a flop, is very cynical, but there is an element of truth in it, because the competitive element in acting is inextinguishable. That is why what we in our vanity call 'the profession', which in its unionised manifestation alone boasts 90 per cent unemployment at all times, still attracts the huddled masses.

Schools of acting fleece them, producers seduce them, the press spit-roasts them, managements exploit them, nobody pays them, but still, as Schnozzle Durante so truly observed, everybody wants to get into the act.

Before the show closed, much drama took place offstage, and out of ken, because the producer vanished. He was incommunicado, his whereabouts known only to his lady love, who wasn't telling nobody nothin', so the stage manager said.

The said stage manager posted a week's notice on the board, to protect the management in case it was decided to close after the first eight performances. But that didn't necessarily mean nothin', neither. He had a theory that for the producer to retain certain rights, it was necessary to have twenty-one paid performances. Having paid performances without paying customers is not an easy trick, unless you interpret the phrase to mean that the actors are paid for their performances.

Either way, the show went on. We had one highly appreciative audience of Irish and British publishers, returning from the Chicago Book Fair, who kindled the faint hope that this was a second *Grease*. *Grease* in its time had been a real bummer, which suddenly took off and made millions for somebody. But the publishers were not the vanguard of a vast *Fearless Frank* movement — just decent, good-natured tourists, with a jar or two aboard.

So the producer started to scatter briefs about, which meant that we had to play to senior citizens in throngs of ten or twelve, glaring sullenly at us, wondering when the coach would come to fetch them back to their cheery nursing-homes. The word went round the old folks' homes: stay put until the Ringling Brothers' freebies arrive. Then, one night, a coachload of 'cerebrally challenged' kids from a

Bronx institution, forty-six in all, took over the front of the house. One of these kids was an enthusiast; his enthusiasm was for enthusiasm itself. I estimated that he was about fourteen. He was black, uninhibited, and liked the show. On my first entrance, he gave me a standing ovation.

Quite early in the piece, Frank Harris has a line to the effect that the surest way to a woman's heart is to gaze into her eyes and 'put a stiff cock in her hand'. 'Right on!' roared the enthusiast. 'Yeah, yeah, yeah, Frank! Stiff cock! You're the man!' This went down very well with his buddies of both sexes, so he treated one and all to regular encores, whether the scene contained any sexual content or not. Thus, a solo song, or a dance routine, or a wistful sigh, evoked loud cries of 'Big stiff cock! Right on! Good ole Frankie!' I was later asked, far from coyly, by a lady of indeterminate age, but easily determined motives, if the plaudits for my sexuality should be confined to my stage persona. I was too gallant to point out that it would make no odds to her, which or whether; so I smiled enigmatically.

# TWELVE

I gave pride of place to *Fearless Frank*, not just on the principle of first-the-bad-news, but in order to build up good will for what follows, namely a feast of self-congratulation, euphoria, nostalgia and theatrical sentimentality — the story of *Borstal Boy* on Broadway.

In 1970 Frank Grimes arrived into the Haymarket Bar on 8th Avenue (before it became the Gaymarket) to find me roaring my head off in song. He had just got off the plane from Dublin. I was in the elated company of Mike McAloney and Helena Carroll, a daughter of the great Irish playwright Paul Vincent Carroll. Also present were Tom Signorelli, Bruce Heighley, Mike Cahill, Terry Lomax, Phyllis Craig, Gino Giuliani and Roslyn Dickens, not names that would be familiar to even keen students of the Broadway scene of the time, but which I mention to show that I recall every detail of those early days.

Grimes looked at me and just shook his head. 'Jasus,' he said. 'Like a duck to water in one week.'

And he was right. Ella Fitzgerald's 'Manhattan' and Sinatra's 'New York, New York' rattled around in my head, intoxicating me as 'The Bells of Shandon' never had. It was to be a few weeks before my wife Judy and our five kids, ranging from eleven down to two, would join me, so the town was there to be painted red. The legendary brushman of the Brooklyn Bridge allegedly takes one year to apply one coat to one side of one tier, by which time he needs to start all over again. I applied more urgency, with ample help, to my own mission, which I continued in other towns in other climes until enthusiasm and stamina parted company some four years later. In the meantime, set 'em up Joe.

I first met the above-mentioned Michael McAloney in Groome's Hotel after the first night of *Borstal Boy* at the Abbey in 1967. Joe Groome and his wife Patty ran what was in theory a hotel, in practice a shebeen frequented by the Fianna Fáil party at play. It was the only safe after-hours house in Dublin, and although I knew many who slept there, the only one who ever claimed to have booked in there in advance as a resident was an English actor whom the Gardaí probably suspected instantly as an MI5 agent.

Mike was as twisted as a ball of twine, and he assured me, before collapsing backwards onto a couch in the bar, that he would make me the biggest star on Broadway. He was the only American theatre producer who kept his promise, if you allow that 'the greatest actor on Broadway' is a matter of personal definition. For this reason, if no other, I have never lost my edgy admiration for his persistence, without ever quite believing his subsequent promises.

Life with Mike about was never very predictable, from the day we sat into a stretch limo in Kennedy and drank pink champagne all the way into Times Square. I was whisked from one unlikely talk show or lunchtime radio show to the next. Jet lagged and hung over, I was catapulted into the *Bill Mazer Sports Show* 'from the Cattleman East Restaurant at the New York Stadtler-Hilton at Madison Square Garden. I'm Bill Mazer and I'll be right with you after this message.' With hardly a pause he looked across the table at me. 'I've been to your country. I loved it. Friendly, kind, hospitable people. So what happens to you guys somewhere out there in The Pond that turns you into fascist racist bastards by the time you hit Manhattan? . . . Welcome back, my name is Bill Mazer. . .'

That interview was not a great success. I thought Mazer was bloody great. Mike dismissed him as a liberal.

We tried to crash the *Merv Griffin Show*, then the second big TV showcase after Johnny Carson.

'You don't have an appointment!' snapped the receptionist.

'I think you may be mistaken, my dear young lady . . .' Mike began.

'Go shit in your hat,' interrupted his dear young lady, smiling.

'God-damned stainless steel dyke. Just our luck,' said Mike philosophically.

We made the *Barry Farber Show*. This was a biggie — a late-night radio spot chaired by a Liberal Republican candidate for the State House at some level, who was consequently barred from hosting a talk-show for one month before polling. His stand-in was Malachy McCourt, actor, of Limerick and Greenwich Village, Mike's best man at one (at least) of his weddings. On the panel was Mike, myself, Joe Flaherty of *The Voice*, and another writer. Farber watched from the wings.

A bottle of Jack Daniels circulated in defiance of Federal Communications Commission regulations. Vietnam cropped up. Four-letter words in our play were mentioned. Flaherty said, 'There are only two four-letter words — Nixon and Agnew.' A good crack, but we were now back with Vietnam again. Draft-dodgers cropped up. Mike said he would forgive his young sons anything except growing up to be fags or refusing to join the army to defend their country.

Flaherty was near apoplexy, McCourt was well pleased with the shenanigans, but the FCC officer came in and confiscated the Jack Daniels. The debate became confused, and our cause was lost. Farber asked me to canvass an Irish district with him. 'With that voice and that accent, you could swing me hundreds of votes.' I declined. I'm glad I did. I would hate to have won the election for him. He had, and still has, a great TV career.

They assigned me to Stanley Kaminsky, of the Solters and Sabinson Agency, a charming bespectacled six-foot-four overtly gay caballero who sported an ankle-length fur coat, carried bouquets of flowers and a handbag. He swept me along to studios with dizzying efficiency. We got on very well. Mike liked him also, which puzzled me. He inveighed against faggots in general as a matter of course, yet seemed to get along just fine with individual practitioners. I appeared or talked on so many shows to plug the play, that had I been able to get a few dollars for each, I could have taken it up full-time and let someone else play the part.

The Really Big Deal came when after the first few previews we were on the *Dick Cavett Show*. They'd built a replica of the prison set, and Grimes and myself played a scene before being invited to join the panel. This was all recorded in late afternoon for transmission at 10.30 p.m., which disappointed us as we would still be on stage then, and miss our big début on American Tee-Vee, ohmigod.

The panel discussion, after the play had been lauded and recommended, moved on to drugs. Sandor Vanocur, a commentator then, as still, famous for being famous and very clever at being clever, was explaining the Methadone treatment for heroin addiction. I heard the same proposals on a radio show here only twenty-five years later, which goes to show how these Americans panic. After the theatre, we went to Downey's steak-house as usual, to find that we would be able to see the *Cavett Show* after all. It had been put back because, while we'd been on stage, Richard Milhous Nixon had decided to come on TV and let the folks know as how that very day he had invaded Cambodia (later called Kampuchea).

He was still talking on Downey's large screen above the bar, his face bright green because the colour control had gone wallop. Later we watched the *Cavett Show*, but couldn't hear a word because by now the anti-war faction were raising the roof.

During the run we had a few Black Panthers, a liberation movement of the time, in at the show. The first act curtain came down just after young Brendan had written his name on the cell wall to join a list of earlier occupants, saying as he did so, '*Breandán Ó Beacháin, óglach* (Brendan Behan, IRA), up the republic!' Three of the Brothers rose and, with clenched fist salute, roared, 'Right on!' A day or two later, in the deli across the street, I saw one of the Panther pamphlet-sellers finishing off a can of Rheingold. The deli-guy said, 'You want another beer?' 'Shit man, I don't have no time for another beer. I got me another Revolution to fight.' The deli-guy shrugged. 'Suit yourself, pal. Have a nice day.'

*Borstal Boy* won the Tony Award for Best Play, which is the equivalent of First Prize at the *Feis*. We went on to great acclaim. I didn't have to pay for a drink for donkey's ages. When I was mugged going home one night, the story made the front page of both the *Daily News* and the *Caracas Times*. There were countless rave reviews. Only Walter Kerr, then retired as head-butcher of the Abbatoir of Broadway, dissented seriously, comparing Behan unfavourably with de Valera. 'No claim on our sympathy' was his verdict.

Jack Deacy's 'Night Owl' column in the *Daily News* is an accurate description of the day we opened:

**Man Into Boy**
In the morning, there was Niall Toibin in his hotel room at the Great Northern telling you that his nerves were bad. In the afternoon, there was Niall Toibin at a table in Downey's working to put a ham omelette into his stomach. And in the early evening backstage at the Lyceum Theater, there was Niall Toibin excusing himself because the ham omelette wasn't going to stay down.

But at curtain time there was Niall Toibin standing quietly in the wings with his hands in his pockets and looking straight ahead as the house lights dimmed. And then there was the transformation, the strange lovely moment when Niall Toibin shuffled out of a smoky shadow into a spotlight and became Brendan Behan. It is a personal resurrection that happens at every performance of *Borstal Boy*, the Frank McMahon adaptation of Brendan Behan's raw autobiography.

You listen to the slow sharpness of his Dublin accent and to the punchy way he slams words into sentences and you watch the way he moves across the stage with his stomach pushing out through his old brown jacket and his baggy cuffs falling onto his shoes and his head tilted at an angle and you think for a moment that it is that October night in 1960 when Behan broke out and went on stage after a performance of *The Hostage* at the Cort Theater.

But this visit with Behan lasted only over two hours and after the curtain went down you found yourself backstage in a narrow dressing room with pink walls and red carpeting with the man who becomes Behan every night. Standing there in the middle of the room in his underwear and horn-rimmed glasses, Niall Toibin did not look much like Behan any more. Now he looked more like some violated cherub trying to get into a tuxedo. He talked about the man he becomes.

'I knew Brendan very well myself,' he said, 'and when I first created the role at the Abbey and realised how much like him I became in the role, I wondered to myself whether I should be doing this thing at all.'

The door of the dressing room then went ajar and the red-mustached face of Michael McAloney was staring in at Toibin. McAloney, who co-produced *Borstal* with Burton Kaiser, has the physical and spiritual properties of one Blazes Boylan, the roguish producer-seducer of Molly Bloom in James Joyce's *Ulysses*.

Deacy introduced me to the Lion's Head in Greenwich Village, which was like being pushed into a pool of alcohol infested with the entire cast of all the Damon Runyon books, along with more journalists than I would publicly admit to knowing, including Pete Hamill, Jimmy Breslin, Frank McCourt and, on occasion, Ulick O'Connor.

O'Connor pulled a nice one on me just after our opening night, by calling me at some unearthly hour like 9.00 a.m and identifying himself in a New York accent as the Head Cross-Burner of the Friendly Sons of St Patrick, or some-such, and pouring righteous abuse on my head for peddling blasphemous filth etc, etc, before he finally collapsed in laughter. He took me in completely.

Deacy was my New York sponsor or Godfather, despite being years my junior, and we have maintained a friendship since, both sides of the Pond, as he likes to make an occasional pilgrimage to the ancestral home in Leitrim, that Lesser Brooklyn beyond the wave.

If Deacy was my godfather, Bill Ross was my guardian angel. He was the production stage manager. He had been on the Cort Theatre production of *The Hostage* a few years earlier. He looked me up and down. 'This is what I have been waiting for. Where did you get that schnozz? The Jewish Brendan Behan.'

Bill himself was the quintessential Jewish New Yorker, sardonic, unsurprisable, a walking anthology of theatrical lore. He endeared himself to me forever by his pithy evaluation of Brendan's contribution to the *Hostage* production. Some of the younger actors in their indefatigable search for the irrelevant trivia they were convinced would add texture and depth to their characterisations, pestered him about Brendan's behaviour, and he would respond with such masterful statements as, 'Some days he showed up and talked and sang and told stories, held us all in the palm of his hand, with all that booze and Blarney and Irish charm — he just created this magic atmosphere. Then there were days when he didn't show up at all. That was pretty good too.'

He was unfailingly courteous, humorous and gentle, could spot trouble a mile off, and ward it off diplomatically. When the pace got too hot for me, he would lead me to some cool sequestered spot and calm me down over a Chivas Regal or two. He swapped the anti-Catholic jokes of his boyhood for the anti-Semitic jokes of mine. He would not have got by too comfortably today among the politically correct. He would like, he said, to be remembered as the Last of the Straights.

While the previews were taking place, Bill stood at his desk in the wings, calling the cues, head bent, half-moon glasses slipping down his nose. During the intermission one night, an actor named James Woods (yes, that James Woods), came to Bill and spoke as follows:

'Mr Ross, I was out front during the first Act.'

'You shouldn't have been. You could get fired for that if I got to hear of it. However, since I didn't, tell me your story.'

'Well, you know the cell scene, where they beat up our Brendan.'

'Yes. I am familiar with that scene, strangely enough.'

This was a particularly violent scene, frighteningly realistic, magnificently choreographed, where two warders, not to put too fine a point on it, hammered the shit out of the pathetic boyish figure in the narrow cell.

'Well, I looked over this direction from where I sat and I could see you standing here. You're in full view. I just thought I should let you know.'

'Thank you. I appreciate your concern. But let me tell you this. Young man, during *that* scene, anybody looks over *here*, we're closin' anyway.'

He was active always in American Equity and in fostering racial harmony. At times of special horror in the North of Ireland, Bill Ross would drop a line, just as I felt it right to send him my congratulations when Arafat and the Israelis started talking. He died in 1994. I miss him.

A couple of years ago when I went back to New York, I was saddened to find that three places where I had many hours of alcoholic happiness were gone with the wind. One was called the Kyoto, a Hawaiian-Japanese restaurant situated right behind the stage door of the Lyceum Theatre, run by a man called Walter Endo and his wife Margaret.

On the first morning of rehearsal of *Borstal Boy* in 1970, I had a dreadful hangover. At coffee-break, I stood at the stage door and looked round for a bar. I went into this restaurant and sat down. There was a guy sweeping the floor.

'Give me a large Scotch and soda,' I said.

'We're not open yet.'

'I don't give a shit. A Scotch and soda, please.'

He looked long at me, and shrugged, and went and poured a large Scotch and soda, and put it in front of me. I polished it off and said, 'Give me a beer.' He shrugged again, and he gave me a Japanese beer called Kirin, and I polished it off, and it tasted great, and I said, 'Thanks. How much do I owe you?' He shrugged again, and nodded towards the till. 'Still locked,' he said. I told him I was rehearsing in the theatre next door. He said, 'OK, see you later.'

At lunchtime I went in, bringing a couple of others from the cast with me, and in no time the Kyoto had become our watering-hole.

About two years later, when I went back, they had my photograph still up on the wall. (They'd only had two photographs ever, myself and Lauren Bacall. She was still playing in *Applause* at the Palace.) Margaret said, 'Your photograph stays on that wall because you brought us luck. You came in here in the morning, and you came back in the afternoon with other people, and all those people in the theatre started to come in. Up to that time we were doing very bad business. So for us, you're a lucky man, and we keep your picture on the wall.' I was deeply moved.

Next time I called, the joint was closed, and friendly Walter and Margaret were gone.

Right across from the front of the theatre was the Palace Bar and Grill, which was run by Harry Kaplan. He was a huge Jewish guy who smoked a big cigar and ran a great bar, and had first-class food. 'Why don't you eat more?' he would complain. 'What's the matter with our food, eh? Come on, you're like all these Irish bastards. You drink and you don't eat.' During rehearsals, I discovered that the Palace Bar and Grill had three different sets of clients. In the morning, because there was so much rebuilding going on around Times Square, the place would be full of 'hardhats', the construction workers, drinking beer and eating hot dogs. You went in there before the theatre, and there were people who were having pre-theatre hamburgers and that sort of thing, and then after the show the place was full of whores — by which time Harry Kaplan was home in bed in Staten Island.

The man he admired the most, he said, the greatest Irishman that was ever in this city, was Bill O'Dwyer. 'He was dead nuts on narcotics and prostitution, but otherwise this city was wide open.' Harry and I got on very well. He would lecture me about my drinking, and stuff 'toona sammidges' under my nose. Again, when I went back there, it was no longer the Palace Bar and Grill. I just said to the lady behind the bar (and that was unusual enough, to see a lady behind the bar there), 'Is Mr Kaplan around?' She said, 'Mr Kaplan, I regret to inform you, is deceased. I am sorry to be the bearer of this bad news.' She was stoned to the eyeballs, of course. The whole place had changed, and when I ordered just a Coke, she put it up and waved away my money. 'This one is with me. My condolences on your bereavement.'

The other place that I loved was Downey's steak-house. Jim Downey was dead, but it was run by his son, Archie, and he sold it while we were there. 'He sold it to the Mob,' they said. Every place that was sold was sold to 'the Mob'.

To get back to the *Borstal Boy* first-night party. Now this was a wonderful occasion, and every time I see a re-run of the *Godfather*, I think of the scene where Luca Brassi was strangled, because the bar in that scene reminds me very much of a bar in a place called 'The Tin Lizzie'. The Tin Lizzie was on 51st Street, across the Avenue from Radio City Musichall. They had a genuine, antique, restored, Ford Tin Lizzie, polished up, anchored, cemented probably, into the middle of the floor in the main bar. The main attraction of this place was that at the Happy Hour, the Rockettes, from Radio City, came in, and they would sit on the bonnet of the Tin Lizzie and kick up their legs, and drink, and entertain the customers, or just be there, and say 'Hi fellas!' These simple things provoke people into buying drink.

Mike McAloney, the producer, had decided that the Tin Lizzie, rather than Sardi's, would be the place for the first-night party. His explanation for this was, 'We've got Chicago money in the production.' This euphemism was accompanied by an explanatory gesture; he tweaked his left ear with one hand, and bent his nose with the index finger of the other, indicating extensive pistol surgery. The Chicago money says it's got to be the Tin Lizzie, and in all fairness, since they've got so much money in the production, it's got to be the Tin Lizzy. We had a wonderful opening. It really was a huge hit. The feeling was there — it was great. We went to the Tin Lizzie, and waited for the papers, and all that, and when the reviews came, it was a case of unanimous raves.

I wanted to communicate this to Judy at home; so I got on the phone to Dublin. I must have been on for the best part of an hour. Long-distance calls were not cheap then. I mentioned to Mike McAloney, 'By the way, Mike, when you get your bill, you may have one very long telephone call, to Ireland. It could be quite expensive.' He looked at me incomprehendingly, and then he said, 'Oh, don't worry about that. By the time that bill arrives, this joint will be closed.'

He was pretty accurate. The place did close. Now, I want to point out that the food in this place was very good, but apparently there was a little illicit gambling operation going on — and various other things. The restaurant account showed a balance of $600 when the FBI examined the books; and it was plain to anybody, even looking at the front door, that there were several hundreds of thousands of dollars going in there every week. It was closed for a Federal offence known as 'Undisclosed ownership' — so I've heard on fairly good legal authority. To close off the thrilling saga of the Tin Lizzie, I met Bill Maxwell from Aer Lingus, who had been at the first-night party, about four months afterwards, and he said, 'Well, how's the show? Still going strong?' And I said, 'Oh yeah, yeah.' He laughed. 'Well, you can boast about one thing. It ran longer than the Tin Lizzie.'

I think every Irish person in New York arrived in on that night. Of course, this has all become commonplace now. Irish people are always having big hits in New York. But you have to throw your mind back to 1970. Then it wasn't an Irish occasion at all, really; it was an American production, and Tomás MacAnna, who directed, and Frank Grimes and myself, were the Irish input. The rest were all New York actors, though not all American. Some of them were English, in fact, who, happily for them, happened to be available and kicking their heels, because they had gone over with a production of *Chips with Everything*, and it had closed sooner than they had expected — like after a week or two. They were all in their early twenties, but they could all pass for teenagers.

It was just the end of the sixties; the air reeked of pot, everybody doing their own thing.

*Hair* was running on Broadway, and you just had to go and see *Hair*. It was a must. It was even claimed that Ragni and Rado, the co-authors, masturbated in the wings during 'The Age of Aquarius'.

In the same vein, one stage director enthused to me about his arrival in 'The Big Apple'. He had come by train from Colorado, and as the train pulled towards the Port Authority, 'I see this guy standing on a lean-to roof, floppin' his dick at us in the train. Blew my mind. I said, "This is the place to be." '

Another Broadway thing at that time was resentment of interlopers from the movies. There were two stagehands in the Theatre Bar on 45th Street one morning, and they were very agitated about this. They were talking about, 'What's on in your place? Who's in it?'

'Oh, we got James Whitmore.'

'James Whitmore? What the fuck is he doing in Broadway? He's a movie star. He doesn't have no right to be in a play. George Grizzard, Barry Nelson, Jerry Orbach — they are Broadway stars. Jimmy Whitmore? Why do they bring him in here?'

There was this definite cleavage between the big Broadway personalities and the film people, which reinforced the sense of community.

Being Irish in New York meant that you were at home already; and on Broadway, not being a movie import helped as well.

Manhattan had eight million inhabitants, and yet in that theatre square mile, after a couple of weeks you knew everybody who was in any way connected with your business, because they all operated at ground level. The other people all lived fifteen or twenty storeys up in various blocks, but the people you were likely to want to see were in the bars at ground level, in this very compact area. You kept meeting the same guys. Leonard Lyons was the gossip columnist of the *New York Post*, and I would meet Lyons at least three nights a week in one or other of the restaurants or bars. He would sidle up and say, 'Hello.' He introduced me to his son Douglas and told me proudly that Brendan Behan had been at his Bar Mitzvah. He knew everybody's name, remembered everybody he met, and he would have a little conversation with them, and maybe the following night you would be mentioned in just one line in his column; and you began to understand how the system operated — you knew they kept plugging you, and so you fed them the little titbits to keep the party going.

You also realised, after about a week, that the same restaurants were going to be plugged. Leonard Lyons would never let two columns go without plugging the Russian Tearooms. All Leonard's celebrities were reported as 'enjoying dinner at the Russian Tearooms', 'because of the gourmet food' or because 'his grand-mother slept with Rasputin'. For many, the buzz of Manhattan is like *herpes simplex:* it sets up a tingle that may die away, but keeps coming back, like a song.

The same buzz almost put paid to myself. I always had money, which was undeniably a difference between Heaven and Hell, on that glittering block of real estate. I went at a pace which nobody could ever maintain.

But it still weaves the same old spell, ensnares me in the golden web. The beat on the streets sets the adrenalin pumping. In countless ways it has deteriorated appallingly, but, as Behan, probably among others, said, 'the man that hates you, hates the human race'. *Die Lorelei* still warbles her siren song down those steel and concrete canyons. As long as you've got bread, that is.

# THIRTEEN

When I left the Rep, in 1967, after fourteen years of devoted, loyal and distinguished service, I felt like a nun who had vaulted the convent wall — a well-paid nun, I grant you, fat and alcoholic.

It was at least fifteen years before I was invited back to partake in official dramatic activity, having committed the cardinal sin of leaving. But between the script-writing and an odd vocal contribution, I did maintain contact with the station. Because, you see, there was another side to broadcasting, to which I now had more access.

One didn't allude to it much, as it was infra dig, really. It came under the general and contemptuous heading of Sponsored Radio. Pleasantries were cordially exchanged between the Real Programme people and the Commercial crowd, but cross-pollination was rare enough.

Niall Boden was the King of sponsored radio, and lest you didn't know that, he let you know. He was, after all, an advertiser. He also, in turn, looked down his nose on the non-sponsored, calling them 'sustaining programmes', as they were known in the US. He had an Americanised Newry accent, which all serious artistes affected to despise, but which in my opinion has never been equalled for an ingratiating persuasiveness, never brash, never strident. He was Mr Soft Sell. In a bar he was something else, before that phrase was even invented. Brandy, champagne, Black Velvet and Havanas, taxis from the front bar to the lounge, if possible, and thence to Shelbourne Park Dog-Track to support the Bookmakers' Hardship Fund.

Boden and his less flamboyant confrères produced a very wide range of shows. *The Kennedys of Castlerosse* must, all other things being equal, have been the most successful show in Irish radio history. Apart from Boden, whose name was synonymous with Donnelly's sausages, others were busy hammering careers out of the clippings of Tin Pan Alley, which was the mainstay of all these programmes: Gay Byrne, Jimmy Magee, Harry Thuillier, Larry Gogan, Cecil Barror, Bart Bastable, Denis Brennan, Frankie Byrne, Bonnie O'Reilly, Noel Andrews, Leo Nealon, Val Doonican and many others, all durable, some great.

I contributed scripts to some of Boden's shows and later lost touch with him completely. When I left the Rep I played a police inspector with the unlikely name of Ó Briada in *The Kennedys*, scripted at that time by Lee Dunne. He told me, without blushing, that I was a 'memorable Ó Briada'. If I was, it's only because the incredible tends to be memorable.

It's likely that some of our fondest memories of radio's great days are inextricably linked with Bird's Jelly de Luxe, the *Tayto Family Show*, the O'Henry Short Story. Any fan of post-war sponsored radio will be able to sing along, if you try the following to the air of the 'Mexican Hat Dance':

> Oh it's true they're the talk of the nation,
> A sausage excitingly new,
> So new that they've caused a sensation
> And Donnellys make them for you.
> With two wrappers, for double protection,
> The best that your money can buy,
> The last word in Sausage Perfection,
> They're fresher and faster to fry.
> So the next time you visit your grocer,
> Tell him no other sausage will do,
> To his other suggestions say 'No Sir',
> It's Donnellys sausages for you.

Let us without condescension salute the unsung soldiers of the sausage machine, and the simple sausage likewise. They don't make 'em, either of them, like that any more.

There had always in my time been a distinct anti-performance bias in Radio Éireann. One felt it was run for the convenience of people in offices on that mile-long corridor, regardless of how the people who made the programmes were affected. This attitude must have carried over to TV, when they left the inner city to set up in Donnybrook. There is a tale of a visitor expressing admiration for the administration block.

'What a magnificent studio,' she said.

'No, ma'am,' said the porter, 'This here behind you is the studios. That is the admin block. You see', he added helpfully, 'in here there's about three hundred people making programmes. Over there, there's two thousand people trying to stop them.'

But an easement had to come. The radio heads had consistently refused to allow the inmates out on parole. However, if only because of sheer dearth of personnel, never mind talent, people had to be released to do odd bits of television. After all, it was one organisation, if that's not too strong a word. Even RTE could not declare its own front garden to be foreign territory, so an occasional television part cropped up.

Then I began to get more offers of theatre work. I had done some for the Damer Hall. One exciting piece was *Spailpín a Rún*, written by Seán O'Riada, based on the life of Eoghan Rua O'Súileabháin, the eighteenth-century poet. This was a splendid opus and could have swept all before it, but for the ingenuity of director Frank Dermody. MacLiammóir called Dermody 'a genius without talent', a savage shaft, falling barely short of the truth.

Dermody, to use his own favourite description of almost everybody at one time or another, was a monster. Even sober, he would gibber with excitement as some new inspiration struck him, spewing out ideas and directions in a crowing, triumphant cackle, scarcely one syllable of which was intelligible. He was not helped by his vocal gymnastics, zooming from inaudible muttering to blood-curdling shrieks. Once, while he was lecturing Donal McCann as they left the Abbey and strolled towards O'Connell Street, the traffic noise drowned out his mutter. At the traffic lights, McCann bent his head slightly, the better to catch the words of wisdom, only to get a resounding whack across the back.

'Ah, come on, boy, straighten up. You'll never make an actor if you can't even fucking stand up straight!'

Pissed, he was like a small rogue fireball, threatening spontaneous combustion, backstage or out front. During *Spailpín*, he appeared in the wings on the first night, muttering encouragement: 'Attaboy, Niall, attaboy! By Jesus, you are a most . . . under . . . rated . . . actor.' Oddly enough, this encouragement was not very helpful, especially as he then proceeded to readjust the angle of the spotlights, leaving acting areas dark, and illuminating irrelevant details.

Niall Buggy's debut at the Abbey, at the tender age of seventeen, was made memorable for the entire profession by Dermody's intervention. It was during that era of preposterous religiosity and pietistic interventionism, when John Charles, by the Grace of God (and Éamon de Valera), Archbishop of Dublin and Primate of Ireland, issued proclamations on subjects as diverse as attending Trinity College, the use of Tampax, and reading the *News of the World*. He was also alert to the dangers which priests, nuns and brothers faced by going to public theatre shows. On the silver screen, Sonja Henie's frilly-clad buttocks, or Marilyn Monroe's billowing skirts, not to mention Clint Eastwood's tight denims, posed no threat to faith or morals. But a visit to even a George Shiels melodrama in the Abbey, for a man or woman of the cloth, was fraught with eroticism and the pull of heresy. Except, of course, at dress rehearsals. Not paying in seemed to sanctify the occasion of sin.

So the Abbey allowed the religious into dress rehearsals. It helped the performers, in those days before previews.

Buggy had a walk-on part in a play called *The Conspiracy*, about the Parnell forgeries. He had to cross the stage, dressed as a newsboy, newspapers under his arm, calling out 'Freeman's Journal! Freeman's Journal!'

Dermody, well tanked, stood at the back of the parterre, in the Queen's Theatre, where the Abbey had a home after the fire of 1951 destroyed the old theatre in Abbey Street. He glared malevolently at the stage, as Buggy put his best foot forward.

'Freeman's Journal, Freeman's Journal!' chanted the boy.

'Ah, Freeman's testicles,' roared Dermody. 'I can't hear a fucking word you're saying!'

The effect on the assembled religious personages can only be imagined; but the dress rehearsal invites still went out, so John Charles can hardly have been apprised of this outburst.

During a pantomine rehearsal in the same theatre, Frank was screeching, justifiably, probably, in this case, at a group of dancers. Dressed in gauze and organdie, they galumphed around the green-lit stage.

'For Christ's sake, you're supposed to be fairies and leprechauns. You're like bulls and elephants, steamrollers! Go back to the start. Bring in the curtain.'

After the restart, about fifteen steps into the dance, the screeching resumed. 'Cows! As gracious as a herd of flatulent fucking cattle! Stop, stop!'

When this performance had been gone through for the umpteenth time, the stage manager, Joe Ellis, intervened to point out that this was only the opening scene, and at this rate of progress, a four a.m finish was probable, with huge overtime bills for the stage crew. 'Mr Blythe won't like that, Mr Dermody,' he added, as a clincher.

Dermody threw up his hands. 'All right, all right. Once more, from the start. And no matter what happens, I will not interrupt, I swear. I *promise*. He folded his arms and waited. The house lights dipped, the curtain went up. The music of Grieg's 'Solveig's Song' stole out through the green gloom. The *corps de ballet*, with the grace and delicacy of a buffalo stampede, pounded onto the stage. No sound emerged from the darkness of the auditorium. The routine concluded and the dancers stole back into the shadows. As the last glimmer of green light expired, there came a strangled cry of anguish. 'Horrifying! Nevertheless, carry on!'

Like everyone else, I had become accustomed to Frank Dermody's antics. The theatre is a strangely charitable world. Idiosyncratic behaviour, well beyond the border of lunacy, is tolerated, if not exactly welcome. It sometimes needs a view through the eyes of a non-combatant to realise that one's existence does not conform to established norms.

The doubtful privilege of affording such a view fell to Arthur Frewen, a gentle, scholarly man who wrote a play, *The Man in the Green Coat*, about the days of 'The White Boys' in Tipperary. His forbears had been benevolent landlords, who had nonetheless borne the lash of agrarian unrest.

Arthur's play was intended to set the record straight about his calumniated ancestors. Frewen taught at a prep school in Wiltshire, and had a deep devotion to Chekov and all his works. He held actors in high esteem. He was in total awe of Dermody's reputation, and regarded his agreement to direct the play as a belated but Heaven-sent reward for his own patient literary endeavours over the years.

The first reading was held in the lounge of the Shelbourne Hotel, with refreshments such as sandwiches and drinks laid on. This was highly unusual, very promising, and indicated pretty generous funding of the production. Dermody was strangely deferential, abstemious and, as the Catechism said, 'modest and clean in dress'.

The reading went very well. The cast loved the play, as the cast always does in the first flush of new employment. Frewen was entranced. He headed back to England, happy in the knowledge that his play was in safe hands.

He was not to know that Frank was going through a period of restraint, and maybe even of atonement (because he was very religious bytimes). Nor was he aware that Dermody tended to familiarise himself with the text of a new play during rehearsal, rather than in pre-production study.

There were aspects of the play that had begun to get Frank's goat. He was out of sympathy with Frewen's revisionist drift. 'There simply were no bloody benevolent landlords,' he declared.

Poor Gerry Sullivan who played the hero had a line which finished, 'Your Honour, Sir', which seemed to escape Frank's ear for a few rehearsals. Then one day he exploded.

'What did you say?'

Gerry repeated the line.

'Stick to the text. I don't want that stage-Irish craven forelock-tugging nonsense.'

'It *is* the text.'

'Jesus,' he spluttered, with an apoplectic splatter of saliva. 'No Irishman ever said that. How dare this Anglo-Irish upstart caricature the Irish peasantry. Cut the line! Cut it! I've had enough of this man's goings-ons.'

Poor Arthur, all unsuspecting, came to join us again two weeks after the read-through, at a crowd-effects recording session at Peter Hunt's studio on St Stephen's Green. The call was for 10 a.m., but through some mix-up we had to wait on the pavement outside for the door to be opened.

'Morning all! Hello again! Good morning Frank!' cried the author's cheerful voice. St Stephen's Green took on an eerie silence. The cast shifted from foot to foot in apprehension. Then the volcano erupted.

'How dare you! How dare you insult a nation that was civilising Europe, spreading the light of culture centuries before your land-grabbing forefathers defiled our soil . . .' And it went on, and on.

Anybody could write the script. The catalogue of wrongs was heaped like coals of fire on Frewen's head. (Twelve years later, I met him in Tipperary, and he trembled at the memory.) The cast then went through one of the most grotesque charades in theatre history. The play had been booked into the Olympia Theatre for a six-week run. It never had a snowball's chance of that, and the reviews, containing words like 'worthy, scholarly, historically intriguing', put the kibosh on it.

But Arthur was proud. In fairness, he was upset at the thought of putting actors out of work prematurely, so he refused the theatre's offer to replace his play at the end of two weeks. At the same time, he told everybody he met, in pub, club, or elsewhere, to stay away from the play — which 'that frightful man Dermody' had eviscerated, ruined.

I did various other productions, including *Design for a Headstone*, an excellent play by Seamus Byrne. Then in 1967, out of the blue, I got a call from Hilton Edwards about a new play, *Lovers*, by Brian

Friel, which was to go on at the Gate. I read the script, and I did the full Molly Bloom: I said, 'Yes, yes.' I said, 'Yes, now the time has come. I am not going on my bended knees to ask for permission. To hell with them all, I'm going to do this.'

I resigned. I went into rehearsal, and it was a huge success. I learned more from Hilton Edwards in four weeks than I had assimilated in radio in fourteen years.

I played 'Andy' to Anna Manahan's 'Hannah'. The second part of the play, which was ours, lasted no more than thirty-five minutes; but it used to take off like a rocket. I have never enjoyed a part so hugely since.

The play was in two separate parts, with an overall theme — winners and losers. Eamonn Morrissey and Fionnuala Flanagan played the young couple who have a very brief romance, and are found drowned. Then there were myself and Anna, who after an unhappy, rancorous, middle-aged love affair, get married, and who are not drowned, except in their own bloody misery. Andy has this religious fanatic of a mother-in-law who insists on saying the Rosary every night and has a special devotion to St Philomena.

Andy's great moment — Andy's only moment — of glory comes when he hears in the pub that St Philomena has been declared non-existent, by Papal Decree. Some of the biggest laughs I've ever heard on stage came when Andy arrives in drunk, insults the mother-in-law, horrifies everyone by interrupting the Rosary, picks up the statue of St Philomena, and waltzes around the bedroom with her, shouting 'You're sacked!' It used to take the house down. It probably wouldn't mean a button today, but at the time it was very daring . . . blasphemy of a high order.

Nowadays they would say, 'Philomena who?'

It was a huge success. I felt it justified my leaving Radio Éireann; but it had its sour moments.

Morton Gottlieb, a Broadway producer, came to see the first night. Hilton told me that Morton was going to put it on on Broadway and 'Dear boy, you'll be going, get ready. A wonderful experience, it's going to be enormous! But keep it to yourself, because the problem is, with all these Equity regulations, we can't bring everybody, you see.' All this went on.

What happened finally was that everybody in the cast went *except* me. The reason for this was very simple: they needed a big Broadway name. The only part big enough in the play to attract a 'name' was the part that I was playing. The two young lovers were only teenagers and wouldn't attract established names. Anna was irreplaceable.

As it happened, Art Carney, who had had a long struggle with the demon rum, was coming back on top form and was looking for a launching-pad, and he seemed ideal. So he got the part, and it ran for about a year and a half, between Broadway and the national tour. I read the reviews, leaning on a shovel in my back garden in Dundrum, and sighed, 'Fuck 'em anyway.' But two years later I went to Broadway with *Borstal Boy*, and if I had gone with *Lovers*, I wouldn't have been in *Borstal Boy*. Some you win, some you lose — and to hell with them again.

At that time, when I left the Rep, to have had a pensionable job was esteemed a very valuable thing. You didn't throw it away lightly. But I asked Judy about it and she said, 'Well, I think you should leave, because if you stay, you're going to be so unhappy that they'll eventually fire you, because knowing you, you won't put up with it, so you might as well leave now.'

I did, and have never regretted it for one minute. In fact, I have never been out of work since. I had the very lucky break of doing a one-man show at just the right time to propel me into a vacuum which must have existed, and which I seemed to fill; so I have never been out of work for the simple reason that every time things got bad, I could fall back on the one-man show.

To call it a one-man show is not really accurate any more (nor correct, if it comes to that), and it hasn't been for a very long time. It just became an extended cabaret act, and it changed, according to public taste, quite a lot. There's stuff I do now that I would not have done fifteen years ago. I became far less arty in my approach to these things, less theatrical, shall we say. I realised that you've got to follow the bread. If that means doing a hotel show, you do a hotel show. If it means doing it in a pub, you do it in a pub. And if a theatre is available, you do it in a theatre.

I had never thought of doing a one-man show, though I had seen, and loved, Emlyn Williams' *Dickens Show*, Mícheál MacLiammóir's *Oscar*, and a few others. The evolution of the one-man effort was fortuitous. I was doing a spot at the Embankment at Tallaght, for the one and only Mick McCarthy. He had seen me in *Borstal Boy*, and in some other Behan stuff, and he thought it was very good. He wanted me to do something of that nature in the Embankment.

At about the same time, director Noel Pearson had come to me with the idea that I should do a one-man show at some stage. I'd never heard of Pearson. He was a band promoter. But I liked him. I said 'OK', and I got some stuff together. I had about an hour of material, and we put this on at the Embankment. While I was running there, Norman Wisdom, then a big star in Britain, was at the Gaiety, doing a show which didn't really click. He had an option on another two weeks, which unexpectedly he decided to forgo, and that left, at about a fortnight's notice, the Gaiety faced with going dark, because they couldn't find a replacement show.

John Lovatt Dolan, who used to drink in the backstage bar in the Gaiety, came to the Embankment and saw me for the first time. He suggested to Fred O'Donovan (then 'Mr Gaiety'), that if my show could be extended to the right length, I could certainly do two weeks in the Gaiety — which was a pretty formidable proposition at the time. Fred came to see me, and when I said, 'I don't know', and demurred a little, he made a reasonable point. He said, 'The way to look at it is this. If it takes off, it's going to be great. But if it doesn't, nobody's going to turn round and say, "He can't act". They'll just say, "Well, he can't carry a one-man show". So what? How many can?'

Looking back, I find Fred's faith in the softheartedness of the punters touching beyond belief. If it were anyone else, I might even have suspected a scintilla of insincerity.

As it happened, I did the show. It was called *Confusion*, and we packed the place for a fortnight. I came back and did another one six months later, and we did equally good business. From there it just took off; and over the next few years I think I did a total of five fully produced theatrical shows.

Then I went on to doing it during the summer, in the Shelbourne Hotel, which used to put on theatre nights.

Soon, invitations began to come in, to perform it in places where obviously you would need to schlepp along a set if you wanted to do the kind of show I was doing. You would have to travel a stage manager and sound operator, lighting and sound equipment, setting up the equivalent of a theatrical company, in order to do a one-man show. This was neither feasible nor economically sound; so gradually I discarded the costumes, the props, the light changes, and got out in a dinner jacket and delivered the stuff. I found it made not the slightest difference. People couldn't care less, so long as they could see your face and hear you properly. I began to do more hotel shows, played marquees during festivals, went to bars, anywhere . . . and that's the way it's been for over twenty-three years.

All these one-man shows, as well as the last one, *Taking Liberties* in 1992, were directed by Donall Farmer. 'Directed' hardly does justice to his contribution. ('Input' had not been coined yet.) He edited, suggested, listened, laughed (mostly quite sincerely, I'm sure, but occasionally by way of encouragement also). We seemed to be almost automatically on the same beam, sharing a background in Blackpool (which should really be spelt Black Pool to convey the equal stress laid on each word), Gaelic culture, drinking habits and many other things. Doing a solo show is a scarrifyingly hazardous undertaking, so it is essential to have a shoulder to cry on; which is another way of saying, someone who will put up with your ego, your foul bad temper, hangovers, vituperation and four-lettered frenzies.

Every now and then it occurs to you that you are once again going to take on up to eleven hundred people. You are going to suggest that, on the basis of almost no evidence, you can keep them laughing, or otherwise entertained, for about two and a half hours. You need no shrink's advice; you're ready to sign yourself into the puzzle factory, pronto.

They play the Anthem. Always make 'em play the Anthem. It announces that you are ready. This is a National occasion. The Anthem takes twenty minutes. The clatter of seats being resumed takes twenty more.

As the house lights go down, and the rag begins its laborious ascent, you murmur the Prayer of Serenity and shit bricks.

Then somebody laughs. Ten minutes later, it's half past ten.

Sometimes.

# FOURTEEN

I first met Brendan Behan in or about May 1952 at a party in Ma Martin's in Stamer Street, off the South Circular Road. It was, as I mentioned before, a fundraiser for Con Lehane's election. In the middle of this party, a man arrived, wearing only trousers and singlet. The shirt had been discarded somewhere. He was grossly overweight, reeking of porter, streaming sweat, with black, tousled curly hair, and he was roaring his head off singing. He went from one song to the next, pausing only to grab a swig of porter and hurl a tirade of political abuse at all his nearest and dearest — because he would have been very close to all these people, politically.

He was a friend of Con's, because Con had represented him legally. I didn't even know his name, but we began singing together and drinking together, and by the time the night was out, we were very firm friends — very drunken friends, but very firm friends, and the next time I met him, it was as though we had known each other for years. We saw a lot of each other, in Searsons of Baggot Street, Tommy Devine's on the corner of Mespil Road, Joe Dwyer's of Leeson Street, the Winter Gardens on St Stephen's Green, which is now the Bank Nationale de Paris, *s'il vous plait*, Jerry O'Dwyer's in Moore Street, and MacDaids, of course. I went to MacDaids very rarely, but that became his permanent watering-hole, along with the Bailey, and many other places with a literary cachet.

Joe Dwyer was a good friend to me, from time to time. On one occasion, Brendan came in to Dwyer's, almost at closing time, and he had under his arm a cooked chicken — a rotisserie chicken, to be exact, a very new invention then. It was in a tinfoil bag. He was very drunk. Joe said, 'I'm not serving you, you've had enough. Go home before you do any damage.' Brendan muttered, went over to the door, then turned, and seemed to become conscious of this parcel under his arm. He took it in his hand, and, roaring aloud 'Fuck you and your chicken', he threw it across the pub, and it landed with a crash among the bottles on the shelves. Needless to say, he was barred from Joe's as a result.

On the evening after his funeral, I was in Joe's.

'I suppose you were at Brendan's funeral.'

'I was.'

'Ah sure, poor old divil, he was an awful fucking nuisance.'

I think it was one of the most honest epitaphs uttered that day, because people came out of the woodwork to pay their tributes, who wouldn't have given him the time of day when he was alive.

The one thing that can't be emphasised enough is that Brendan was very, very funny. He was a splendid raconteur, and he had an infectious blasphemous humour. In fact, Brendan Gill of the *New Yorker* used a very accurate phrase in describing him 'with some ambitious blasphemy teetering on his pursed lips'. You could see him, drunk and all as he was, trying to find just the right phrase that would offend the greatest number of people, so that they'd shut up and listen to him.

That became terribly sad in his later days — if fifty-one can be called anyone's later days. A few months before his death, I was in the house with his father, and himself, and Beatrice, and his mother, and Judy, my wife. He had got to the stage where he was barely able to hold a drink at all. He kept up a stream of name-dropping. It was pathetic. He would fall over, and then he would appeal to his father to verify that he had been a great soldier in the IRA, and so on. He also only barely recognised people, from time to time during that period.

But it was before that deterioration that he really was very funny. What spontaneous laughter he could evoke, and cause to spread and ripple through crowded bar or public street.

One St Patrick's Day, Judy and myself were going to the races at

Baldoyle — not that we were interested in the races *per se*, but it was a good day out, and the bar would be open, and you would meet people there who were having a jar. I am of course speaking of the time when the pubs were kept shut to honour the 'Snake Harmer', Saint Patrick.

We got the bus from Eden Quay, and were joined by Brendan and Beatrice, and by Paddy Darcy and Nuala Morgan. We all went upstairs and sat across the back row. Brendan proceeded to deliver a travel talk to the entire bus. He gave a yard by yard description of the territory we were passing through, and I can remember, it was just nonsense, but it was off the top of his head nonsense, and it was spiced with songs of course. It was on that occasion that I first heard a line that occurs in *Borstal Boy*, about Kilbarrack graveyard: 'the healthiest graveyard in Ireland, it's so near the sea.' He used that little gag as we went by Kilbarrack. 'Clontarf retains a curious, unpleasant odour, because it was here that Brian Ború beat the shite out of the Danes.'

Fairview Park was much more sparse in trees than it is now. One very large one in the middle stood out on its own, and he said, 'Now there's a very interesting landmark, that tree in the middle of Fairview Park. It stands out there on its own, because it was there that my grandmother and James Connolly spent New Year's Eve dancing around that tree, singing "When the red, red robin, comes bob, bob, bobbin' along." '

That was the kind of nonsense he was able to trot out, and the bus was in uproar. A holiday crowd going to the races, they loved it. And he produced a paper from his pocket. 'I want you all to listen to this.' And it was to the best of my recollection one of the first articles he had had published in the *Evening Press*. It had been published that day, and he had got the early edition. He read it aloud. It was about St Patrick's Day, and about going to the Dog Show in Ballsbridge, where the bar was open. Dog-loving tended to verge on the idolatrous in Ballsbridge on St Patrick's Day. The article included the story of a guy, pissed out of his mind, who trips over a dog at the Dog Show, and says, 'What a stupid effing place to bring a dog!'

At the races, we went to the bar, and he would send his bets down to the bookie. He stood on a bench inside the window of the top bar and gave commentaries on the races. All this was done with an enormous sense of gaiety, a feeling of friendship and joy about it all. The whole world was his friend.

When he would come down from those heights, he would be depressed, and that was how I often met him, in Searson's. I'm trying to describe what it was like to have an ordinary, day-to-day jar with him. He had an odd snobbery about certain pubs — Jerry O'Dwyer's, in Moore Street, for instance, where he would occasionally drink with Seamus Kavanagh. But when all was said and done, Seamus Kavanagh was from Aungier Street. He was from the South Side. 'This is Seamus Kavanagh's fuckin' Dublin,' he would say. As far as he was concerned, this kind of pub was invented for the likes of Kavanagh, who, being a teacher, was not quite working class. There was always this little rub of enmity. What in the country would be parish rivalry, in Dublin I suppose was inter-street rivalry.

He was constantly being hailed in the street by fellow-citizens. Any acclaim was like mother's milk to him when well, or well pissed, but not when he wasn't feeling the best. He went on the dry one time, and I was in Madigan's with him, and he was slapped on the back by a cheerie chappie. I swear this was the actual phrase the man used: 'Good man Brendan, never a dull moment, wha'?'

'Oh, for fuck's sake, let's get out of here, away from these ballockes.'

These of course were the same ballockes he would have had in stitches when he had a few jars. But when he was off it, well, *sin scéal eile*.

He had his own sense of the fitness of things. For instance, he discovered that I used to go to Dalymount Park.

'What are you doing going to Dalymount? You're a Corkman. You're a country man. Croke Park is the place for you.'

I reminded him that Cork teams had won the Free State Cup, the FAI Cup, and the League, in their various incarnations as Cork City, Cork Hibernians, Cork Athletic, Cork United, and in earlier days as Fordsons, also as Evergreen. He conceded the point, but he still thought it was wrong for me to be stepping above myself, or below myself, or outside myself. In many things he was very traditionalist, not exactly conservative, but he felt that in cultural matters you should know where you stood.

We had in common that we were both contributors to *Comhar*, at that time edited by Riobard Mac Góráin. Mac Góráin, gently spoken and quietly humorous, showed great determination and resilience in furthering the ideals of *Comhar*, and of Gael-Linn. He gave that organisation, whatever his actual office or title, a catch-all attraction. He specialised in corralling mavericks, could cajole and mollify such diverse talents as Behan, Dermody, Seán Maguire, Seán O'Riada, Breandan O'hEithir, Ian Henry, myself, Sonny Knowles, Len Clifford, Louis Marcus and Gene Martin; and he could treat all with exquisite courtesy, usually getting what he wanted. He once confirmed to me that the only people ever paid in advance by *Comhar* for work which had not yet been written were Brendan Behan and myself. He was probably on the better bet for deadlines with me, and certainly on a better bet for value from Brendan. *Comhar* first carried Brendan's *Jackeen, Guí an Rannaire, Omós do Joyce*, and a serialised diary of some of his IRA exploits.

Brendan could speak French. It was pretty basic French, but he lived in Paris on and off, and he certainly could get by in that language. I heard him speak French to my brother Tomás, and it was quite fluent. It was street French — picked-up French rather than learned French. *Caint na ndaoine*, as distinct from *Gaeilge na leabhar*, or *Fraincís na leabhar*.

The first chapter of *Borstal Boy* appeared as an article in the Paris magazine, *Points*, almost word for word.

His first real mark was made in Ireland with those articles in the *Evening Press*, one of which he read out on the bus to the races. I had an incidental involvement in the genesis of that series. Our mutual friend Eamon Martin was running a photo company, and he ran out of photo paper before he had completed an order for about three hundred prints. It was Friday evening, nowhere was open, so he and I and Brendan went in search of photo paper. Having tried many pubs, we resorted to the more obvious sources, the newspaper offices. We drew a blank with the *Indo* and the *Irish Times*. Then Brendan suggested we go down to the *Irish Press*. He asked to see Pearse McGuinness, the name by which he knew Jim McGuinness, the editor. He was put through from the front desk, and explained his case. 'I'll see you in the Scotch House in a few minutes,' McGuinness said.

Waiting in a pub was neither a novelty nor a hardship, so we repaired to The Scotcher. McGuinness joined us fairly soon. He had fixed up Martin's problem by arranging for a loan of some papers, to be replaced next day. He hadn't seen Brendan for a while.

'I'm glad you came in, because I wanted to get in touch with you. I want you to write some articles.'

Brendan said, 'About what?'

'About anything you like. We could do with a regular article of some kind, with a Dublin slant.'

So Brendan said, 'OK.'

Within a couple of weeks the series started, and later became *Hold Your Hour and Have Another*.

It was on *The Balladmakers' Saturday Night* that Brendan first sang 'The old Triangle'. At that time he used to say, 'Well, this is a prison song, written by Scolara Corbally', though afterwards that accreditation was discarded. Whether it was in fact written by Scolara Corbally, who was one of an entrepreneurial Dublin family, historically familiar with the ambience of corrective institutions, or whether he lacked confidence that the ballad would stand up on its intrinsic merit, or whether he was just shy, which is highly unlikely, or whether it was really Corbally's or a combined effort, I don't know. It is now generally ascribed to Brendan himself.

While he was working on *The Balladmakers' Saturday Night*, and I was working on some broadcast with Tomás MacAnna in the Radio Éireann Studios, we met under the portico of the GPO. Brendan accosted MacAnna and said, 'I have a play for you. It's called *The Twisting of Another Rope*. The first play ever produced in Irish was *Casadh an tSúgáin* — *The Twisting of the Rope*, by Douglas Hyde. *The Twisting of Another Rope* was about capital punishment. It ultimately became *The Quare Fella* (or *Fellow*, as they insisted on spelling it, though nobody who would say 'Quare' would then say 'Fellow'). As is well known, it was rejected by the Abbey and was done by Alan Simpson at the Pike. So obviously Brendan was busy working at that time. He was also translating Merriman's *Midnight Court* — but then, so was everybody else.

*The Quare Fella* was eventually done by the Abbey, in the Queen's Theatre. It had great topicality, because of the Bentley case. Bentley was a teenager who was hanged for allegedly urging his accomplice during a robbery to shoot a policeman. To this day, efforts to establish his innocence continue.

Brendan wrote a column in the *Sunday People* every week, for two or three years. Liam Robinson of the *Irish Press* was trying to assemble some of these articles later, but failed, because the column was carried only in the Irish editions. Maybe Brendan didn't feel they were worth keeping, because a lot of them were gossipy pieces about people he knew in Dublin. In any case, they were not included in the archives with the London edition of the *People*.

He had a poem published in *The Irish Workers' Voice*, a paper I used to take in preference to the *Irish Times*. It was edited, to the best of my knowledge, by Michael O'Riordan, of the Irish Workers' League, as the Communist Party was coyly known. Not surprisingly, it was somewhat left of centre. Brendan's poem described the American bombing of North Korea, and their use of napalm. The only line that comes to my mind now is 'As we jelly-bomb and flame-throw the screaming yellow dog'. It was a propagandist piece, designed for the paper that was going to publish it, and none the less meant for that. And I quoted this line to Brendan quite a few years later. He got very upset.

'Where did you fuckin' find that? I never wrote that.'

'Yes you did, in the *Workers' Voice*.'

'How the hell do you know that?'

I quoted another couple of lines to him, and then he grinned, and said, 'Oh well, I probably did, but don't be talking about that.'

That would have been about the time of the Kennedy inauguration, which he was going to America to cover, and the visa application was in, and things like that surfacing obviously wouldn't have been very welcome. But it shows that when some of his left-wing mates came and said 'Give us a poem', he was prepared to produce, and his interest in writing was not entirely mercenary.

To talk about the Behans without mentioning the Kearneys, the Furlongs and the Burkes, would be a distortion of history. Brendan himself acknowledged the Burke interest. He had a special fondness for his author-cousin Seamus de Burca, normally known as Jimmy Burke. 'He's the only one of the Burkes who can write,' Brendan said. 'I mean, his name,' he added jocosely.

Jimmy Burke has been kindness itself to me, over many years. His knowledge of the theatre in Dublin is legendary. Every now and again, I get a scribbled note, a pamphlet, a photo, a memoir about some long-forgotten production, a scrap or a souvenir, as a keepsake, or a reminder of joyous days. Jimmy ran the theatrical costumiers and dress hire service with Con Kearney, his cousin.

It was well known, and the Burkes ensured that it remained so, that Eamonn Andrews, the celebrated TV star, was married to Lorcan Burke's daughter, Gráinne. I witnessed once a stunt they must have pulled many a time on the punters in the dress hire section. A burly client, broad of shoulder but short of stature, had tried on every jacket in the shop, but rejected the lot. Jimmy bore all this with a patient shrug. The customer is always right. Finally he said, 'Well, it looks as if your physique has got us licked.'

Con, with ostentatious secrecy, beckoned Jimmy towards him.

'There's just one chance,' he said, in a stage whisper you could hear in Dollymount. 'Remember the suit Eamonn Andrews left in to be pressed? He doesn't need it until Tuesday.'

'Great idea, Con,' said Jimmy, in an equally loud stage whisper.

They gave each other the thumbs-up, good-man-yourself, saved-the-day routine. Jimmy returned to the client.

'There's one suit that I was holding,' he said. 'I think it may just fit you.'

You bet it fitted him. There was no way this man was going to be denied the pleasure of bragging to his mates, 'See that jacket? See the cut? That was made for Eamonn Andrews. How did I get it? Ah now, that's another story. But look at the jacket. That's quality, what?'

Pearse Kearney and his brother Con were near neighbours of ours when we lived in Raheny. We tended to foregather in the Manhattan Bar, a single-storey old inn with stone floor and open fires, and a Belfast landlord, Jim Maguire, who served the best pint in North County Dublin, of which Raheny was then most definitely a proud part. His excellence as a publican notwithstanding, 'Jem' was admired for his talent for telling whoppers so outrageous that they were accepted as true, on the grounds of their sheer unlikelihood.

The Irish National Anthem, 'A Soldier's Song', was written by Peadar Kearney, father of Pearse and Con. One could not be around Brendan for very long without having that fact drummed home. One of Jim Maguire's more successful lies was that the brothers met in the bar occasionally, to drink the royalties on the National Anthem, inherited from their father.

Kathleen Kearney, Brendan's mother, was Peadar Kearney's sister. Her second husband was Stephen Francis Behan. Stephen was alleged to have studied for the priesthood, with aspirations towards Jesuitry. The tale sits well with the Kearney nickname for him, 'Rosie the liar'. He was indeed rosy-cheeked. One thing has always puzzled me about *Mother of all the Behans*, Brian Behan's play about Kathleen, which was so memorably played by Rosaleen Linehan, accurate in every gesture and inflection. She refers to her husband throughout as Stephen. I never heard her address him as anything but Frank, which he was, by nature as well as by name. I mentioned Brendan's 'ambitious blasphemy', as described by Brendan Gill, but for sheer quality nothing could match Stephen's outburst when someone spilt a pint over his trousers in Jerry Dwyer's: 'Well, that the Lamb of God may stick his hind leg out through the golden canopy of Heaven, and kick the ballocks off ye.'

There was only one Lorcan Burke. It is unlikely that the Almighty ever saw the need for another. His theatre pedigree was beyond question, his father an actor, a playwright, a theatre manager, a theatrical costumier. Lorcan's involvement was universal.

Brendan recalled a visit, as a child, to the Queen's Theatre, when Lorcan was stage manager there. They shook hands in the parterre bar, then the Behan party went up to the gallery, where they were again greeted by Lorcan and asked to have a drink. He'd nipped up the back stairs, a short-cut of which Brendan was unaware, planting in the kid's mind the idea that Lorcan was everywhere, like God, only better, because unlike God you could see Lorcan.

He was unembarrassable, unabashable. 'Who', he asked a friend in the Gaiety bar, 'is that bird comin' in with the huge tits?'

'That', said the friend haughtily, 'is my wife.'

'That's right,' said Lorcan, as if confirming a correct answer on *Mastermind*.

'I see our cousin is the toast of Broadway,' he said to Pearse Kearney when *The Hostage* opened well. When Brendan hit the headlines again after a drunken brawl, he told Pearse, 'That cousin of yours is no credit to you. He's bringing disgrace on the whole bloody country.'

I did a take-off of Lorcan in *If the Cap Fits*, a TV series of mine which RTE consigned to the knacker's yard by jet. Facially not unlike him, I had, like most actors in Dublin, been impersonating the distinctive, bubbly Burke lisp for years. Wearing the Burke blazer, I strolled along Dollymount Strand as Lorcan, delivering a travelogue on the sights of the bay, pointing out the famous residences and noting that Fred O'Donovan of Eamonn Andrews Studios walked along the strand here while Charlie Haughey walked on the water.

I was standing at the Parnell Monument in O'Connell Street the next day, waiting to cross the road, when a familiar voice hailed me from the pavement.

'I saw you on the television last night. You weren't half as good as me.'

Lorcan's son Jack owned the City Theatre in Limerick. Due to what was a simple misunderstanding that was allowed to get out of hand, there was bad blood between myself and Jack, not to mention the entire population of Limerick. In fact, *The Chronicle* ran a gently censorious editorial, calling for my blood, and a pastor, protective of his flock's sensitivities, read me from the altar.

Some year or so later, Lorcan tackled Noel Pearson and myself in the bar of the Olympia, where he held court when not on circuit at the Gaiety.

'When', he demanded of Pearson, 'are you going to bring this man to our place in Limerick?'

'What place?'

'The City Theatre. My son Jack's theatre.'

'Your son Jack ran us out of town. Toibin is lucky he wasn't lynched.'

'Now just wait a minute, Mr Pearson,' said the unfazeable one. 'What transpired between Niall Toibin and my son Jack is a family feud, and has f... all to do with you.'

The Prodigal Son never had it so good.

When jarred, which may have been a fairly frequent, though not obvious condition, he was musical, lapsing rather than bursting into song — usually 'Mother Kelly's Doorstep'. At one Variety Club dinner and dance in Limerick, which I, in the words of one speaker, was 'attending in happier circumstances', Lorcan filled in with a spot of solo singing, while Art Supple's band took their break. When they returned, Lorcan was still giving it stick, so the band politely sat on their hands, awaiting the end of his set. Someone decided to help, as

Lorcan launched into 'Mother Kelly's Doorstep' once more.

'That's enough, Lorcan.'

'*I sit alonga Nelly, Nelly sits alonga Joe,*' sang Lorcan. Then he said, 'What?'

'OK, Lorcan. Finish it off.'

He sprang to attention, throttle wide open. '*Soldiers are we, whose lives are pledged to Ireland . . .*'

Before the guests got fully to their feet, Supple brought the boys in with a mighty crash of 'The St Louis Blues', and invited one and all to cut the rug.

The Burkes added great colour to the theatre in Dublin. Rick and Lorcan between them filled what one might call the Sam Goldwyn role. Just as dubious witticisms of a rude kind were attributed to Brendan, any amusing malapropism, mispronunciation or verbal confusion was laid at Rick's or Lorcan's door. Thus Rick, who spent most of his leisure helping the Variety Club children's charities, was quoted as saying that the new swimming pool for the blind children's hospital was a sight for sore eyes. Lorcan, who as deputy lord mayor was alleged to have welcomed visitors to Dublin for the Tostal Festival with 'I wish you all a hearty *Slán Leat*', and to have reprimanded some opponents in debate, saying 'I know yous. The Three Musketeers. A right pair of hooks, if ever I saw one.'

# FIFTEEN

When I saw the first production of *An Giall* (The Hostage) in the Damer Hall in 1958, it struck me as a simple story of love, naïve and undeveloped, but cleverly set in an era and location unfamiliar to the Gaelic theatre, such as it was. The very idea of a half-whore running a half-brothel, with the half-help of a wholly embittered, half-crippled half-husband, and all through the medium of the sweet and kingly tongue of Erin, was enough to arouse public curiosity. The introduction of an innocent British Tommy as a prisoner of the IRA, who had only half commandeered the house, and were so lax they allowed their prisoner to fall in love with Teresa, a country girl from an orphanage who is just newly hired as a maid, strained credibility. However, the quality of the playing sustained the show.

The ludicrous figure of Monsewer was tolerable only in the atmosphere of the period, when the IRA had come to be regarded as a bunch of inept idiots, pantomime patriots.

This is not just my view; I remember when I was doing research for The *Bells of Hell*, meeting Cathal Goulding in Sinnot's of South King Street to get some stories about Brendan's prison days. Dave Gold, a decent musician, MD of the disaster *Crock*, whose father was Harry Gold, of *Harry Gold and His Pieces of Eight* fame, joined us at the bar, and upon introduction to Cathal, he greeted him with 'Wotcher mate!', or some such cheery Cockney salutation, before the penny dropped with a loud clunk in the rear of his brain. Like the Brett Harte character, 'He smiled a sort of sickly smile, then curled up on the floor, and the subsequent proceedings interested him no more.'

Well, not quite, but he did sport a fixed, uncomfortable grin. In due course Cathal went for a piss.

'That's the IRA bloke, isn't it?'

'Yes,' I said, 'Well, ex-IRA, I suppose.'

'Well, you will tell him my heart's in the right place, and all that? I mean, with my fucking accent, I don't want to get fucking shot.'

But as the chat resumed, Dave relaxed, and began to ask an occasional question. 'How many members would you have had?'

'Well,' said Goulding, 'you have to understand that in those days everyone was in the IRA. I mean, everyone. We had thousands of members.'

'And how come you did so badly?'

'Ah well,' said Cathal, looking him straight in the eye, 'what happened was, some fucker let off a forty-five up in Glasnevin or somewhere, and within a week we had about a hundred and thirty members.'

When Joan Littlewood got her hands on *The Hostage*, she superimposed Cockney jokes, pub piano, musichall gags, Miss Gilchrist, Mr Meleady, Rio Rita, the African queen, the Russian sailor, Ropeen, and other assorted whores, on the simple story. But in the Behan way, it worked. I played the IRA officer in the Dublin production of this Littlewood text, and it was like being in another play, a parallel, simultaneous production, if you like, where your lines or moves bore no relation to what the actors in the more enjoyable piece said or did. David Kelly played Pat, Marie Kean played Meg, Celia Salkeld was Teresa, and Colin Farrell, Leslie.

The showstopper was provided by Martin Bradley, who brought the house down every night with his strangely affecting, but side-splitting rendering of 'The Captains and the Kings'. Martin was a middle-aged, middle-class, middling to excellent English rep actor, benign, beautifully spoken and fastidious. He carried his England around with him like a cultural cocoon. During rehearsals, if someone arrived in with some such Irish greeting as 'Jaysus, the rain is a whore', Martin would likely nod in sympathy, then he would add, 'The weather's appalling in Melbourne too, you know.' Then, sensing our mystification, he would continue, 'Well, rain stopped play in the Test.' There were no satellite transmissions in those days, so he could only have found this in his *Daily Telegraph*.

He had never seen, and for all I know never heard of *The Hostage* before he took the part. Because it was so soon after Brendan's death, people got quite emotional and anecdotal about him, and Martin himself got quite hooked on the Behan personality. He confided in me one morning that he had been thinking about the play.

'You know Niall, old Brendan may have been a rough diamond, but he was a pretty sound judge of people. I see in the *Dramatis Personae* he says the IRA officer is a teacher by profession, and the volunteer is a railway porter. That's pretty shrewd, you know. Poor working chap, having his discontent stoked up by this arrogant fanatic — teachers are like that, you know, get carried away with their own intellectualism. My own brother's a teacher, and he's just like that. Red as they come. Works for the Labour Party.'

Like the rest of the cast, I would never miss his 'Captains and the Kings'. I would watch from the wings as he walked into his downstage spotlight in his saffron kilt, a balding, bullet-headed, squat figure, exuding a ridiculous dignity:

> I remember in September,
> When the final stumps were drawn,
> And the shouts of crowds now silent,
> And the boys to tea had gone.
> Let us, O Lord above us,
> Still remember simple things,
> When all are dead who love us,
> O the Captains and the Kings.

He delivered the piece in a rich baritone, straightfaced and full of emotion, with no hint of mockery or lampooning, his eyes misting over with the pain of lost summers and vanished glories. I took the liberty of complimenting him on his rendition.

'It's wonderful,' I said, 'Nobody but you could do it justice.'

'But, you see,' he said, in patient, kindly explanation, 'That's why I love old Brendan. IRA man or not, he knew his England. His time in Borstal wasn't wasted, you know. He absorbed the very spirit of the English countryside:

> Cups of tea, and some dry sherry,
> Vintage cars, these simple things,
> In our dreams we see old Harrow,
> And we hear the crow's loud caw.
> At the flower show our big marrow
> Takes the prize from Evelyn Waugh.

These things do mean a lot to an Englishman. He was a genius, you know, was our Brendan, bless his heart.'

When he learned that I was from Cork, he beamed with pleasure. 'I have happy memories of your beautiful city. When I left the Army and went back to the theatre, I toured with a play, and Cork was on the circuit. I had a very kind landlady in Summerhill, and I loved that riverside walk down Tivoli. One afternoon, when I came back for tea, she said, "Well, you have a night off, Mr Bradley, tonight." "What do you mean?" I asked. "The whole town's closed down," she said, "Shops, cinemas, the Opera House, pubs, buses, the lot, in protest against the hangings." Well, I knew nothing about any of this. She told me about these two chaps being hanged in Belfast, and the public mourning. So I thought I'd better get this cancellation from the horse's mouth. I went to the Opera House, and sure enough, there on the front steps was a sandwich board, announcing "No performance this evening". I went round to the stage door, only to find it locked. But there was a typewritten notice on the door, which said, "To the visiting company: we regret any inconvenience or loss to you due to the protest against the Belfast hangings. Please be assured that no personal animosity is intended. We wish you a pleasant stay." And it was signed by some IRA chappie. I thought it was jolly civil of him.'

Bless his heart.

My next *Hostage* was at the Lyceum in Edinburgh, in 1971, or round about that time, directed by Richard Eyre, then one of the resident directors, along with Bill Bryden. This time I played 'Pat'. May Cluskey played 'Meg', David Blake-Kelly, 'Monsewer', Anthony May, the hostage, and Zoe Wannamaker, 'Teresa'. It was an immensely effective production. Eyre got the designer to provide a set which at the flick of a switch could be transformed from a realistic, shabby, Dublin shebeen, into a tatty musichall stage, where serial carnival lights ran along the foots, and up and over the proscenium arch. Thus, when each character went into his or her solo 'shtick', they took the centre spot, while the others became an impromptu chorus. It followed the Littlewood text pretty faithfully, and Owen Dudley Edwards, then at Herriot Watt University, weighed in with background advice and information on Brendan and the Troubles, for the enlightenment of the English and Scottish, and, lest I offend Zoe, American members of the cast.

I fell for Edinburgh instantly, its genteel accents and austere beauty. It may have been a touch of *La Vie En Rose* provided by a new-found acquaintance with single malts and 'McEwan's Heavy', a sure shield against the bitter east wind that singed your ears with frostbite as you trudged along Prince's Street. A glass of 'Glenmorangie' made the whole world glow.

One unscripted line of mine, on the first night, had a galvanising effect on the house. The lady who played Miss Gilchrist, the wacky preacher, 'the servant or ghillie of the Lord', while excellent in the part, tended to crowd one a little; and in a scene where I, as Pat, sat at the table, glowering and resentful, she leaned in over me, stuffing one of her pamphlets almost up my nostril. I attempted to indicate gently, by facial contortion and gestures of dismissal, that enough was enough, but she persisted, and I felt I had no choice but to deliver a rebuke, while staying in character. So I said, barely above a whisper, 'Would you ever fuck off?' There followed that most theatrical of reactions, an audible gasp. Then, after what seemed like four minutes of shocked silence, the entire upper portion of the auditorium exploded into ecstatic cheering. The university students of the 'Athens of the North' went for Pat in a big way.

Three years later, Peter Zadek decided to stage *The Hostage* — 'Die Geisel' — in a translation by Heinrich Böll, at the Schauspielhaus in Bochum, in the Ruhrgebiet, in collaboration with Westdeutscher-undfunk, who were to film the stage version and transmit it as a four-hour television play. I have never quite lost faith in German efficiency (I still prefer German cars), but a nation which can stretch *The Hostage* to four hours invites enquiry as to its grasp of reality.

Zadek had seen rehearsals for the first production of *Borstal Boy* at the Abbey, and was greatly taken by my performance and by the workshop approach Tomás MacAnna had adopted with the Frank McMahon adaptation. Rehearsals were generally exciting, good fun, if hard work; and, of course, frequent pauses for replenishment of the porter level helped the general gaiety. Zadek's memory of me must have been firmly placed in that milieu when he advised Volker Canaris, the producer for WDR, to invite me to join the Aufnahmeleitung as an adviser, and the cast as narrator. My German was about adequate for the latter, and since all the heads of the production spoke English, the former seemed to present no difficulty, and a preliminary flying visit to Bochum, and two days' discussion on the production, went very well.

Unfortunately, in the years since 1967, a few things had changed. I had now been two years or more on the wagon. When I explained that I was off the sauce for health reasons — mainly the mental health of those closest to me — Zadek was at a loss to understand this. He said I was listening to quacks — as he opened another bottle of brandy. At the same time, he aggressively declined the offer of a *butterkek* because he distrusted its cholesterol content. He was also listening to quacks. Anyway, I was not the all-singing, all-dancing, wild Irish piss-artist of his imaginings.

My advice was dismissed as 'a shitty bore'. 'I can't get over you,' he said, 'You were a bloody marvellous Brendan. Then you turn up here in a sharp suit and overcoat, and gold glasses. You look like a fucking German.' (Zadek himself had been reared in London, after his family had escaped from Nazi Germany.)

On the performance level, however, he was happy enough with me. The idea of the adaptation was as follows: as I leave a Dublin pub with a brown paper carry-out, there's a bomb alert. I climb through the window of a derelict building to sit and drink until the all-clear. Then I recognise my surroundings as the burntout shell of Pat and Meg's old place. Flashback, and we are in the typical Dublin shebeen of the fifties . . . well, not quite.

There seems to be an insurmountable obstacle among strangers, to understanding the Dublin word 'kip'. 'A kip-shop' may mean 'a brothel'; likewise a 'kip-house'. But 'a bit of a kip', while it could, to certain Anglo ears, convey 'forty winks', to the Dubliner means a place that falls short of acceptable standards of hygiene, comfort, service, decor or furnishing. When someone says, 'I spent the night drinking in that kip,' he refers, probably, to an after-hours house where the whiskey would take the paint off the door and the porter would scour the lining off your bowels.

So, the resuscitated Belvedere Hotel (oh, but yes), as Meg's old place was renamed in the German version, was not just 'a kip', as in the sense of the original in *An Giall*, but a full-blown brothel, with a spiral staircase, corridors of whores' cubicles, some with Sacred Heart lamps, others with May altars, for such as had *Eine religiösen Tick; 'vor jedem Trick das Nachtgebet, hinterher die Danksagung'* — which translates as, 'Before each trick, the night prayers, afterwards, the thanksgiving'.

As for *The Hostage*, far from the bewildered National Service conscript of the original, he was a brawny, mustachioed replica of the Kitchener 'Your country needs you' World War I poster. For all that, Zadek was a genius. But geniuses in the theatre usually interest critics more than they do actors. He was always courteous to me, after the initial frankness. Canaris was kind and encouraging, and Gottfried Greiffenhagen, the 'Chauspielhausintendant', with whom I kept in touch over the years, did show a genuine appreciation, not just of the play but of my own difficulties.

The television version preceded the theatre presentation; at least the recording of it did. The party scene, which even in the Littlewood version consisted of a few bottles of Guinness and a sing-along to the piano accompaniment, became an absolute extravaganza. Seven cameras, if memory serves, covered about forty minutes of improvised drinking, dancing, singing and general fuckology. It had all the curious, non-erotic, schoolboyish, bum-smacking, tit-rubbing high-jinks beloved of the Teuton. The highlight was when the Russian sailor descended the spiral staircase with a semi-nude whore thrown over his shoulder, her bare arse uppermost. The sailor hit the floor level beside Pat, who was pouring himself a bottle of Guinness as this pale posterior crossed his eyeline. He raised the bottle and emptied the rest of his Guinness into the passing rectum, and the foam bubbled over the adjoining buttocks. Nothing, quite obviously, could follow that.

The play opened in the Schiller Theatre in Berlin shortly afterwards, *ohne mich*, since I had declined the honour. I have never seen the TV version either, since it preceded the days of video cassettes. I am torn, to this day, between curiosity and the fervent hope that it has perished in the stampede of technology.

Máirtín Byrnes was a legendary figure among Irish folk musicians, even before his death. Through some good luck, Zadek had secured him to do the soundtrack fiddle music for the play. He was due at Düsseldorf airport a week after my own arrival, and I was on hand to greet him. We had never met before. He was instantly recognisable: small in stature, with a flaming red beard, and carrying a coffin-shaped wooden fiddle case under his oxter, and in his free hand a very large bottle of dutyfree brandy.

'That's for you,' he said.

'No thanks, I'm off it.'

The leprechaun brow clouded over and the bright blue eye flashed. 'Does that mean I'll be drinking on my own? And me without a word of German?'

'No,' I reassured him, 'I'll be with you every step of the way.'

It was a promise I was to regret, and failed to fulfil. He had the leprechaun's facility for vanishing as soon as you took your eye off him.

'Welcome to Germany,' I said.

'Welcome me arse. The bastards lost my suitcase, and it's not even mine. I borrowed it off Carol, His Honour's secretary.'

'His Honour' was Garech de Brun, of the Guinness family, for whom Máirtín worked, at least nominally, as a gardener, when not providing music for the guests at Luggala.

'We'll get your case,' I said, leading the way to the lost luggage office, followed by Máirtín expostulating on the shortcomings of the Bundesrepublik's baggage handlers. I explained our plight to the youngish man at the hatch, who kept looking past me at Máirtín.

'You're Máirtín Byrnes, the fiddler, aren't you?' he said. Only the final 's' of 'Byrnes' gave him away as not being English.

'I'm a folk music fan,' he explained. 'I love Irish traditional stuff. I've got an LP with your photo on the cover. Never mind, Mr Byrnes, we will have your bag at the hotel by afternoon.' (Which they did.) Máirtín bowed graciously before we left.

'Well,' he said with great magnanimity, 'Aren't they a cultured people?'

He entranced most of the German crew, from director down, but posed a big problem for one young trainee floor manager, Detlev. Máirtín was a chain-smoker. Smoking was not allowed in the studios, a fact announced in notices on every wall, door and window. Máirtín puffed away, unperturbed, Detlev trailing after him, remonstrating, 'Herr Byrnes, bitte, haben Sie die Schilder nicht gesehen? Rauchen verboten.'

'Christ, Niall, this young fella has me persecuted. Is it my body he's after, or what? He puts chat on me the minute I'm in the door.'

From sheer badness, I didn't explain.

'Rauchen,' intoned Detlev, a shade more desperately, 'ist verboten. Es ist nicht gestattet, hier zu rauchen,' he spelled out. Finally the word 'rauchen' lodged in Máirtín's ear, and he cottoned on.

'Listen here to me, you, goss'n,' he said, 'I'll rauch when I like, and where I like, that is fuckin' that.'

Zadek, on being apprised of the crisis, solved the problem at a stroke. 'Oh, Máirtín can smoke on the set,' he ruled, 'because the musicians would smoke anyway, so technically the cigarettes are props.'

Máirtín enjoyed the victory. 'Didn't I know well that little upstart was getting too big for his boots.'

We had adjoining apartments on Schillingstrasse, near Eigelstein, on the edge of the Turkish quarter, in Cologne. He made friends with the lady who ran the *Kneipe* at the street's end, and he played the fiddle for her and her customers, which saved me the chore of escorting him as minder and interpreter. 'I'm off down to the little womaneen on the corner,' he'd say.

One morning at about two o'clock, my bell rang. I went to the front door to find two members of the Polizei standing behind Máirtín, his fiddle in its coffin beneath his arm.

'God save all here,' said he, 'these fine gentlemen want to meet you. They're great fans of yours.'

*'Erkennen sie diesen Kerl?'*

*'Ja. Er ist ein Freund von mir.'*

They had found him wandering on the Autobahn, a few miles out of town. It is illegal to walk on the Autobahn, so they had arrested him. They'd found a WDR security pass on him, but it didn't have his address. Their competence in English fell short of the dialect of east Galway, but eventually they'd got the Schillingstrasse part of the address out of him. When the *Hostage* company heard this story, Máirtín was elevated to near sainthood. No German, they said, would have gotten away with less than a week in the 'slammer' for a similar misdemeanour.

During our curious sojourn in Cologne, the Ronnie Scott Quartet, featuring Louis Stewart, played at Gigi Campi's bar-cum-café in the Hohestrasse. They did a four and a half hour gig, at the end of which Ronnie Scott said, *'Danke schon*. We hope you enjoyed our music. If you did, please tell your friends, if you didn't . . . fuck you. Goodnight.' And he was cheered to the echo.

Máirtín inevitably produced his fiddle, and a minute *fleadh*-cum-jazz session ensued. The following evening I went with the quartet for a meal. Kenny Baldock, the bass player, was proud of his proficiency in German, and proceeded to order for everyone in that language. As he listed each item, the waiter nodded and said, 'Yes, Sir,' or 'Certainly, Sir.' Máirtín Drew, the drummer, tired of this showing-off, said, 'Oh, turn it up, Kenny, the cunt speaks English.' 'That's right,' said the waiter proudly, 'I do.'

In 1990, Michael Scott and I co-operated in a new translation and adaption of *The Hostage*, based on the Irish text of *An Giall*, and sticking to the Dramatis Personae thereof, but incorporating some of the songs of later versions. It was enormously successful and very well reviewed. It subsequently ran into difficulties when objection was expressed, belatedly, by the Behan copyright holders, and permission for any further production was withdrawn. A pity, because, modesty bedamned, I think we had concocted, finally, the *Hostage* Brendan meant to write.

# SIXTEEN

R*yan's Daughter* hit Ireland in late 1969, and the only way to talk about it is the way folklore has it now. At that time, a reconnaissance party arrived in mid-winter, in Dingle. They scouted around, and one of them went into a hardware store. He said, 'Can you supply hardboard?' And the businessman, being a Kerryman, looked at him, and he thought unto himself, 'Now this man has an English accent. He looks like an ex-British Army man, he has other fellas outside there with him in a van, and they have a trailer and so on. He's not looking for hardboard just to plug a hole in the tent.' And off the top of his head, he said, 'I can supply all the hardboard you want, twenty-four hours a day, and all other supplies of any nature whatsoever that you want. That is what I am here for.' So they said, 'All right. Good man. We want delivered, by the next couple of days, five hundred sheets of eight by four hardboard (which he duly ordered, and on which, allegedly, he put an extra mark-up of fifty pence per sheet). And there he was, £250 richer, without moving outside the counter.

That's apocryphal, but has more than a grain of truth in it, I would say. This man had spotted immediately, without being able to identify it in precise terms, that this was a film unit, and that it was going to be a big one. And he was proven right, because one and a half years later he was still supplying everything bar mother's milk to this enormous operation, beside which the invasion of Normandy pales into a mere manoeuvre.

*Ryan's Daughter* spawned many more stories than Robert Bolt's endlessly amended screenplay. Over the ensuing quarter century, these stories have grown into colourful legends, and they come back to me, mine own involvement in them totally unrecognisable. People say, 'Do you remember the day you told Bob Mitchum to fuck off?' Which of course I never did, nor would I — it would be a dangerous thing to do, even today.

But I want to tell a story of, shall we say, somebody getting his just desserts.

There was a man whom we shall just call Reg. He was of the Cockney persuasion, very abrasive and aggressive, and very good at his job, which he tended to redefine frequently.

On the first day of filming, there were people sitting on upturned currachs, or *naomhóga*, as they call them in that part of the world, on Coominole beach. Reg arrived like the wrath of God, and screamed, 'Get up off those fucking boats, you're fucking up the continuity of the picture.' Now, they hadn't shot a single frame at this stage, but the simple folk of Corcaguiney had not yet got the hang of this movie caper — a failure they very soon rectified, need I say. So the locals shifted as requested. That night, an Atlantic gale shifted the boats, making smithereens of them against the cliffs. Reg was not very popular at the outset, nor did the populace warm to him to any noticeable extent.

One night he was involved in a fracas outside a pub in Dingle. He had a top-of-the-range automobile, which he ostentatiously drove around. After an altercation with his wife, he threw her into the car, jumped in himself and proceeded to drive off. She tried to wrest the wheel from his hands. He was trying to close the door, and the car was spinning around in circles, while oaths of varying quality rent the air.

In due course police were called, and this gentleman very soon faced about eighty-five charges, including public affray, rioting, use of abusive and obscene language, driving without due consideration, driving while drunk, dangerous driving, reckless driving, common assault, aggravated assault, and God knows what else.

Since Reg was indispensable to certain operations in this venture, the wheels were set in motion to get these charges dropped, because if he were to be sent to jail, or held for any length of time, it would seriously disrupt the filming. The film company went to various authorities, all the way up to the Department of Justice, but were informed that the only person who could withdraw any of these charges was the arresting officer. And this arresting officer's superior officer explained: 'You know, I could try to use my influence with him, but unfortunately it's up to him, whatever he says. I have no power to order this man to withdraw these charges.'

And when they had gone, he who had no power to order anyone to withdraw these charges, said to the arresting officer, 'Now, what you are going to do is this. You will withdraw the charges on condition that this man goes and apologises to all the people who were discommoded or in any way embarrassed by his behaviour on the night in question. And you will draw up a list of the people who were offended. And this man will go and apologise to them, accompanied by two Garda officers.'

And this came to pass. They chose about seven streets, most of them well out of earshot of the incident, and they chose houses where there were elderly people who spoke very little English. And this man had to go and knock on doors where elderly women came out and said, '*Cad tá uait?*'

'I've come to apologise for my bad language, and what I've done.'
'*Cad é?*'
'She can't fuckin' understand what I'm saying.'
'Don't use that kind of language in front of a lady.'

With a sizeable crowd following, he had to traipse round, apologising to people who had never seen him in their lives, who didn't know what he was saying, even as he didn't know what they were saying. But justice was done, and the law satisfied, which doesn't always amount to the same thing. I feel that this heartwarming tale could only have originated in Kerry — if, that is, it ever did happen. And if it didn't, it should have. In the words of the storyteller, '*Má tá bréag ann, bíodh.*' ('If there's a lie in it, so be it.')

I landed the Dingle gig because the word went out that David Lean was making a film and that he was interviewing people. As it happened, the day I went to see him I was doing some work in the garden. The heavens had opened, and I had Wellington boots and an oilskin coat on. I was about to change, but then I thought, 'Ah, what the hell, he just wants to see people.' So I went as I was.

A giggle went round amongst these people when they saw me, and they said, 'How did you know what we were looking for? You look as if you're dressed for the film.'

They told me it was about a group who were landing arms on the beach during the Troubles. I got the part.

With the inescapable irony of the movie business, I spent all my time in hat and overcoat, wearing glasses and carrying a square briefcase, standing on the beach like an idiot, in the pissing rain, waiting for the Germans to land the arms.

I was what they called 'The Political'. (That was the part.) There was a whole subplot cut out of the film because (this was the folk memory again) the rumour was that at the end of filming, when he had edited it down as much as he could, Lean still had something like nine hours of a story. In fact, the landing of the arms by the IRA, and all that, was a bit disjointed in the film, anyway.

There's a scene in the film where the British Army are lying in wait in the heather to ambush the IRA men as they come up from the beach.

There had been a lot of protest, as there always is when films are made in Ireland. Somebody who has never seen the film, for the simple reason that it hasn't yet been made, decides that the morals of the community are being threatened. The fair name of Ireland is being sullied by all this carry-on and the nation is being made a mockery of, and brought into ridicule. Noises of that kind, I think, have been made from the pulpit, and local councillors have being saying the same thing for as long as I can remember. But in this case, I remember watching, after this ambush scene, all these extras (who came from the Bullring in Tralee, which wouldn't exactly be the Foxrock of that town), some of whom were in the habit of consoling themselves for their long hours in the wet grass with bottles of red wine, and so on.

After the scene had been shot, they were straggling up the hill in their ill-fitting uniforms (the size of which didn't matter, because they had been lying down in the grass anyway), with their wooden rifles. They really looked a sorry bunch, with their trousers sagging down around their knees, and boots that were three sizes too big or too small, and shirts coming up around their ears.

This big, rather jovial English lighting man, leaning against a five-kilowatt lamp, surveyed this bunch going by.

'There goes the British Army,' he said, 'Fine body of men.'

I laughed.

'You know, you lot are complainin' that *we're* bringing *Ireland* into ridicule. Well, fuck me, what about this lot then, eh?'

Every movie needs a publicity gimmick, preferably of the 'continuing saga' variety, with inbuilt sensation reactivators. Lean's publicity men thought up a beauty: THE STORM. This film would contain the storm to dwarf all storms. The storm in *Man of Arran*, till then Ireland's most celebrated celluloid tempest, would be as a linnet pissing in the breeze, compared to the seething deluge that would crease the cliffs of Kerry, like the Crack of Doom itself.

If it came, like.

The meteorological portents were not encouraging. Veterans of filming tornadoes in Florida dismissed the kingdom's best as mild flatulence. Old folk in chimney corners and pub snugs donned the mantle of an extra half-century to reminisce about the 'Night of the Big Wind', but held out little promise of a repeat in the foreseeable future, such not having been foretold in either Old Moore's Almanac or the Prophesies of St Columcille.

And nothing dramatic materialised. The Irish weather, notoriously uncooperative, scuttered around in its usual way. It conjured up mist, fog, rain, sunshine, sleet, hailstones, and permutations in eternity of all these — but divil a storm.

All the better for the press boys. Paragraphs abounded in the Irish and British papers, speculating on the dread consequences of continued calm, with headings like 'Lean times for David in Dingle doldrums' or 'Guinness the only draught as movie-makers hope for hurricane'.

Nonsense from beginning to end, needless to say. All the *Jaws* sequences which leave *Moby Dick* for dead, were shot in six feet of water in the Universal Studios back lot; but the saga of the storm that never was rolled on.

The storm sequence was an inspired publicity stunt, because nobody was responsible if the storm didn't happen, and the publicity could go on forever. Eventually, the storm was manufactured with giant hoses and wind machines, just as one or two of the screen sunsets, which lured the trippers to Coominole, were imported from South Africa.

While we were all waiting for the storm, we tried to drink ourselves to death. And some, it must be said, succeeded, later rather than sooner, to invert a meaningless phrase.

I have spoken about the cloistral conditions in Radio Éireann. *Ryan's Daughter* produced a similar irksome mood. The contract specified that no one could travel beyond twenty-five miles from the base, without permission. Since permission was not forthcoming, it was not sought, and people regularly went the thirty miles to Tralee, or the forty-two miles to Killarney, to whoop it up, in breach of contract.

Furthermore, because of a curious clause, one's commitment could be unilaterally extended — by them only, not by oneself, by up to a month at a time. Since most reasonable people do not object too loudly to being highly paid for doing nothing but drinking porter and playing poker, with an occasional gawk at the lens of a multi-million dollar camera thrown in to break the monotony, this arrangement was considered equitable. (Indeed, today's film producers would consider it lunacy. Not to secure all performers to the set with stage screws, until the completion of principal photography, would strike them as extreme eccentricity.)

I, predictably, was the exception. I was, just like everybody else, trying to drink myself to death, but I was also going frantic to get out of Dingle — though not for lack of love for that demi-paradise. I was due to go to New York in January to start rehearsals for the Broadway production of *Borstal Boy*. The date seemed more and more like being firmed up, and *Ryan's Daughter* looked more like pissing around the peninsula until Tib's Eve.

I made, or rather, my then agent, Mr Tommy O'Connor, made appeals for a release date, but to no avail. They had me over a barrel, and I could yodel my larynx off, unheeded, as long as they gave seven clear days' notice of intention to extend the contract. I was becoming quite paranoid about their insistence on emptying barrelfuls of lolly into my unreceptive lap. Where others might have grovelled in gratitude, I suspected a British plot to deprive America of seeing me perform on Broadway.

Fate took a hand, in the form of Mr Douglas Twiddy, a very high up one of Them, who was flying out one Friday from Shannon to London. He was entrusted with an armful of letters, to be mailed on arrival in the Big Smoke, on the reasonable assumption then, and perhaps even now, that that would be quicker than lobbing them into a postbox on the peninsula of Dingle. One of the letters was the habitual intimation to Mr Tommy O'Connor, of the intention to extend the employment of the indispensable N. Toibin. It was a Bank Holiday weekend, so the letters rested in the London postbox until Tuesday morning. This three-day delay ensured that there was not seven clear days' notice, and with one bound, I was free.

But first, a song.

O'Connor called the boys and said it was time to say 'Goodbye' — the notice was too short.

'OK, *touché*,' they said, sportingly, recognising that it was they who were now over the barrel. 'How much does the bastard want?'

'Nothing. He wants out.'

'Oh, sure, we know that. But how much does he want?'

'He wants out. Stuff the money.'

They were now floundering in unfamiliar waters. Surely I wasn't looking for *billing*?

No. Just out.

They finally accepted that the Dingle climate, over-indulgence in whiskey, and too much salt fish, had driven me round the twist. Why else would I spurn money?

A hasty rethink of the schedule showed that I could be 'wrapped' in four days. They managed this with grace and dispatch, and on the fourth day, in the late afternoon, I sat into my car and took the Golden Road to Samarkhand.

Well, not the road to Dublin, anyway.

Still paranoid, I thought they had been too bloody nice, too sweet to be wholesome. So I went first to Cork, and thence to Dublin. I found, when I reached home, that they had indeed asked the Gardaí between Dingle and Limerick to try to intercept me, as there was one shot they had overlooked.

What the hell, it would have only ended on the floor, with about six hours more of filmic genius.

Strange things, inconsistencies, happen in any movie that is spread over a long period of shooting, and one of the very first scenes that we shot was when the IRA men arrive in from the beach. They rush into Ryan's pub, sou'westers dripping. Emmet Bergin is first, you see him thundering on the door to be let in. And some one year and three months later, they did the reverse shot, of the door being opened, and Emmet coming through. In the meantime, he had put on three stone in weight. So, between the knocking on the one side of the door, and the opening on the other, the man's face was twice the size it had been. Since they flashed through the door, nobody in the cinema would cop it, but for anybody watching the editing, it must have been hilarious.

During the fifteen months while the cast were putting on weight, some investors were losing confidence. Mr Lean was obviously not the kind of man who could be told by anybody to wrap it up, or to get the finger out. One must remember that *Dr Zhivago* and *Lawrence of Arabia*, his last two films, had been enormous successes, *Zhivago* particularly. Nobody was going to turn round to the maker of *Dr Zhivago* and say, 'Come on, get a move on.' They would say, more likely, to comfort themselves, 'Trust David. Of course he knows what he's doing. This is going to be wonderful.'

But one man, Mr Peter O'Toole, when visiting the set, expressed the opinion that David Lean had approached all the people who had refused to back his earlier films, and had offered them the chance of backing this, and that he was now busily feeding their money into the Atlantic. Stranger things have happened in the film business.

There were some horrendous near misses. John Mills almost drowned in Coominole, during a tricky filming sequence. They managed to get him out, and as he passed David Lean, who was looking a little anxiously, though not all that anxiously, maybe, at his star being carried on a stretcher, Mills, in true-blue, stiff-upper-lip fashion, said, 'Sorry, Guv, ruined the shot I'm afraid.' All the British chaps thought that was wonderful, and all the Irish thought: 'Fuckin' eejit. Why doesn't he sue the bastard?'

Lean was rather cold in manner. I didn't have that much to do with him, but he was always very civil. He had an automatic smile, which flashed on, teeth only, no eyes. He was one of the best film-makers ever. My own favourite film to this day is *Great Expectations*, which was one of his.

I heard Robert Mitchum being interviewed outside his caravan one day during a period of strain between himself and David Lean. It was a rookie reporter from one of the local papers. He got off on the wrong foot by asking, 'What kind of director is David Lean?'

'He's a tall director,' said the poker-faced Bob.

Did he not agree that David Lean was, filmicly speaking, a genius, whatever one thought of him personally?

'Yeah, sure. Give me fifty-four takes of any shot, and *I'm* a genius.'

Mitchum was a genial man, and very affable with other actors, because he just liked them. He would ask after people he had worked with years before, Irish actors, people like Geoff and Eddie Golden. And it wasn't just 'And how's old So-and-so?': there was a genuine affection there.

John Mills was very kindly, very English, chatty, pleasant, keeping the party going, in an awfully 'nice' way.

Leo McKern was liked by everyone. He was a wonderful eccentric. He would sit on his own, drinking pink gin, at any hour of the day. Pink gin, in fact, seemed to be his only tipple. But once he knew he wasn't on call the following day, he would board his yacht and pull out to sea — and stay there until he was required to come back in. He also had a Dormobile, stocked with guns and fishing gear, and he would go up Mount Eagle and shoot and fish, and perhaps drink pink gin, and come back down again. When he did go into the pub, he tended to drink with the local fishermen, or with the actors, of course.

*Ryan's Daughter* had a huge and lasting impact on the economy of an entire area. There can be no question about that. For instance, the

200

*Contd on p. 217*

17. *The Hostage*, Edinburgh, 1971

*Left to right:* Bill McCabe, Jenny Lee, P J Stephens, Niall Toibin (sitting) and May Cluskey.

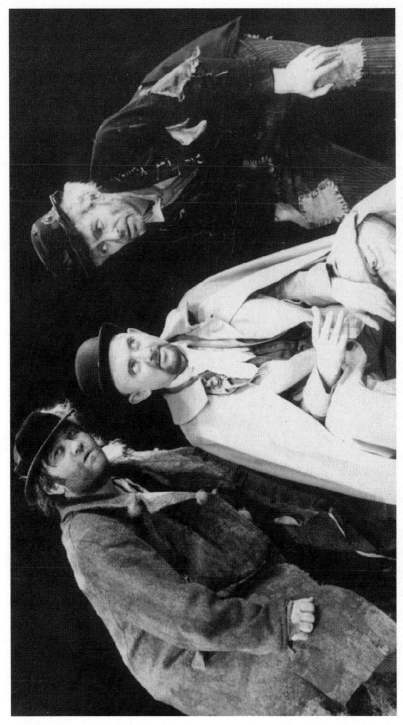

18. *Waiting for Godot* with Donal McCann and Peter O'Toole, Nottingham Playhouse, 1971

Ah, yes, I remember it . . . well, most of it.

19. Niall Toibin and Liam Sweeney in a production of *Patrick Pearse Motel* by Hugh Leonard, City Theatre, Limerick, 1971

20. Niall Toibin as Captain Boyle and Brendan Cauldwell as Joxer Daly in *Juno and the Paycock*, Toronto, 1972

This was a season done by Siobhán McKenna for the 'Irish Arts' of Toronto, featuring *Juno*, three plays by Synge, Siobhán's *Here Be Ladies*, and *Confusion* with Niall Toibin. Jack MacGowran was to join us with his Beckett one-man show, but he died in New York on the night of our *Juno* dress rehearsal. Bob Bahl, the designer, died shortly after the run, and Seán Kenny, who had directed, died soon after his return to London. Connoisseurs of superstition may be interested to know that a 'Good Wishes' telegram at the outset of the season contained a quote from the 'Scottish play'.

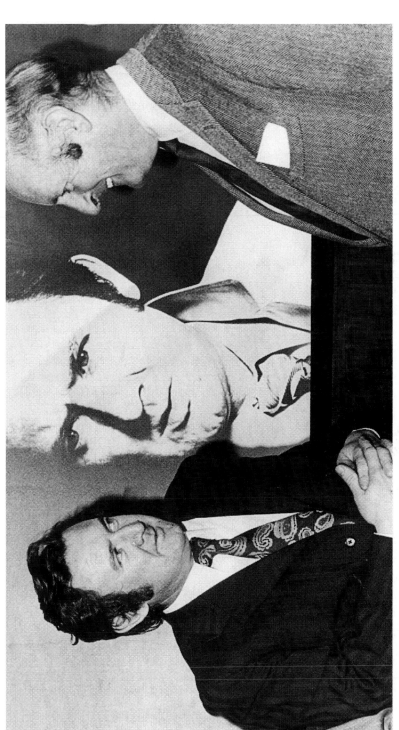

21. Niall Toibin chats to Bill Twomey, manager of the Cork Opera House, 1972

Bill asked me once before curtain-up to cut any references to hanging in *First Confession* by Frank O'Connor. A woman whose husband had hanged himself was in the audience, her first night out since the tragedy. I managed to do as asked. Re-reading 'First Confession' now, it seems impossible, but no one complained that the story was distorted. But then, Richard Burton told me that on a whim, when he was playing *Hamlet* on Broadway, he delivered the 'To be or not to be' speech in German. If anyone out front or backstage noticed, nobody mentioned it.

22. Judy and Niall Toibin at Christy Brown's wedding, 1973

23. *Left to right*: Gay Byrne, Noel Pearson, Ulick O'Connor and Niall Toibin, 1973

Only Byrne and I never stopped talking to each other, I believe. But the stars of this show are missing; Christy Brown, whose wedding it was, and Charlie Haughey, with whom I danced on the lawn, both of us clutching a bottle of brandy — the same bottle.

24. Niall Toibin, Anna Manahan and Des Keogh in rehearsal for *Twigs* by George Furth, Gate Theatre, 1974

This photo was taken in the Gaiety Circle Bar, where we rehearsed. During the run of *Twigs*, we sold our house. The clincher to the negotiations was six tickets for *Twigs*.

25. Niall Toibin and Marie Kean in *Crock*, Gaiety Theatre, 1974

Cecil Sheridan and Séamus Healy were relieved of their choral duties by Dave Gold, the MD, on grounds of idiosyncratic harmonising. As they went down for coffee, Séamus said, 'I'm sad about that, Cecil. That opening chorus haunts me.' 'Why wouldn't it?' said Cecil, 'Didn't ye murder it.'

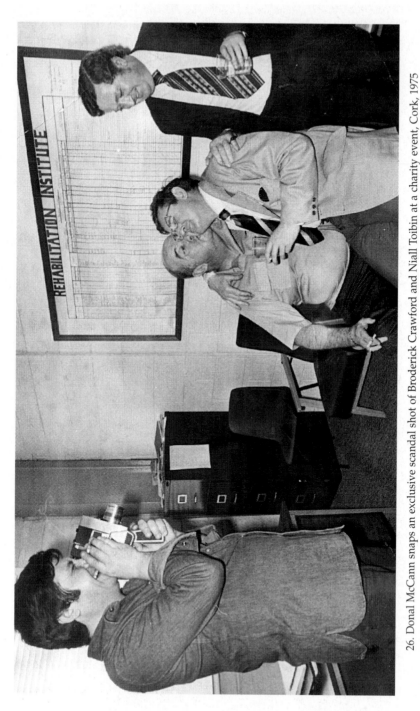

26. Donal McCann snaps an exclusive scandal shot of Broderick Crawford and Niall Toibin at a charity event, Cork, 1975

Broderick Crawford took over as director of *That Championship Season* by Jason Miller when John Mahon took ill. He had been playing the coach for two and a half years on tour, and inevitably an element of paraphrasing had crept in. When pulled up by a prompter who knew no better, he growled, 'What d'ya mean it's not the line? It's the only god-damn line you're gonna get. It's not Shakespeare, it's not goin' into the Library of Congress, nor the Smithsonian Institute. . . it's only Jason Miller.'

27. Charity event in aid of the Equity Benevolent Fund, Gaiety Theatre, c1975

Extracts from six one-man shows were read.

*Left to right:* Micheál MacLiammóir, Noel Nagle of the Wolfe Tones, Marie Kean, Eamonn Morrissey, Niall Toibin, Noel Warfield (Wolfe Tones), Maurice O'Doherty, Siobhán McKenna, Derek Warfield (Wolfe Tones), Eamonn Andrews, Tommy Byrne (Wolfe Tones), Anna Manahan, Hilton Edwards.

28. Niall Toibin and Laurie Morton in *Liam Liar*, Hugh Leonard's adaptation of *Billy Liar*, Gate Theatre, 1976.

29. Luke Kelly, Niall Toibin and Danny Doyle, *c*1976

They were probably laughing at my collar and tie during the launch by Plough Records, a Noel Pearson enterprise, of *Toibin Being' Behan* and Danny's umpteenth LP. The label was so exclusive it issued no more records.

30. Judy and Niall Toibin, An Taibhdhearc, Galway, c1977

31. Beatrice, Blánaid and Kathleen Behan with Niall Toibin at the opening of *Borstal Boy*,
Gaiety Theatre, 1978

Kathleen Behan was irrepressible, probably quite fearless in her younger days, certainly so
in age. She and Stephen Francis Behan, her husband, were a great double-act. She never
called him Stephen in my hearing, always Frank. After a full evening's consumption of half
pints of Guinness, her stock reply to 'Will ye have another?' was 'I'd rather have a bit of
lovin', if it's all the same to you.'

32. A scene from *Long Voyage Home* by Eugene O'Neill, National Theatre, London, 1978

*Left to right*: Bill Owen, Jack Shepherd, Dave King, Niall Toibin, Trevor Ray, Brian Glover, John Tams, Mark McManus and James Grant.

Bill Bryden, the director, assembled a brilliant company at the Cottesloe to produce ensemble playing in the Abbey tradition. Other members of the company were Bob Hoskins, Oliver Cotton, Edna Doré, June Watson and Derek Newark.

'There are no stars, each of us is already a star in his own right,' said Bryden. 'Nobody has to prove anything anymore.' Well, what can I tell ya? Frederick Treves, on joining the company from the Littleton, said, 'I'm thrilled. I've never done any pick-your-nose acting before.'

Contd from p. 200    NIALL TOIBIN

only places in Dingle you could eat in when we arrived, in early 1969, was Benner's Hotel and The Skellig Hotel, only just opened. There were a few guesthouses. There was one restaurant, Kenna's, which operated full-time, along with a couple of chip shops, and the fast-food place right beside the production office. Within a few years there were ten or twelve, and now there must be twenty restaurants.

This is the kind of mushroom growth you would normally expect to have faltered after five or six years, but it seems stronger than ever.

Dingle became known, not just as the location for the filming of *Ryan's Daughter*, which after all has by now faded from public memory, but as a gourmet's paradise — or at least, a trencherman's delight. Later, of course, it became famous for the dolphin, Fungi — so-called, maybe, because he was a mushroom growth too?

# SEVENTEEN

After a couple of years of the one-man show, RTE offered me a comedy series. Noel Pearson, who was my manager then, considered it a good idea, and so indeed did I. I was not unaware of the perils. Being offered a show of the quiz variety, where contestants can win a car for guessing the colour of the compère's knickers, is a licence to print money. Your very own comedy show could mean a poisoned chalice clamped to your gob. You won't know till you've swallowed.

We assembled a great team. Chris Curran, Derry Power, Emmet Bergin, Barbara Brennan, Eileen Murphy and myself, Earl Gill, Johnny Curran and other distinguished heads on the music end, Wesley Burrows, Eoghan Harris and myself on the script, with contributions from Brian MacLochlainn who directed.

MacLochlainn was clever and opinionated, as a good director should be. He was very good in fact. Some of the time we got on like a house on fire, sometimes the studio near went on fire. One way or the other, it was a productive partnership. We were both prepared to take on any subject, nothin' was too hot or too heavy. Them was days, Joxer. And them was nights. A so-called coffee break the next morning was like refloating a beached whale, assuming those mammals could wallow in porter.

Looking back over some of the scripts is the only way we can judge the series now, as the archives contain no more than a few flitters of tape, amounting to no more than ten minutes, if that. The series was called *If The Cap Fits*. By the general reaction, the ratings, the press reviews, it was pretty good stuff. By the standards of previous or subsequent Irish TV efforts it was a smash.

What follows is the sketch from the second programme of 2 July 1973, which caught the public fancy and set the series alight. It is a send-up of the *Late Late Show*, an obvious enough target, but just as surely a very deep pitfall. Emmet Bergin played Gay Byrne, Máire Hastings was Lady Doolan, I played Matt Goulding (these latter characters based on Lady Valerie Goulding and Matt Doolan, a serious-minded campaigner, who got on the real *Late Late* panel through constantly writing to the papers letters of unimpeachable worthiness, on subjects bereft of any hint of controversy). I also played Bishop Eamon Casey and the Dutch Dominican, Vivian Van Damm. Derry Power was the right-winger.

I have made a few cuts, but nothing has been added to the original text, no name, reference or gag has been changed. Remembering that it was performed, and never repeated, almost twenty-three years ago, I think the following sketch stands up well enough to confirm that the show's reputation was well-earned.

(Extract from *If the Cap Fits*)

**MATT GOULDING:** I'm glad this subject of the Third World has come up. Because, Gay, I feel we've all become too flippant, too glib, too much out for a laugh. Some people don't even believe in the existence of the Third World. We don't respond to the needs of others the way we should. We're selfish. We talk about the North and that kind of thing — as though nobody else needed our consideration. Wouldn't you agree, Lady Doolin?

**LADY DOOLIN:** Yes I do, indeed. You have a very fertile brain if I may say so.

**MATT:** Because tis well-watered, Lady Doolin. I never touch the hard stuff. No. Never. Thank God.

**LADY DOOLIN:** Well, I must confess that my husband and I are rather partial to the crayther, because I feel we can promote the best in Irish industry by drinking Irish wiskey. Even the kitchin staff have a bottle of stout at Christmas. That's another great Irish industry, of course. A small gesture to Desmond, too, I suppose, for saving all those delightful Georgian houses.

**MATT:** Jools. Jools, gems of architecture! Part of our heritage as a pluralistic society.

**LADY DOOLIN:** Yes, absolutely. Ghastly to live in, of course.

**GAY:** The houses or the society, Lady Doolin?

**LADY DOOLIN** (haughtily): Both, if necessary, I presume. (She bows.)

*LOUD, PROLONGED STUDIO APPLAUSE.*

**BISHOP CASEY** (To stage manager, in the wings): Is that my cue to go on?

**GAY:** Not yet, Eamon, not yet.

**CASEY:** Ha, ha, ha . . . too late Gay. Too late. I have the oul' music wit me an' all tonight. (He looks about.) No sign o' Mick Cleary, I see. I s'pose he's on UTV is he? Or in the Daddy's place in Mullhuddart? (HE SITS AT GAY'S RIGHT, LEANS IN.) Well, my boy, an' how long is it since your last confession? Ha . . . ha . . . ha . . . Ach, sure 'tis all in fun, all in fun. D'you ever see Dave Allen at all, Gay, taking off the clergy?

**GAY:** Oh yes. Very amusing.

**CASEY:** Tunderin' blackguard, if I had my way I'd have him off the air, the hoor.

**GAY:** Ah, now you wouldn't.

**CASEY:** I'd do worse, I'd convert him. Ha . . . ha . . . ha. O hananamdial, are my old peepers playing tricks on me — is that Mosheen Tom Breshnihan I see there? Glory be to God, isn't it a small world.

**MOSHEEN:** Hallo Ned!

**CASEY:** Wisha how are tings in Tangmalangmaloo? I met your Aunty Abbey at Puck an' she told me you were in Australia.

**MOSHEEN:** She's behind the times faith. I'm only jesht home from Nebraska. Jack is in Hackensack, Noo Jersey, now you know.

**CASEY:** Did he get the parish?

**MOSHEEN:** He did. But he isn't all that thankful to the place they're sending him. You see, he was very happy in Canastota (that's Noo York o'course) and subsequently in Chittenango.

**CASEY:** Chittenango, oh yes, yes. Mairead Sheehy from Melodeonstown has a married daughter there.

**MOSHEEN:** She hov. Jack baptised her eldest. But Hackensack was agreeing with him fine when he got the lift up and the transfer — oh, to a horrible place.

**CASEY:** Where is that?

**MOSHEEN:** Sullivansville.

**GAY:** Matt T, you were saying?

**MATT:** Yes I was. I always am. (Pause) Oh yes. I was saying, do we do enough? No. Certainly not for the Third World. I was down in Whiddy in West Cork during the week, and I met a man connected with the refinery. (And let me say, by the way, there's no pollution, not at all.) But this man, he's home on a charter flight from the Third World, and do you know he was telling me that you can't find a place in Bankok to park your ostrich. Isn't that a fright? We could train traffic technologists — send out traffic wardens and parking meters to Rangoon and Libya — the Third World in general, like. After all, in a less materialistic age we did it for Europe — with our missionaries — we did our bit then — wouldn't you agree Bishop?

**CASEY:** Bleddy sure we did, and more than our bit. And there's no need for the formality, ha . . . ha . . ., all that Bishop business. Just call me Your Lordship. But Gay, there is so much nonsense talked about the Third World. The notion is very prevalent that we whites are in some way superior, a cut above the rest of the world. This is just not true.

**POWER:** With all due respect to your cloth, your Lordship, I oppose you there. Diametrically, actually, and categorically. Am I on camera? If God had intended everybody to be equal he'd have made us all white. That's obvious. But perhaps you'd answer a question.

**CASEY:** Oh willingly, willingly, willingly.

**POWER:** When I was at school . . .

**CASEY:** Sad time, sad time . . .

**POWER:** When I was at school I paid out a fortune for the black babies. (I'm going to have my say, Doreen. Stop pulling my sleeve.) Can I have an assurance that this practice, if still in operation, is not just a cover-up to supply arms to the terrorists who want to depose Smudgie Smith's Democratic, decent Christian Government in Rhodesia?

**CASEY:** I'm afraid not . . . As you know, the Church does not meddle in politics — we want to keep religion out of politics.

**POWER:** And we want to keep politics out of sport.

**MOSHEEN:** (CHRIS) And ye want to keep the blacks out of everything.

**MOSHEEN:** I don't agree with looking for Arms Trials in connection with the Black Baby Money. I didn't agree with the first Arms Trial fwin 'twas fwite, and I won't change my coat now and support an Arms Trial fwin 'tis black. I don't agree with this dirty narrow-minded unchristian little *suarachán* from Sunday's Well that we should all have been made fwite . . .

**CASEY:** Mosheen! Not interrupting. But that kind of polemicism reminds me of the priest on the American mission who stopped the car one day to give a lift to a Baptist minister. A black Baptist minister by the same token — very strict: TT, non-smoker, never went to a football match or coursing meeting in his life. But anyhow, Father Mac pulled out the fags and asked *mo dhuine gorm* would he care for a smoke. 'No Father,' ses he most severely and reprovingly. 'If the Good Lord intended I should smoke he'd have put a chimney on my head.' 'Fair enough,' says Father Tom, and he stopped the car and opened the door. 'And if the Good Lord intended you should get into town any faster, he'd have put fweels under your arse.'

*LOUD LAUGHS AND APPLAUSE*

And I think that's about the size of it.

**GAY:** Well done, Bishop. We needed that little touch of common sense there. But seriously, is there really a slight mental superiority in the white races, counterbalanced by a physical superiority in the black? Is it a case of they have their Muhammad Ali, we have Ted Bonner?

**CASEY:** Well, theologically speaking — AD LIB

**MOSHEEN:** More to the point, is Cassius Clay past his best? — AD LIB

**LADY DOOLIN:** You mean as a prize-fighter or as a man? — AD LIB

**POWER:** For Heaven's sake. He wouldn't beat Katty Barry. The best of the whole lot was Ingmar Johansson, and after him Jack Doyle.

**CASEY:** Ara, not at all. Doyle had a glass jaw. Anyhow 'tis time for a song. All together now:

Oh the Garden of Eden has vanished they say,
But I know the lie of it still . . .
Just turn to your left at the bridge of Finea . . .

**MOSHEEN:** (Sings) Can't you sing a Kerry song?
(Starts): *Ar an dtaobh thall den Ghóilín 'sea chonaíonn mo ghrá geal . . .*

**POWER:** (Sings, to the air of 'Sospan Fach'):

Sunday's Well were langers around the town,

Sundays Well were langers around the town.
And Bater Logan got the gawk.

\* \* \* \*

The undoubted success of *If The Cap Fits* can hardly have pleased
many of the programme chiefs, since it took the piss out of them as
much as any other figures of authority. To RTE's credit, there is an
accurate and sharply critical piece on this whole business in their
own publication, *Irish Television Drama* by Helena Sheehan (1987),
essential and fascinating reading for anyone interested in TV and its
social and political effect.

The next series, three years after *The Cap*, was *Time Now, Mr T*.
How ironically prophetic can one get? Someone was calling 'Time'
with a vengeance. The reactions to this show gave me the roughest
ride of my time as a pro. The first sketch in the first show had the
phones jammed with the protesting pious. RTE turned tail and fled,
apologising and grovelling. They admitted that I had been offensive,
as though the writing, production and subsequent transmission of
this lewd assault on the morals of the last bastion of Christian
decency had been carried out by me, singlehanded, while they were
all at Choral Evensong or saying the Rosary.

Bobby O'Donoghue, of the *Cork Examiner*, who has lavished praise
on my efforts from time to time, told me of a reaction to my *Time
Now, Mr T* programmes, which he, so to speak, intercepted.

He was in the habit of making his way to work through the
English market, where one of the stallholders greeted him every
morning as Mr Lyons, under the impression that he was Larry
Lyons, the *Examiner* TV critic. On the morning that Larry Lyons
wrote an unfavourable, more-in-sorrow-than-in-anger review of the
show, she hailed him (Bobby that is) with special enthusiasm. 'Good
morning Mr Lyons. I see where that boy Toibin is disgracing us
again. But you didn't let him away with it. And you're quite right,
Mr Lyons. Slam the bastard.'

It was a lonely time. My wife and kids took the flak as much as I did. The letters of the affronted caused me not to repent but to vomit. They were quite literally sickening. I managed to flush most down to the spiritual home of their senders before anyone else got to see them. One crusader had gone to the trouble of enclosing a sample of excrement in a plastic satchel. I noted the postmark, foolishly, because every time I pass through that town I recall that someone there hated me to that extent.

However, I applied the advice of Ernest Blythe to all subsequent bouquets. He'd once explained that if the opening words of a letter were abusive, he burnt it without looking at the address or signature. That way he could meet the writer at any time and greet him warmly, taking the wind out of his sails without even knowing it. So someone thinks he's cut you down to size when you don't even know he wrote you a stinker.

We had the poison pens and hate-calls, as I say. But I had one call that nullified the lot. Gay Byrne rang and simply asked 'Are you all right?'

I probably said, 'Yerra fuck 'em.'

'You've started getting the letters? Did you get the one about being flushed down the jax along with Frank Hall and Gay Byrne and whoever?'

I had got an identically worded letter. 'I could quote them all for you,' he said. 'No one knows the virulence of the Catholic lunatic fringe as well as I do. To hell with the lot of them. Just carry on.'

It was a short call. It was to the point. It was almost congratulatory — you've really arrived when this shower are on your back. This was in 1977. I managed to shrug it off publicly. When one paper asked if my show could now be written off, I quoted Kathleen Behan's stock rejoinder, 'Carry on with the coffin, the corpse will walk.' A sense of betrayal hovered in my mind. RTE was out from now on, it seemed to me. So increasingly I turned to British television. Bill Bryden had written a play about Benny Lynch, the Scottish flyweight world champion. Gordon Flemyng, that Judaeo-Hibernian Glaswegian genius, directed, casting me as the priest who ran the club where Benny was trained. This was an early instalment of the compulsory series of priests, IRA men and drunkards that were the lot of your middle-grade Irish Thespian before it started showering Oscars from Heaven. These included Father Mackey in *Brideshead Revisited*, a soup-serving monk in *Knife-Edge*, IRA big-shots in *Confessional*, a series, *Shergar*, drunks in *Thin End of the Wedge*, *Heel of the Hunt* and *The Irish RM*. The balance was redressed by playing the Commissioner of the Metropolitan Police in *The Detective*, *Mitch* and *Dempsey and Makepiece*, and a university chancellor in *Miss Morrison's Ghosts*. Then came *Stay Lucky*, which lasted three years.

When I was offered a contract with the National in 1977 I accepted, more or less resigned to the prospect of moving out in due course. I had no deep feelings about this aspect of the job. As things panned out, I didn't need to move, but for twenty years I have been semi-detached, a foot on either side of the Irish Sea. As luck would have it I found myself involved immediately in a succession of co-productions between Irish and British companies. Little Bird and Channel Four did *The Irish RM* in association with UTV. It was popular all over the world and is still repeated far and wide, thirteen years after its production. It went down better in Northern Ireland than anywhere, especially with Protestants. I know this, not from a survey of viewers' affiliations, but because on my frequent visits North, any interviewer from an 'establishment' source, such as the *Newsletter*, the BBC, or UTV, will ask me first about 'Slipper' in the *RM*, where a nationalist would ask about Brendan Behan.

The *RM* hit the screen in the early eighties, when sectarian murders vied with hunger strikes for the headlines, a grim time of palpable hatred and unrelieved tension. The *RM*, I suspect, tugged at the heart-strings of some who cherished memories of a golden past full of galloping hooves and gorgeous girls. It tells of Major Yates, an Englishman appointed as Resident Magistrate in West Cork, who is duped and tricked by the wily peasantry, who for all their misdemeanours, know their place and come up trumps when the chips are down. Slipper is the perennially tipsy whipper-in of hounds, schemer, adviser, trickster, lovable at a distance but odoriferous close up.

Rose Mary Sissons, who adapted the series, thanked me for

investing Slipper 'with an extra dimension of horror'. I mulled over this compliment for all of a minute, probably, before deciding it meant I even *looked* smelly. Most viewers, needless to say, simply take a series like this at its face value, and enjoy it fairly uncritically. But there was a hard-core of resistance on 'our side of the house', who deeply resented the whole Somerville and Ross circus. George Colley, one-time contender for the Fianna Fáil leadership, a man of whom nobody ever spoke ill, told me he enjoyed the programmes, though they grated a bit. 'Still,' he said, 'I suppose we're mature enough to be able to laugh at ourselves now, or at their idea of us, anyway.' In my warped way, I might translate that as meaning, 'Well, now that we've won, it doesn't really matter.'

For myself, I find the series, and the books, bitter-sweet and ambiguous about the relationship between Anglo and Aborigine, or, if you like, between the Real Irish and the Planters. Peter Bowles was superb as Major Yates. The spirit of the whole series, though, is expressed in an exchange between the major's wife Philippa, and Slipper, when she dances with him at the Servants' Ball:

SLIPPER: Didn't the Major do very well, all the same, and him an Englishman?

PHILIPPA: Maybe a bit too English, Mr O'Mahoney?

SLIPPER: No. There's nothing we dislike more than an Englishman pretending to be Irish. The English are the English and the Irish are the Irish, and they understand each other like the fox and the hound.

PHILIPPA: And which is the fox, Mr O'Mahoney, and which the hound?

SLIPPER: Ah now, Ma'am, sure if we knew that, we'd know everything.

# EIGHTEEN

We hear that of all movies made, only ten per cent secure release, and that up to sixty per cent of the footage of those released ends up in the actors' Limbo, the cutting floor. Mr Big-Bankable-Megabucks may have some contractual protection in this respect, but otherwise we may say that the profession in general wastes most of its time, even when working. In my own case, there were three examples of prolonged involvement, by turns lucrative, enjoyable, or infuriating, which I consider not untypical of filming as it was, but no longer will be, now that films are made as a means of avoiding tax, first and foremost.

Two of these films starred Richard Burton, and were never commercially released, which somewhat colours my relationship with Mr Burton. He was a man I liked very much. He had a dark, indeed, a morbid streak to him. He could be very depressed. He wasn't drinking during either of the occasions when I worked with him. The first was for seven weeks around Munster and Connemara, on the film *Tristan and Isolda*, in which I played Sir Andred and he played King Mark, and we rode the same horse, simultaneously, in several scenes, which gave rise to great merriment. Even depressed, he always managed to be good company.

He was incredibly well read, quoting Yeats and Dylan Thomas at enormous length, and obviously with great affection. He talked a lot, compulsively almost, about Elizabeth (never Liz), in a tone as of respect for one who had bestowed a great honour on him. He related some unexpected experiences. He would hardly have been overwhelmed by any figure in the Western world, though he did recall staying up all night discussing poetry with Bobby Kennedy. But working actors can find themselves in situations which nobody else would ever be in. Burton was a house guest of President Tito of Yugoslavia when he was playing the Marshall in a film about the Yugoslav resistance. They had dinner together every night for a week. He was the perfect host, Burton said. He didn't have much interest in the film; he just thought it was a good idea that the film was being made.

Now I am not very likely to play any living president, least of all Mary Robinson, but I have in my time played people who were known to me personally. I played Brendan Behan, and also Tony Murphy, who was still alive when we made *Murphy's Stroke*, whose comment was, 'Well, it was good. I liked it. Enjoyable like.' He died not very long afterwards. In *Children in the Crossfire*, I played Vincent Lavery, who started a scheme for bringing Protestant and Catholic kids together, and taking them to various parts of America to share vacations and get to know one another. Lavery's organisation was called 'The Children's Committee Ten', because for ten years he would carry out this experiment in the hope that in time the idea would have borne fruit, and that that would be the end of his involvement. And it was.

He then went on with 'The Children's Committee Ten, Part Two', in which he took Arab and Jewish children from Israel to the States; and that experiment is still going, as far as I know. Vincent Lavery went to America and joined the American Army, and is now a soccer coach in Fresno, California. A story factually based on experiences of Irish kids and their adoptive American families was worked up by Frank Prendergast, the producer, and the film was directed by one of nature's gentlemen, who was also a gifted film-maker, George Schaefer. Schaefer's approach to me was not an unusual one except insofar as he actually started by offering me the role. 'I want you to play this part. It's not a very big part, but it is an important key role.'

They always say, 'It's a key role', or a variation would be to say that it's a great showcase, and that although the part is small, it is a great chance which, taken at the flood, will lead on to fortune, because everyone will see at last how brilliant you are. You finish up, of course, being asked, 'By the way, what were you in that film, anyway?' But with Schaefer, it was different.

'Now, this movie will be shot in Dublin, mostly. Unfortunately, you will have to come to California for three days' shooting.'

'Well', I said, 'that is very unfortunate, but I'll try. I'll do my best.'

He smiled and said, 'Look, I don't want to drag you over for three days, but if you come over, you'll have three weeks before you're due back in Dublin, so you can come as our guest for the rest of the time, and bring your wife.'

And that's what we did. We were set to do the first scene, and they said, 'By the way, Vincent Lavery has come down from Fresno. Have you any objection to him watching the filming?'

'None whatsoever. Why should I have?'

Lavery came to our motel for breakfast. Physically we didn't look alike. Our colouring was about the same, that's all. But the odd thing was that he and I, who had never met before, were wearing identical grey shoes, identical blue slacks and identical light blue shirts. We could have bought them off the same rack. And to crown it, we both had black sunglasses sticking out of our breast pockets. That's standard gear, but nevertheless, it was the final touch.

Then I spent the day with him, and produced a reasonable facsimile of his voice, because it was an American voice overall, naturally enough, but there were slight Dublin things in it. He took my performance very well. Most people don't recognise themselves, however accurately they are portrayed by someone else, just as their first reaction to hearing their recorded voice is one of disbelief.

Vincent had quite extraordinary views, and strong opinions. How, otherwise, could he have thought up, and carried through, the Children's Committee Ten project. He tried to persuade me, years after the film (which incidentally was very effective), that the Tiananmen Square affray was a myth of Western propaganda. He had been to Beijing, he said, and had the assurance of the Chinese Government that the incident never took place. Shortly after the film was shown on American TV, there was a very sad outcome. David Huffman, who had played one of the American leads, was murdered when he left the studio in Hollywood to get something out of his car. Nobody knows why.

*Tristan and Isolda* was a disaster for many reasons, none of which we'll go into here, because they don't concern us, and as we know, nine out of ten feature films that are shot never get released, so it's no disgrace. You're among the majority if you never get shown. I asked Burton why he had accepted a part in the film, and he said, 'Because I was very well paid for it, and it meant spending seven weeks in Ireland, and I love Ireland and Irish people. It was an attractive prospect. And also, I suspected it would never be released.'

It never was released, so he was right. I'm not saying he contributed to that, but he was in decline at the time. It is no slander on the man, or diminution of his talent, to say that he wasn't in the best of health. By the time Wagner was finished, his health had deteriorated quite a bit more. His physiotherapist pestered him about exercises he'd prescribed for some kind of spinal trouble, but it all seemed to fall on deaf ears.

A spoof book called *The Golden Turkey Awards* gave Burton a hell of a time. He got all the turkeys, and Worst Film of the Year was 'anything with Richard Burton in it'.

Well, that's all right by me. Actors don't look on other actors the way critics and the general public do. I've pointed out that a movie takes almost three years, from insemination to unveiling, to coin a phrase. So an actor can no more command or foretell success than anyone else. In any case, since we tend to judge a script's merit on, firstly, the number, and secondly, the quality, of our own probable scenes, objectivity scarcely enters our vocabulary. Big stars have their wounds licked for them, because it is in the producer's interest to blame exterior influences, or a hostile climate of public opinion, or some such nonsense. But in the case of a good run-of-the-mill pro, who might have been going through a lean spell and might have accepted something because the money was OK, or because it looked like a good opportunity, he signs a contract, and two months later he knows this is wrong. He knows it is garbage, but there is nothing he can do about it. He's got to go through with it. And just when the embarrassment has all but faded, and the lines are hardly even a memory, they release this 'turkey', and some smart-ass apprentice laptop-abuser reviews it.

Almost as bad as the whiff of failure, is the sour smell of success, or reaching the top of the billing. A good and fairly carefree living can be made by always playing second or third below the title. Aficionados will recognise your name, while the majority of viewers will refer to you as 'Ah, you know, your man . . . what's his name?' The big trouble starts when you get a lead in a series. Thereafter, casting directors will think of offering you only leads in series — specifically, parts identical to the lead you have just played. You get mentioned for a juicy character role, and the suggestion is immediately shot down. 'Oh, he's far too big now for anything like that. He wouldn't even consider it.'

At least, that's how it used to be. I am still apt to confuse the present with what I knew.

Perhaps, now that no qualifications are deemed necessary, and the Warhol Fifteen Minutes of Fame is becoming the norm in the business, they offer everything to everybody. Maybe we now face full employment in the acting industry, with everybody working for a fiver a day. Bring your own sandwiches, no specified meal breaks, provide your own transport . . .

I mentioned sharing a horse with Burton. This was not, as it might be today, due to budgetary restrictions, but because the plot required it. Andred, having lost his steed, climbs up behind his King.

We were filming outside Oughterard, in Connemara, a scene in which Kate Mulgrew stood on the bank of a stream, a tiercel perched on her wrist. I had to approach on a horse. I am not an accomplished horseman, but I was able to get by in this little scene. I had to trot in, the last fifty yards, dismount, say, 'My Lady', or something, and then 'cut'. The rest of the scene was on foot. Each time I came within less than a donkey's roar of this lady with the tiercel, the horse shied, and it was 'cut' every time.

'What's wrong?'

'I can't control her. She's fine until she comes to this point here, and then she just shies.'

They held a conference about this. Experts appeared from behind the rocks. One guy said, 'I'll tell you what's wrong. The trouble is, you see, that this bird is a bird of prey. And it is a well-known fact that all horses are terrified of birds of prey — eagles, hawks, falcons, tiercels, and all like that. They hate them. They're frightened to death of them. This one here senses the bird of prey, and she shies when she comes near it. That's what's wrong, boy, I'm telling you.'

The director wasn't party to this conversation, nor even interested. 'Can we get on, please? Can we do it again?'

I tried again, and again the horse shied, and this patient American man said, 'What's wrong now?' I lost my rag, I'm afraid. 'This fucking mule is afraid of that fucking parrot.'

Indignantly, Garrett Dooley, the kindly owner of the mount, cried, 'Don't you call my horse a fucking mule.' And the man who owned the tiercel said, 'Don't you call my falcon a fucking parrot.'

Now we had a whole new political situation. All this time, Burton was in his caravan, looking out at this scene, which appealed immensely to his sense of humour.

Finally, another local wiseman produced what became the accepted explanation of the mare's odd carry-on. 'This part of this field is a quagmire,' he intoned. 'It's under water nine months of the year. The soil beneath that grass may feel firm enough to the human foot, but a trotting horse would feel that wobbling like a jelly under her. That's why she shies.' I apologised to the bird, the beast and both proprietors, and we moved to a more solid part of Connemara, where the wobble was confined to the after-lunch jelly.

Burton talked much about the theatre, about playing on stage, so I think he must have regretted his abandonment of it, because there's no question about it, that he decided when he was quite young to go after the money; and the money was not in the theatre. He was scathing about London first nights. 'I didn't want to do this, because these people didn't listen. They were only there to show off their fur coats.'

He told me one fascinating story about doing *Hamlet* in New York. He had just completed the legal procedures in the adoption of his daughter, who was a German citizen. He invited some people from the German Embassy to the theatre to see the play. In drama school he had learnt the 'To be, or not to be' speech in German. And on a whim, on the night of the German visit, he spoke it *auf Deutsch*. He waited for the whizzbangs from all quarters, but nobody ever mentioned it. Nobody. The stage management said nothing about it, the director wasn't there, the Germans possibly accepted it as a compliment, and the rest of the audience may have asked each other, but nobody asked him about it. Perhaps they thought it was the normal thing. Or is one to infer that they, too, were just showing off their fur coats?

# NINETEEN

I have been embarrassed hugely, from time to time, by being asked to speak about acting. Some enthusiastic teacher persuades me, after a performance, to address her pupils and to explain my technique. The honest answer, which I am at liberty to give here, though not to her, is, 'Madam, I'd love to, but I can't, because I don't know how I do it.' I've usually got by through subterfuge, spicing up a few generalisations with personal anecdotes or performed examples.

There are actors who are brilliant at exposition of this kind, like Ray MacAnally, or Simon Callow, or writers like Richard Hornby, who can expound, explain, rationalise and analyse, to such effect that I find myself wondering how in the name of God I have made a living out of acting for over forty years, when I plainly don't know the first thing about it. What's even more confusing is that I can listen to, or read, conflicting claims about the purpose, impact, execution and effectiveness of various Methods, Techniques and Approaches, and concur wholeheartedly with the whole bloody lot. An actor I know, once, when he was young and knew no better, accosted an illustrious star of the London stage and offered his thanks and congratulations on this man's performance in his current success.

'What night were you there?'

'Last Thursday.'

The great man's brow furrowed as he summoned up the recollection of Thursday. Then he said, 'Ah, yes, yes, thank you so much. I was very good on Thursday.' Which was either arrant bullshit or this man inhabits a world in which I have never set foot.

All acting is a trick, I suppose, to some extent. It's got to be, if you are going to produce the goods, even when you're dying on your feet. So there is a trick involved — or at least a skill as distinct from an art. As for my own way of doing it, I have no theories, because I've never had any formal training, so I don't know.

I still shiver with horror at the memory of a week in a one-man show at the Opera House in Cork, when my bowels were open twenty-four hours a day. I went from bed to stage, then back to bed, subsisting on brandy and port, which failed to cement the sundered sections of my anatomy in the reputed manner. The shuttle from bed to bathroom lasted from Sunday to Thursday night; but although I stayed loose while at large, I dried on stage, without missing a line. And that was not technique, it was not know-how, it was . . . somebody's prayers, as they say. Certainly it was an intervention from somewhere, over which I had no control.

Film acting is a happy hunting ground for Method freaks, Theoreticians and Approach Enthusiasts. All I am certain of is that it happens behind your eyes. It's all up in the head, and the camera is so sensitive that it can register a thought, or at least a change of thought, and as long as there is truth in the line of your thought, the camera will register that.

There is no explanation as to why one can do it and another can't. Gary Cooper was by all accounts as emotionless as a wooden clothes horse; yet once you looked at him through a camera, he was transformed. He himself had no magnetism, but this was somehow conferred on him between the lens and the screen. I doubt very much if Gary Cooper could have explained how he did it, but he was able to do it, and he was aware of what he had to do in order to achieve it. There was a standard joke about him that he had two emotions: 'hat on' and 'hat off'. For 'hat', read 'magic'.

Alec Guinness's great trick, they say, was to have an utterly blank canvas on the close-ups, and let the audience put in the thoughts. I think the camera anticipates the audience.

In my own experience, the less fussy you are, the more helpful people behind the camera will be to you, and the kinder they will be. They will ensure that you look good. The acting has to come from you.

Back to Wagner. Wagner had composed *Lohengrin*, and arranged a special production for King Ludwig, on a lake somewhere. This scene was being shot in Hungary, on Lake Tata. They had constructed an enormous swan out of polystyrene. I am not familiar with the plot of *Lohengrin*, but I gather that the swan self-immolates in the opera. Well, at any rate, it goes on fire, or ascends to Heaven. It was a night-time shoot, a lovely summer's evening, very warm, and it was pleasant to sit there watching, because it went on forever, to the terror and discomfort of a Viennese actor, Arthur Danburg, the swan-jockey. At the time, the first trickle of Western tourists were coming into Hungary, and there was the inevitable American lady with camera, introducing herself to various people, none of whom spoke her language, until she got near enough to Burton. 'My God, Richard Burton! Oh, what a wonderful pleasure this is — to meet you! What a romantic life you've had. Oh, I don't mean about your wives, but the wonderful romance of your travel, the places you've been.'

Burton listened to this with patience, and then he said, 'Yes, I suppose you're right. After all, what other profession would afford you the opportunity of sitting in the moonlight with a drunken Irishman, on the shores of a Hungarian lake, surrounded by hordes of howling Magyars pretending to be Bavarians, while a megalomanic Englishman incites a bunch of demented Italians to incinerate a plastic swan.'

She considered this for a while, and then said, 'Yeah, I guess.' (I was not, for the record, a drunken Irishman at that time. That was in another country.)

We did a scene with Olivier and Gielgud in the Hofburgkapelle. It was the wedding of King Ludwig, and this took the whole day to film. I, as a member of Ludwig's cabinet, stood on a step behind more senior members of the cabinet, including Gielgud and Sir Ralph Richardson. We were surrounded by choirboys, cardinals and officers in Ludwig's army.

Ralph Richardson turned to the other noble knight. 'I'm getting awfully bored. Do you think we'll film anything today? Oh, my God, not more music. Oh, dear, oh dear, dear, dear.'

Gielgud, however, disagreed. 'I'm enjoying this immensely. I love panoply. Costumes, cardinals, altar-boys, all this fur, ermine, red hats. It's wonderful! I've always been like that. Even as a boy, I was very fond of dressing up. I remember at school I got diphtheria, or something . . . scarlet fever . . . I'm not quite sure. I know I wasn't confined to bed. I was left to wander around the school, and I was in a games room of some sort, looking out over the cricket ground. There was a red carpet there, a strip, I don't know what it was for, but it was on the steps, and I took up this red carpet and wrapped it round my shoulders, and there I stood, with a cricket stump, commanding my army. I had a wonderful time. It was lovely being sick. Surely you must have done things like that?'

'What?' said Richardson, 'Good God, no. I had a sailor suit, I do remember that. I must have been about six.' He shot a slightly anxious sideways glance at Gielgud. 'I never wore a carpet, no.'

And similar conversations went on all day.·

'What are you doing next, old man?'

'I don't know. I did that semi-porn thing. A lot of trouble over that . . . Caligula. And I've done a lecture tour. I didn't enjoy that very much. Nice money, though.' Then he began to list other film offers. Richardson, indifferent but not quite dismissive, shrugged. 'Hm. Of course, you'll take anything, Johnny, won't you.'

During the *Tristan* film, there was a perfect example of the totally wacky world of the cinema. We were outside Oughterard in an old castle. King Mark and Sir Andred charged out of the castle gate, swords in hands, scattering hens and other farmyard occupants in all directions, with many a squeal, and squawk, and a flurry of feathers.

Again, not quite. Connemara poultry are phlegmatic. An odd pullet may have vouchsafed us a cursory glance, as we hurtled headlong out the door, but generally, apathy prevailed.

'Cut! What happened the hens?'

'Divil a bit, they're still there.'

'Goddamn it, they should be squawking with terror.'

'Well, they don't give a shit.'

'Well, make them give a shit! We can't have hens ignoring the King. It's gonna look silly.'

Take after take, we burst with bloodcurdling oaths and clanking hardware, upon the courtyard. Not a chicken cheeped, not a cock crew.

'Hens can't act,' Burton pointed out, 'Notoriously.'

We began to compile a list of histrionically unendowed creatures of our experience: cows that will not moo, pigs that will not grunt, horses that shy at parrots, donkeys that stand absolutely still when required to budge — an endless list of recalcitrant, time-wasting, non-Thespian fish, fowl, bipeds, quadrupeds and amphibians.

Eventually, an invisible nylon fishing-line was flicked under the feet of our unfretful feathered friends, which evinced a slight irritation at the King's fury, that was very far short of Oscar quality.

* * * *

Playing Tony Murphy in *Murphy's Stroke* was very amusing, because Tony Murphy was a great friend of my younger brother Colm. I remember them playing pontoon. They formed a terrible duo, who would rook everybody else, because they played in cahoots, without appearing to. I had lost all contact with Tony until this film was mooted. When I played the part, I had to guess what he would have grown up like. He was to have turned up on the set, but didn't bother — he went to the races instead. After transmission, I met him in Cork. Overall, he was quite pleased. 'One thing, anyway, you flattered me. You have a fine head of hair, God bless you. I'm gone as bald as an egg.' (Which he was.)

*Murphy's Stroke* was a really good story. Murphy and a group of others, about eight of them in all, entered a horse in a race at Cartmel in Cumbria. This horse had been secretly trained in Ireland, to a pitch way above his known form. They had a Scottish trainer named Collins looking after him. They had picked the Cartmel course deliberately because it was an obscure track, there was no blower system and there were only two telephones on the course, both public payboxes. This meant that they could get bets on horses other than Gay Future, to bring their prices down, so that Gay Future would drift out in the betting, and by tying up the two phones, they prevented information from getting back to the big bookies' HQ in time for them to take remedial action. All the bets placed in the London offices were in the form of doubles or trebles, Gay Future with Ankerwyck and Opera Cloak, both also trained by Collins, and entered at different meetings. An hour before racing at those meetings, he withdrew those horses, which meant that all the bets that had been placed as doubles and trebles, now became singles. When a horse in a multiple bet is scratched, a treble becomes a double, a double becomes a single. If two horses in a treble don't run, the treble is treated as a single bet.

Hundreds of bets of twenty-five pounds or less had been laid all over London. None of them was big enough in itself to attract attention. Besides, bookies often don't even look at doubles and trebles. They are the original 'mugs' bets — money in the bank for the bookie. The trick here, however, was that you were putting in mugs' bets (trebles) and then, by withdrawing the two horses that you controlled, you now had one red-hot thing going.

Of course, there was the slight difficulty that the horse had to win. Because of his hidden form, and the out-of-the-way meeting, and the poor quality of the opposition on a Bank Holiday, when there was racing at some fifteen venues, it all came off beautifully. Gay Future romped home. The bookies stood to lose £375,000. Murphy and others were charged with criminal conspiracy. The judge on the case raised a very good point: 'If it is criminal for a punter to conspire or to co-operate with other punters to keep the price of a horse up, why is it not a criminal conspiracy for bookmakers to conspire to bring the price of a horse down, which they do?' Was there any legal or moral difference between the two positions, or were they two sides of the same coin? Gambling, after all, is gambling, and it is part of the game that you bluff. He advised the jury to throw the case out, but the jury did not oblige. The suspicion was that it was because of anti-Irish prejudice — that these Paddies were getting away with murder.

To Murphy's credit, he went back to England to face trial, which the judge considered jolly upright of him, and for that reason he was fined only £1000, which was very little, really. But it made a tremendous racing story, and of course Murphy became a popular hero.

Frank Czitanovich, who directed the film, said at the very first reading of the script, 'The whole point of this is that we are on the side of the punters. We're not on the side of the bookies, or the trainers, or the Racing Board, or anybody else. I want everyone in Britain who has ever had a few bob on a horse, standing on their chairs, cheering Murphy, at the end of the film. And that's the attitude with which this film has got to be made — that this man is doing what every punter dreamed of doing, and he's going to succeed.' And that was the spirit of the piece. It worked very well.

I also played another living person, whom I met only once — Paddy Hill, of the Birmingham Six. I went to visit Hill in jail. Leslee Udwin, who was the producer, had herself a very remarkable history. She was an actress and an Israeli citizen, and she read about this case and got hooked on it. She became obsessed by it, and she began to write to all six prisoners. She gathered petitions, and she decided she would try to make a film. She finally got Granada Television interested, after Yorkshire TV had made a documentary on some of the obvious discrepancies in the Crown evidence. Granada decided to go ahead with the film, and to their eternal credit, be it said, in the face of very severe pressure from lots of influential sources, they stuck with it and showed it.

Again, it's to the great credit of people like Leslie Phillips, John Hurt, Alan Badel, Martin Shaw, Terence Rigby — big names, people who had nothing whatsoever to gain, maybe a lot of credibility to lose with producers, who might feel 'This guy's gone very political, now. We don't want that.'

Like it or not, somebody like Leslie Phillips becomes a very Establishment figure, very comic, silly-ass image, certainly, but very much in the Establishment mould. I'm sure he would count many titled heads and top lawyers, maybe judges, as his personal friends. For him to go in, there must have been a sense of personal outrage involved.

I think everybody who agreed to do the film had some sense of helping to rescue the fair name of British justice — much as most Irishmen might leer at the very idea. Terry Rigby (a smashing actor) played the policeman George Reade, although he expressed some misgivings to me. 'It's unbalanced, because people like George Reade are not allowed to give their side of it.' I said, 'Well, they gave their side of it in court. It's the people who weren't able to give their side in court that we need to represent.' He still did it, though. More power to all of them, they put their reputations at stake, to some extent, in a way that almost no politicians, here or in Britain, did.

I went to visit Paddy Hill with Gerry Conlon, a week after Conlon was released. Leslee Udwin had arranged everything. I met her in London and we drove to Gartree prison in Leicestershire. She told me, 'You're going to visit a man called Peter Keogh, who is in for housebreaking, and we are going to visit Paddy Hill.' These were the passes that she had secured. Keogh and Hill were good mates in jail.

Conlon, remember, had been released a week previously, and he was going back as a visitor into the prison where he had spent a lot of his fourteen years' stir. As we came within sight of the prison (it's a flattish landscape, with a good view of the exterior of the jail), he began to tremble. He rarely shuts up, but he suddenly went very quiet. He was really upset and emotional. Leslee, who was driving, asked, 'What's wrong? Are you afraid to go back in?' 'Ah, no, it's not that. But all the time I've spent in that fucking place, and I've never seen it before. I've never actually looked at it from the outside. I never knew what it looked like.'

When he was leaving the place, he had been whisked away in the van to the court, and then out of the court, and he was free. He had never actually seen the approach to the prison from the outside.

When we got to the entrance there was no problem. Leslee had the passes and the visits had been sanctioned. We went inside, to the big general waiting-room, where all visits were conducted.

Mothers with small kids watched for the Dads to come down, and I would say there must have been about a hundred people there, tables and chairs spread all round the place. It was a very big room, a reception hall really. In one corner you had a café, where you could buy tea, coffee, cigarettes, and an extraordinary selection of things like Cadbury's Snacks and Wispa chocolate bars — nothing of any use — no sandwiches or anything like that. We were drinking coffee and eating all this shit for about three hours.

When we got in, the warders' expressions were a study, some of them absolutely stoney-faced, hiding their outrage that this fucker was back here. Others were smiling at him. One fellow said, 'Good afternoon, Sir', and others said, 'Hello, Mr Conlon', with a friendly grin.

We had come in, ostensibly, to visit different people, but we sat together, waiting for Hill to come down to Leslee, when this other warder came down and said, 'Conlon, what the fuck are you doing here? Upstairs.' Conlon jumped, and said, 'Jesus.' The warder laughed and went on his way. 'You know,' says Gerry, 'he was the best of them all. He was very decent to me. Well, fuck him, anyway, he frightened the shite out of me.' At that stage, other visitors were pointing, and as the prisoners came down to meet the visitors, every one of them made straight for Gerry Conlon, and they were hugging him and bringing over their wives and kids to meet him. The warders were absolutely stoney-faced still. Orders must have been to let it go.

Soon the whole thing just died down. They each went to talk to their own folk. Hill arrived, with my friend Peter Keogh. We started to chat, and Keogh sat back with his cigarette and said, 'Don't mind me. You've come to see him, just carry on.' He took no further part in the deliberations. Neither, come to think of it, did anybody else. Hill spoke for well over ninety per cent of the time. We must have been there for nearly three hours, which was longer than we should have been, but they allowed us a bit of extra time. The first thing Hill said was, 'Have you any fuckin' money? The price of marijuana's very high, you know.' It was well known that he was smoking pot.

He unburdened himself at great length, very humorously, I may say. He was an extraordinary man, the man who jumped around the place and punched the air when he came out. He was like that in there too — and we're talking about a good year before his release.

I want to point out an incident, just to reinforce what I said about the credit due to the actors who took part in that film. I am speaking now of the courage of the English actors. During the filming, I came through Manchester airport. A Special Branch man at the desk said, 'Mr Toibin, isn't it?' And he pronounced the name right — he knew me from other visits.

'Yes,' I said.

'You working with Granada Television at the moment? What are you filming at the moment?' And it was perfectly obvious that he knew exactly what I was doing. 'What about this Birmingham bombing thing? You're in that, aren't you?'

'Yes, I am.'

'You think they're innocent, do you? You think the cops have been telling lies, do you?'

'I have no view on the matter, I'm just playing a part.'

Of course I did have a view on it, but I added, 'After all, I have played judges too, you know, but that doesn't mean that I think judges are always right.'

'Oh yeah. All right.' He waved me through. There was a definite antipathy, I felt. The view was that I shouldn't be doing that kind of thing. He had me marked down. So how much more must the film have offended when one of their luminaries of the screen agreed to malign the police, as they would have seen it. It's all right for a Paddy — you couldn't expect any more. However civilised he may appear, underneath he's only a Mick, anyway.

Now I've always found any of these security people extremely courteous; and even as this man said, or implied, these things to me, he was not being offensive. But the underlying nark was detectable. With someone of their own, the antipathy must have been much greater.

Hill was quoted as saying, some time after he had been released, that he would prefer to be back in prison. Well, one shouldn't pay any attention to what's quoted in the press. Alas, most people do. If he did say it, I can see his point. He had developed a life of his own in the prison. He was making furniture. I saw a bit of the furniture he made. He said he would stay up all night just to finish a piece of polishing. He became obsessed with it — and it kept him sane.

He wrote something like thirty letters a week, asking people to join his campaign and to do things for him. And he also told me a very interesting thing during that interview. He described various people who had come to see him, and what they had done, and said, 'The only man who unequivocally did what I asked him to do was Cardinal Ó Fiaich. He came to see me, and Jesus Christ, you won't believe this, he brought in a box of fuckin' chocolates. Cadbury's fuckin' Roses. I said, "Fuck you and your Roses. Have you any fuckin' money?" And he said, "I didn't know what I should bring." "Well, bring cigarettes, for Jesus' sake." "All right. I'll get you some cigarettes." '

He went for him. He just went for the cardinal. And Ó Fiaich said, 'Look, just tell me what you want me to do.'

'You told me', said Hill, 'that you believe I'm innocent.'

'I do believe you're innocent,' said the cardinal.

'Well, I want you to say in public what you have said to me in private — that you believe the Birmingham Six are innocent.'

'And', he said, 'a week later the cardinal made a speech, and he said he believed we were innocent. And he was the only man who did exactly what I asked him to do. Oh, others helped, but this was a specific promise, which was carried out.'

✳ ✳ ✳ ✳

During the eighties I made a return visit to the Abbey to play Claudius in Mike Bogdanov's superb production of *Hamlet*. It was tough work, and made for very exciting and entertaining theatre. It furnished through its reviews more evidence of the acuity of the Irish critics, one lady castigating Gertrude for not displaying more grief at the death of her daughter Ophelia. I confess it eased my own resentment at the doubt cast by another learned reviewer on my own capacity to convey the nobility of Claudius. I failed to invest him with that quality, just as the wretched Shakespeare did.

I enjoyed the experience but I would not have done another Shakespeare. I was on a hiding to nothing in the face of such profound scholarship.

My next foray on to the sacred boards was in *The Field*, by John B Keane. This was good red meat, and I tore into it. The great thing about 'Janbee' is that while he may have written an odd bad play, he has written no bad parts. The Abbey's production of *The Field* was acclaimed by those who matter — the paying public. I came out of it very well and was very happy to have re-established myself in straight stage and drama. When the Russian trip came up, it felt like winning the jackpot. The USSR was opening up. We would be the first visiting company. As it happened, the USSR was closing down, and at least a dozen other contenders claim the first visitors' honour.

For me, it was an unhappy mess. We travelled without an interpreter, so one was at the mercy of the Russian speakniks. The company contained the casts of *The Field* and *The Great Hunger*, Tom McIntyre's version of the Kavanagh poem. There was a clash, stylistic, attitudinal, generational, within and between the various personnel, as there always has been, is, and should be. But when you shove a theatre company, and a press corps, including the critics, into the same plane, and then into the same hotel, you are closeting the chickens with the foxes. An actor after a show relaxes, but forgets that a journalist is never off-duty till he's dead. I was quoted as having said harsh things about *The Great Hunger*. I was quoted accurately. No point in protesting that I wasn't speaking on the record, or such clap-trap.

I contracted food-poisoning from eating the flying horse which the Hotel Rossya in Moscow put up as chicken. I was weak, expelling solids and liquids from both ends by turn and simultaneously. The two hugest female doctors in the Russian Army, which quartered some of its best and brightest in the hotel, ministered to me in the middle of the night. I conveyed my symptoms by a mime act, which they evaluated silently, like adjudicators at a drama festival. They then drew clock-faces, set for different times, on a large pad — placing the number of tablets to be taken beside each clock. We synchronised our watches and operation Block was all systems go.

I read recently that John B, on learning that he couldn't take the profit from the play out of the USSR, told the cast to drink it. I'm sure he would have, if he could have, but he wasn't there, and we were back home before he could have got through on their twine-and cocoa-tin phone system of the time. Also, there was no profit, and not for any reasons of Communist ideology.

33. Niall as Larry Slade and Oscar James as Joe Mott in Bill Bryden's production of *The Iceman Cometh*, Cottesloe, London, 1978

All the parts are star roles, but it's a six-hour job, everyone remaining seated almost throughout, sometimes drunk, so wool-gathering or slumber can be a threat. In Edinburgh, Alec Heggie played the barman and kept an eye out for possible nodders-off, so he could drift naturally from behind the bar to flick a dishcloth at the table-top as a warning of a cue coming up. Thanks, Alec.

34. Niall as Oliver Cromwell in *World Turned Upside-Down*, National Theatre, London, *c*1978

The first part I played on a London stage was Oliver Cromwell in *World Turned Upside Down*, Keith Dewhurst's dramatisation of Christopher Hill's Marxist history of the Revolution. I told Brendan Kennelly on a train to Tralee that I was to do this part, and he wrote a poem about Cromwell contemplating his being portrayed by an Irish actor. Later, he wrote a second long work called 'Cromwell'. I understood the first one.

35. Albert Finney and Niall Toibin in a scene from *Has Washington Legs*, National Theatre, London, 1979

36. Dana Wynter and Niall Toibin in a scene from *Bracken*, 1979

I am rarely lost for words. Any compliment to Dana would be 'like praising the Lakes of Killarney, a piece of impertinence' (Behan).

37. Niall Toibin and Pierce Brosnan in a scene from *Murphy's Stroke*, Thames Television, 1980

Tony Murphy told me how he got his first big Post Office contract: to rip up Jermyn Street for new cable-laying. Work could only be done on Sunday and with minimal noise, as so many titled and mitred heads lived nearby. He gave all the assurances required, then blew his whistle at six o'clock on Sunday morning, setting some hundred pneumatic drills into simultaneous action. It took well over an hour to get the relevant bureaucrats out of bed to halt the racket, by which time the whole street had been softened up and the remaining work was barrow, pick and shovel stuff. Murphy apologised and guaranteed that there would be no more loud noises. He lost money because of the hire of so much equipment, but the Post Office overlooked the breach of conditions, and many further contracts came his way.

38. Bill Owen (sitting) and Niall Toibin in *Long Voyage Home*, National Theatre, London, 1980

39. Niall Toibin, John Kavanagh and Joe Pilkington in a scene from *Ballroom of Romance*, 1981

Rarely have subject, text, casting, direction and location all come as near perfection as in this gem — adapted by William Trevor from his own story, directed by Pat O'Connor, a co-production of BBC and RTE, with Brenda Fricker, John Kavanagh, Brendan Conroy, Niall Toibin, Joe Pilkington, Pat Leavey, May Ollis, Cyril Cusack and the Tony Chambers Ballroom Band.

40. Niall Toibin in a scene from *Mass Appeal*, Olympia Theatre, 1982

During this sermon, a drunk asleep in the emergency exit woke up and shouted 'Shut up — you're worse than the bloody choir!'

41. Niall Toibin with Cardinal Ó Fiaich on the steps of Armagh Cathedral, 1988

*When I played Peter Lombard, one of Cardinal Ó Fiaich's predecessors as Primate of Ireland, in a play called* Making History *by Brian Friel, the cardinal told a BBC interviewer: 'We are so used to Niall's comedy shows on RTE, it was hard to take it seriously.' His gesture seems to say: 'This you call a performance?' Still, he graciously posed with me on the cathedral steps.*

42. Niall Toibin with Jerry O'Sullivan, Lord Mayor of Cork, 1988

Jerry O'Sullivan was real. He didn't take a jar. When I did his Lord Mayor's Charity Concert at the City Hall, he and his wife Bina made a decent pot of tea in the mayor's office and produced a tray of pastries bought that morning in Dick Tobin's shop in Blackpool. He was a junior minister for a few short months. He knew I had no *meas* on his government, yet he came to my show on his own, paid for his ticket and came backstage to wish me well. He was taken ill soon after. He would hardly have used the phrase *savoir-faire*, but he surely knew what it was.

43. Niall Toibin with Senator Chris Dodds and Teddy Kennedy, 1988

This picture was bought and paid for and is included as a tribute to the Kennedy machine. At a charity function in the Burlington Hotel, Kennedy worked the room, shaking hands with everybody at each table, while a photographer tracked the hero's progress, snapping away in a seemingly haphazard manner. But everyone was offered an opportunity of buying the record of their moment in history.

44. Actor Joe McPartland and Niall Toibin at the Maze Races, Co Down, 1990

From '64 to '95 I have worked in Belfast in radio, TV and stage, oddly enough never with Joe McPartland, my constant companion, in the original meaning of that phrase, on visits north. He regularly took me apart on the rickety snooker table of the Ulster Arts Club, where also Dr Paddy McHugh ministered to many an actorly hangover. Michael Duffy, Davie Hammond, Jerry McCrudden, Jimmy Ellis, Rowel Friers, John D Stewart, were but a few of a great and generous gathering over whom presided the inimitable J G Devlin. When Devlin and McPartland were in top gear, the slaggin' was only mighty, me oul' han' . . .

45. *The Hostage*, Tivoli Theatre, 1991

*Centre:* Conor Mullen and Regina Crowley. *Standing:* Des Keogh, Dolores Keane (in her first acting role) and Niall Toibin.

46. Nick Faldo and Niall Toibin partnered at the Carroll's Irish Open (Pro-am Day), 1992

So well he might laugh. Tom Prendergast, Denis Coffey, Niall Toibin and Nick Faldo represented Killarney Golf (and Fishing) Club at the pro-am. Faldo marking the card entered Tom's par 4 at the second, although my own 4, with a shot, was the better score. Nobody copped this till all was in and signed, so we came seventh instead of fourth.

Despite his reputation, Faldo was friendly and very helpful. It is not true that he thought the 'Fishing' of the club title referred to me. A Kerry onlooker asked: 'How're 'oo getting on with Nick? He's hardly a barrell o' laughs I'd say. Not in the Eamonn Kelly class, I imagine.'

'True,' I said, 'but I wouldn't like to be depending on Eamonn Kelly's tee-shots.'

47. In the Doll's House at the Central Remedial Clinic, Sandymount, a 'Variety Club' fund-raiser, 1993

48. Niall Toibin, Liam Hamilton and Ossie Ardiles at the FAI International Club, 1994

# TWENTY

Early in 1995, I sat thinking in a fourteenth-floor apartment on 72nd Street West, in Manhattan, where Judy and I had been celebrating a reunion with our daughters Fiona, who works in New York, and Aisling, who had taken holidays from San Francisco to come and join us. My brother Colm had been to visit from Richmond, Virginia, as had Judy's sister Kathleen, from Washington DC. We had traded news of our other kids, my son Seán in Swords, County Dublin, my daughter Síghle in Greystones, County Wicklow, my eldest daughter Muireann in Jeddah, Saudi Arabia. The doings of many grandchildren, nephews, nieces and in-laws throughout the United States, in Canada, Britain, South Africa, Switzerland, Australia and Ireland, had been chronicled. Someone had quoted the joke that the truly enchanting thing about small children is that they don't insist on showing you photographs of their grandparents.

We had enacted our own minor acknowledgement of the Irish diaspora, the new politically-correct, positively-thinking name for what used to be called 'the curse of emigration'. It is right and proper that we face the reality of the unavoidable dispersal of our loved and not-so-loved ones, all over the globe. Brian Lenihan pointed out once, palms helplessly outstretched, that we cannot all live on a small island, ignoring the embarrassment that his leader, Charles J Haughey, was literally doing just that.

After decades of claptrap about our most precious asset being our youth, we have bowed to the logic of 'export or die', but being what we are, we shall probably do both, the latter of terminal euphoria.

There is, we are assured, a new confidence about our latter-day emigrants. They are professional, erudite, technologically accomplished; and why wouldn't they be? Are they not subsidised by the Irish taxpayer to a greater degree than any so-called sponger on the Welfare system ever will be?

To me, the definition of an emigrant is still someone who has nothing to go home to, and lacks the wherewithal to go. The 'new variety', who can jack it in and piss off home, are expatriates, not emigrants. What can't be cured must be endured, they say. Perhaps, but it makes no sense to claim that the incurable is also more desirable. The cruel, longing pain of exile is as real as it ever was. Some of us will always look for home in the bottom of a bottle, in Shepherd's Bush or Queens, in Woolamaloo or Etobicoke.

It is chastening for someone of a socialist cast of mind to grapple with the United States. I was once told by a Munster man, flushed with whiskey, rotten with money, that anyone can make it in America.

'Yes,' I agreed, 'provided they're white.'

'Ah, fuck them,' he roared. 'Let 'em pull themselves up by the bootlaces, the way we had to do.'

Who's going to subsidise *their* bootlaces?

It is a common trap to equate New York with the United States. On my first sojourn there, in 1970, it was pointed out rather heatedly by proud residents of Philadelphia and Chicago, that New York is not America. The squalor, the drunks, the junkies one saw all around, would not be tolerated in those more refined cities. That was precisely why they were in New York, which always seemed to find a spot in its heart of steel for the wretches dumped on its doorstep by the anti-Welfare bootlace hauliers of Middle America.

The contrasts are so shocking. I returned to New York in the early Gorbachev years after a month in Russia. The streets of Leningrad and Moscow had yet to benefit from the enlivening presence of the ultimate practitioners of private enterprise, the Russian Mafia, so the bored and listless natives all still had roofs of some kind over their heads. But it was a suffocating atmosphere.

By contrast, 5th Avenue was spotless, bustling, beautiful in the early spring sunshine, and a man dying of gangrene was eating garbage out of a trash basket on the pavement. You could smell the diseased legs at forty paces.

I intend no judgement. New York is infinitely the more likeable place. It is to my mind the greatest city in the world. Why then do I, a self-professed believer in the Welfare State, and in social equality, not find the United States revolting? I believe it is because the sheer honesty of American greed is quite disarming.

In fact, this openness is the great likeable characteristic of the United States. It is true that justice delayed is justice denied, but equally one has to say that injustice admitted must be part restitution. And to an extent unequalled by any other Empire, by Britain especially, the US has admitted mistakes and done repentance, if not made reparation. The simple truth, that the West was won by near genocide, has come to be confessed. The scandalous treatment of Japanese Americans after Pearl Harbour, the awful blunder of Vietnam, the treatment of ethnic minorities, have come to be officially regretted. This struck me very forcibly on a visit to the Ellis Island museum. The first words of the guide were to the effect that those who had been led to expect the US to be the land of freedom and equality, found they had been deceived. It was more free for those arriving with money, less equal for those without.

Again, the violent opposition to Chinese immigrants, to Catholics, Jews and 'Niggers' by the Ku-Klux-Klan, the suppression of organised labour, is detailed without equivocation. It is not the kind of frankness one finds too often in the Green and Misty, where public acknowledgement is rarely if ever made of wrongdoing. The essence of the Ould Blarney is to tell people what they want to hear. The opposite, American idea, is to tell it like it is.

All of which is half-baked theorising, but I have to poke about and probe, to make sense of my own conflicting reactions. There is no conflict, however, in the reaction to the simple Wall of Honour, the monument to some six hundred and twenty thousand emigrants, all steerage passengers, who passed through Ellis Island. Their names are carved on stainless steel panels, along a low wall between the rear of the building and the quay wall on the Manhattan side.

SMILE AND BE A VILLAIN!

All visitors head for the wall, to locate their own relatives' names. We traced Hardimans, Kennys, O'Sheas, O'Sullivans, Sheas and Sullivans, before I scouted for Tobins, Toibin having been declared a non-runner. The result was startling. The list contained, among others, Gunda Koppang Tobin, Renee Djemal Tobin, Rose Sundick Tobin, Solomon Tevlowitz Tobin, Ida Barus Tobino and John Settimo Tobino.

* * * *

Since all this American stuff was triggered off by thinking of our family reunion, of sorts, it's as well to say something about the effects on the said family of my carry-on over the years.

How did my children react to their father's curious lifestyle? I first thought of this when one of the girls was about seven years old, and she brought a young pal to play in the garden, where I happened to be sawing logs. 'Oh,' said the visitor, 'I never knew your daddy did real work.' It was, of course, a dead giveaway on her parents, who must have voiced their belief that I never did a day's work in my life, apart from 'acting the eejit and getting paid for it'.

One might say that I fed and clothed the children, told them stories, not too often, sang them songs, especially in my drinking days, but that Judy actually reared them, and to some extent reared me as well, taught them their prayers, gave them very down-to-earth and earthily-expressed advice.

We were pretty happy-go-lucky, certainly devil-may-care in our early married days. One example of this must suffice. A neighbour who had left us in the pub, noticed, about an hour later, peculiar shadowy movements in our bedroom as he passed the house. He was considering alerting the Gardaí, when I suddenly appeared at the front door to put out the milk bottles. I explained that we were using candles, as the lights had fused. The real reason we had gone out earlier was that the light had been cut off. It seemed logical to go to the pub, the Manhattan Bar in Raheny, where there was light.

I spent a lot of time away during the kids' young days. I missed a few Communions and Confirmations. I know when I sent a cable to

268

Aisling on her First Communion day, the clerk at the telegraph office at Grand Central Station was in tears, reminiscing about the Confirmation of his own daughter, who had later gone to Africa as a missionary.

The kids had compensations, of course. Neither Judy nor myself went to university, and I have never felt that I was any the poorer for that, socially, morally or physically, though I gather that I may have missed out hugely in the matter of sexual diversification. So we were not pushed about whether the kids went to college or not, but they didn't lack for variety in their early schooling. They were, so far as we knew, well-adjusted, well-behaved, if not cherubic, and it was the privilege of schools in Dublin, Limerick, Dingle and Manhattan, to welcome them in, and further form them. In our maturer years, drop by dribbling drop the truth has leaked out, but we have clapped our hands over ears and cried, 'Enough, enough!'

We didn't speak Irish at home. We had Augustinian intentions of being bilingual, but not yet. I was somewhat loth to expose the kids to jibes of 'Ireeshian', I suppose. However, the Gaelic Nemesis arrived for my children in their Kerry school, in the shape of an elderly witch who wore a teacher's mask and was either seriously maladjusted or completely bananas. She would carve a square hole in a cardboard carton, drop it over a kid's head, aperture to the fore, and announce, 'Now you're on the television. Give out the News.' (This in mellifluous Munster Irish.) For failure to achieve a suitable TAM rating, she would administer punishment by drumming the top of the box, and *ipso facto* the top of the head, with a heavy wooden pointer. It must be conceded that it seemed to have had no detrimental effect, but had I known of this pioneering approach at the time, I probably would have had qualms.

I have a feeling that Seán, my eldest and only son, must have been called upon to defend the younger ones more often than we knew. Muireann and Aisling and Seán had the benefit of early schooldays at Holy Trinity School on West 82nd Street in New York City. It was then largely, and is now entirely, Hispanic, though the daily language was still English. Under the influence of a social slug or two, the girls can still be persuaded to perform their cheer-leaders' kick-ups and sing, 'We are the girls of Holy Trinity', and they talk of eight-or-nine-year-old boyfriends called Julio (Hooley-oh) and Santos.

I suppose that absence from the home of a working parent must have some effect on children. I have had more than my share of dubious sympathy, with an implication of dereliction. *'What could you expect from an actor?'* Yet airline pilots, politicians, pro footballers, consular officials, jockeys, Arctic explorers, spacemen, private soldiers, bus-drivers and newspapermen also spend time apart from their offspring, without incurring the reproachful concern of their neighbours. Homecoming often makes travel worthwhile. I still glow with pleasure at the memory of presents snatched from my arms before I was halfway through the door.

A depressing feature of travel these days is that the old joke about the American tourist saying, 'This is Tuesday, it's gotta be Amsterdam', is no longer a joke. The lovely pedestrianised area I admired so much in central Manchester ten years ago has been replicated in Boston, Dublin, Cork, Norwich and Vancouver. Everywhere is looking better, and everywhere looks the same. The same shops sport the same logos in similar cobble-stoned boulevards from South Ferry to Thurso, from Darwin to Hammerfest.

I used to go to Belfast throughout the sixties and seventies, to the BBC studios, or on various other gigs. The very name 'Belfast' caused wild excitement at home. 'Chocolate money, chocolate money!' they howled. Coin-shaped Swiss chocolate, wrapped in foil, packed in a gold-stringed net bag, was a mandatory present from Belfast. It was peculiar to that town. A hundred miles up the road, but a magic memory to my youngsters, to whom the name Belfast only much later carried much sadder and more sinister connotations.

Now there's chocolate money everywhere. You can buy the same clothes, candies, condoms, styling gel, jeans, jelly-babies, beers, wines and Y-fronts anywhere. Drisheen, boxtie, colcannon, and that nauseous, sawdust-textured, green-bile-tinted soda bread, seem so far to have evaded internationalisation, but their day will come.

# NIALL TOIBIN

When one can buy Barry's tea and Galtee rashers in the Bronx, and lash back iced Smithwick in Bangkok, it is questionable whether one should ever bother to shift from home sweet home.

# TWENTY-ONE

I mentioned to someone recently that it was twenty-two years since I'd had a drink. When he was sure he had heard properly, he asked, 'Were you having a problem with it?'

'No,' I replied truthfully, 'I was fine. Other people were having the problems.'

It is usually unwise for a lapsed drunkard to speak about drink, except at AA meetings. It glazes the eyes of the person who drinks in moderation, whereas it really gets on the wick of the more normal Irish drinker.

A pal of mine, long sober, had a houseful of guests in high hilarity, recounting his drinking exploits, which were pretty impressive and hugely funny. Through the shrieks of laughter, one sourpuss grumbled, 'Jasus, Neddy's twelve years on the wagon and he can still describe every fuckin' pint he ever drank. I can hardly remember goin' home last night.'

Many an ex-drunk shares something with the woman who insisted on telling the local curate the same sin of amorous dalliance on every visit to the confessional. Finally, suspicious that such frequency of fornication could not have failed to become common gossip in the parish, he said, 'Is this the same sin, on the same occasion as before, Maudie?'

'Yes, Father.'

'Well, you need not confess it again. You only did it once, and you only need to confess it once.'

'Ah but sure, I like talking about it, Father.'

I would myself have to confess to drinking many pints retrospectively, with much more pleasure than the first time around, often in the same company. At least my tale is true if tedious, and I do not discuss the matter much. A very famous actor once astounded the world with his revelations of his awful addiction. The astonishment, however, stemmed not from the gargantuan consumption of liquor, but from the news that e'er a sup had stirred beyond his sculpted lips. He was a secret drinker. 'This', said the garglers, 'is a job for the Pope. The man is an alcoholic version of the Immaculate Conception. He became an alcoholic without ever buying a drink.'

I want to hark back to the pubs I loved so well, because they were mostly places of great fun, some even of great charm, on the whole, gin-mills pure and simple, rather than the yuppie restaurant-wine bar of these complex times.

My first favourite pub was Tommy Moore's of Cathedral Street, across from the side-door of Dublin's pro-cathedral. It was primarily a GAA house, as Tommy Moore was a Kilkenny ex-hurler, held in high esteem by the Black-and-Amber brigade, who were quite capable of genuflecting as they entered the bar. It had a truly rural atmosphere, not just because of the hurlers, but because Civil Servants from Revenue, Education and the Census office used it as a watering-hole. One famous tax officer, a Mayoman of wild appearance, and vocally memorable, would charge in shortly after opening time, bellowing from the door on arrival, 'A foaming pint — and fast!' He lived out on the north side and travelled by train, the last of which left for his townland at about twenty to midnight. He was reputed to have sued the Great Northern Railway for loss of conjugal rights when the train left ahead of schedule and he had to kip in a hotel. I used to change my Civil Service cheque in Tommy Moore's.

Around the corner in Marlborough Street was Mick O'Flanagan's, the smallest pub in Dublin, if not the world. Mick was a brother of Dr Kevin, the only man capped at soccer and rugby for Ireland, of whom it was told that in his days with Arsenal, a visiting Dublin fan cheered his every move with shouts of 'Well done, Doctor', until

Kevin shot wide of an open goal. 'Flanagan, ye bloody quack!'

A few yards further down Marlborough Street was Doran's Lounge, never called just Doran's, but 'Doran's Lounge Bar', with an intake of breath on the word 'Lounge'. Lounge bars were coming into vogue — they were of course the devil's latest strategy for luring beautiful women with short skirts onto tall stools with red upholstery and chromed tabular legs. The devil appeared regularly in Doran's upstairs, never leaving without giving a fleeting glimpse of the cloven hoof, as might one of his lady clients give a flash of suspender belt to the slavering drunks about her. The visits were not billed in advance, as his schedule was pretty loaded, what with having to appear in 'The Four Provinces Ballroom', (a natural haunt for him, owned as it was by the Bakers' Union, whose president, Jon Swift, was a confessed and crusading Communist), and pay flying visits to the Long Valley in Cork, and several joints in Salthill, Galway. Doran's, a few doors from the pro-cathedral, was known also as the Pros' Cathedral.

The Abbey Bar was owned by Tommy Lennon and Ursula White-Lennon, mother of Biddy. It was not a part of the theatre, but snuggled under the old Peacock Theatre, a 100-seat experimental adjunct to the Abbey and a favoured spot of theatre people. Tommy Lennon's had a great appeal for me. It was dimly lit, and its lounge had been designed by Michael Scott, allegedly free, and perhaps rightly so. It was here, sipping a bottle of Mountjoy stout, that I would watch Bill Foley play chess with Tommy, the proprietor, who looked like a greying Adolf Hitler and who could sometimes leave a game to pour and serve a drink without ever taking his eyes off the chess-board.

The Mountjoy stout was the product of Mountjoy Brewery, and the Abbey was a tied house. For this reason Tommy served Guinness with his own distinctive label, as Guinness refused to supply their official one, which bore the words after the name of the publican 'who sell no other brown stout or bottled porter'. Pubs commonly did their own bottling.

Tommy also had a juke box, and for as long as it was there, one of the records was Bing Crosby singing 'The Star Spangled Banner'.

Someone must have played it fairly often, because I quite unconsciously acquired the words. The other disc played at least six times a night for years was Peewee Hunt's 'Twelfth Street Rag'.

The Abbey bar survived the Abbey fire. Rumour had it that Tommy was holding out for an unconscionable sum for the pub, which it was proposed should be knocked down to make the theatre bigger. It was also claimed that he wanted the franchise to run the bar in the new theatre.

I somehow doubt that latter part, unless it also stipulated a chess-playing area. Tommy didn't last too long himself. After we married, Judy and I patronised the old place, which had really become like a morgue, just what the original Abbey Theatre building had been. Mick Dolan, the manager, once showed us a ledger he'd found under the counter where Tommy had recorded drinks on the slate to customers, identified by such vague names as 'The Captain', 'The man with the Trinity scarf', 'The lad under the stairs' (there was a little cubby-hole there).

The other welcome novelty of Tommy's was a slot machine which yielded to gentle prodding up its posterior with a screwdriver. Gene Martin and I discovered this added attraction and patronised it gratefully.

Picture Dublin in the fifties. 'Fort of the Dane, garrison of the Saxon, Augustan capital of a Gaelic nation, appropriating all the alien brought . . .' said Louis MacNeice. He must have been having a quiet sneer, though he went on to speak of 'Grey stone, grey water and brick upon grey brick'. Well, now you're talking.

Sometimes the only escape from the drabness of those days was into the pub. Perversely, our favourite pub was easily the drabbest and smelliest of them all, Jerry O'Dwyer's in Moore Street, which I have mentioned more than once.

The greatest service I can do for history is to reconstruct, as faithfully as I am able, the events of a glorious Saturday morning in summer on that street of streets. It should be the most famous street in Dublin — it was of course the nearest residential street to the GPO, where the 1916 rising took place. Yet in all my years of drinking in every pub in that thoroughfare, I have never heard a word about the events of Easter week. It seemed that dismantling the chariot of Empire mattered no more than packing away the apple cart in the shed in Cole's Lane.

Rosie, the Queen of Moore Street, had a flower and vegetable stall right at the corner of Henry Street. She visited Jerry's many times during the day, still a handsome woman in her late middle years. She displayed a photo of herself with Schnozzle Durante, 'when he came over to see me'.

Jerry was fond of a jar, seeing no reason why the customers should have all the fun, as they in turn felt that neither should they do all the paying. So when Jerry pushed the boat out, many of them climbed aboard. He was occasionally taken by the men in the white coats to the drying room. He was, I should point out, generous to a fault, even when sober. He was a shy and well-read man.

On this summer's morn whereof I speak, Jerry was sleeping off a hard day's night in one of the cubicles in the rear portion of the bar. This riled Dinny, one of the barmen, because the foreman was out sick, the Saturday trade was very brisk, and there was only a somnolent apprentice rinsing glasses with no detectable frenzy.

It was a con-man's joy. An elderly pensioner entered the front snug carrying a shopping basket. He tapped on the hatch door. Dinny opened it to see this bespectacled man nervously looking over his shoulder towards the street.

'I want a glass of Jameson and a nice slow pint of stout.'

A slow pint was drawn with unhurried reverence in those times. Pulling a good pint was a real point of pride with a real bar-tender. 'You can't rush the blonde with the black skirt,' they said.

'And listen . . .', with another fearful glance doorwards, 'give me the Jameson before she comes — oh, and a small sherry for her, but don't let her see the Jameson.'

Dinny swiftly served up 'the large-wan' and the sherry, then went to perform the initial rites of the Pulling of the Pint. Busy and all as he was, it was not in his training, or indeed in his nature, being a pint-man himself, to hurry the sacred ritual. A few minutes later, having satisfied many orders, he picked up the pint and went to the hatch door. There he beheld an untouched small sherry, an empty whiskey glass, no nervous old geyser, nor indignant spouse in search of same.

It didn't help Dinny's mood, any more than did the arrival of several German sailors from a ship which was paying a courtesy visit from the Bundesrepublik. He had barely sorted out their orders when a screech rent the air. He charged up the bar to find that an elderly regular was sprawled on the floor, foaming at the mouth. The screech had come from Rosie, who was bent over the unconscious man.

'Get him a glass of brandy — force it down his throat!' some medically-minded onlooker suggested.

'Never mind the brandy,' said Rosie, 'think of his immortal soul.' She began to say the Act of Contrition into his ear.

The apprentice had been galvanised into motion, if not action, by this commotion, and halfway through Rosie's prayer he arrived with the glass of brandy.

'. . . and I firmly resolve, never more to offend thee but to amend my life. Amen.'

'Thanks son,' she added, taking the glass and polishing off the brandy.

Dinny had by now got to the phone and dialled for an ambulance. An irate Yorkshireman was surveying all of this with deep disgust. 'Bloody 'ell fire. Place is gone to th' dogs. Last year I was 'ere, we 'ad a fookin' great time. Brendan Behan was singing songs for us an' all. We 'ad none of this fookin' carry on.'

At this juncture Jerry woke up. He stretched himself, looked about to establish his whereabouts, then went forward behind the bar. 'Oh, Dinny, get me a gin-and tonic,' he said.

'Get it your fucking self,' cried the put-upon barman. 'You're asleep all morning, then you wake up and it's fucking servants you want.'

'Don't you use that language with me. Apologise or you're fired.'

'Ah, kiss me arse.'

'I will not be spoken to like that,' said Jerry, now quite agitated. 'I will not have that fucking language in my bar.' And he slapped his open palm down on the bar, under the nose of a naval ambassador of the German Federal Republic.

'What!' roared the sailor, 'You call German fucking language. We speak our own language. Who gives you authority to say we shall not speak the language of our Fatherland . . . you will apologise!'

Jerry looked at him with interest. 'Oh hello', he cried, *'Herzliche Willkommen. Deutschland über alles*. You'll have a little drink?'

By this time the Germans, fearing a diplomatic incident, had begun to edge towards the door. Rosie had begun a rehearsal of a good keening dirge, and the ambulance siren was blasting the glass out of the shop windows. As the German retreat was completed in good order, the ambulance stretcher-bearers appeared in the doorway. Jerry caught sight of the stretcher and backed away. 'I'm not going,' he screamed. 'I'm not going back to the chamber of horrors', and he fled out the back door. The paramedics hoisted the unconscious man onto the stretcher and left, Rosie ordered a Guinness chaser for the brandy, Dinny threw off his apron, poured a whiskey for himself and came outside the counter to sit beside the Yorkshireman.

'Jacked in, 'ave yer, son? Wouldn't blame yer, I must say. Bloody mad-house. Last time I were 'ere we had bloody Brendan Behan here, singin' songs an' all, 'e were. You know Brendan? I like Brendan, he's a gent is old Brendan.'

The Chariot Inn was a friendly but slightly ramshackle establishment on Ranelagh Road, near the Triangle. It had a deserved reputation for its pint, at a time when that was still the main draw in a good pub. Frank Walshe, the boss man, was a progressive and enterprising host, determined to establish the Chariot as a venue for cabaret entertainment, based on traditional music, singing and comedy. He certainly succeeded in putting it on the map. Breandán O'Dúill was a sort of resident *Fear a Tí*, who also sang, with Ronnie Drew, Paddy Reilly, some or all of the Chieftains, Séamus Ennis and Dolly McMahon popping in from time to time.

I'm talking now of the late sixties. Luke Kelly's death left an emptiness in Ireland that has never been filled. I have pondered why that unforgettable and inimitable voice, with its almost chemically caustic power to burn its way through a song, is so seldom heard today, despite his great recording output. Nobody could turn a simple ballad into a rallying cry the way Luke could, and maybe that's too uncomfortable for today. His was the radicalism of Joe Hill.

> In my memory I will always see
> The town that I loved so well . . .

I still feel the tingle in my spine at the memory of hearing Luke transfix the Albert Hall with those lines. It wasn't just the singing, though it was superbly sung. It was a stark, unsparing telling of simple, brutal truth. Luke could so well echo the boast of Tony Bennett: 'When I sing a song, it stays sung.'

One experience I had in the Chariot was being publicly and politely ticked off by a Mr Philip Berg. The show featured Cabaret Gael-Linn, a loose coalition of O'Dúill, Martin Fay, Seán Potts, and possibly Paddy Moloney. It was a very warm summer's evening and the punters, normally numerous enough, had stayed away in droves. We stalled over a pint or two, then decided we'd better get moving.

I went on stage. 'Good evening . . .'

I got no further before being interrupted. 'And about time too. You're late.'

'Yes,' I said, 'we are, but we were waiting for a few more to turn up.'

'So you let those who have turned up sit twiddling their thumbs, eh?'

I probably mumbled some feeble apology.

'My name is Philip Berg. I have several of the young people who work for me here this evening as my guests. I'm a Londoner, as you've probably guessed, but I've discovered the beauty of Irish music, and I want young Irish people to enjoy it too.' He went on in this vein for a while, thanked me for listening, and asked that we get on with it.

I met him and some of his guests later. His appreciation of the music was obvious, and his employees were enjoying the gig immensely. I suspect he was a benevolent despot, a Renaissance man let loose in Ranelagh.

Séamus Ennis was the original Law-Unto-Himself. He was so often given a short time to live, he probably played the pipes at some of his doctors' funerals. At one time in the Chariot, while on tranquillisers, he had a *sean-nós* or gob-music ditty which he sang to his own accompaniment. The words simply ran 'Librium for Equilibrium', with grace notes and change of rhythm according to whim.

He was rarely flush, but had acquired highly sophisticated ways of communicating his need for funds. He would quietly whisper in someone's ear while they were engaged in chat at a bar table, 'Don't let anybody see you slipping me a pound.' No doubt this would be psychologically definable as transferring the preoccupation from performance to methodology. Again, he might peer over the shoulder of somebody about to write a cheque for immediate encashment, and sing in his 'diddle-eye-die-die' fashion: '*Cuir ceann ansin do Shéamus*' ('Put one in there for Séamus.')

He was an incredible performer and a wonderful musician, with a beguiling speaking voice. He could go on stage without, I am convinced, the faintest notion of what he would say or do, and entertain himself and consequently others for as long as might be. One night he began humming as he adjusted the microphone: 'Ditherum doo-dah, ditherum doo-daddy.'

'You know where that comes from?' he asked the audience, then launched into a story of a young girl whose father had the flu and demanded *poitín* punch. No punch was available, but she came across a bottle of rum in the pantry. She mixed the punch and administered same. The father slept and awoke feeling much improved, as the daughter peeped in to see how he was.

'Did the rum do, Da?' she asked anxiously.

'What love?'

'Did the rum do, Daddy?'

A simple, mildly amusing piece of nonsense, but he convinced you that the whole thing was concocted while he fiddled with the mike, and that you were attending its world première.

Madigans of North Earl Street was one of Dublin's finest pubs, ever and always. Their pint was a joy to behold and a pleasure to swallow, which didn't necessarily follow in other cases. It was a very much stand-up-at-the-bar establishment, with a few chairs and a table for the faint of heart at either end of that counter that stretched from Earl Street back to Cathedral Street. There was a lounge upstairs, reachable by lift, where you were expected though not required to take female companions.

The Madigan brothers, Paddy and Mick, were a by-word in the rugby world, which was always a bit of an alien planet to me. Gradually their Empire spread. They took over Grainger's of Moore Street, which became a chapel-of-ease for those temporarily out of favour in the Mother House in Earl Street. Other sanctuaries on the pilgrim route were opened when Tommy Moore's fell to the advancing Madigan army. Guiney's of Burgh Quay surrendered, and put to sea again as 'The Galleon'.

Central Dublin remained the stomping ground of the Home Guard, but we heard of the Madigan Empire's further conquests among the hill tribes in far-flung Ballinteer, and in the flatlands of Sallynoggin.

Running a slate was accepted as normal practice in the taverns of the town. Running from the slate was very perfidy, as monstrous as pleading the Gaming Act. The barman and the bookie had to live too — that was an Article of Faith. It stood to reason, of course, that trying to keep the bookie going meant leaving the barman short from time to time. The etiquette of self-impoverishment could be maintained in the case of the Madigan chain by avoiding the house where you owed more than it was convenient to clear, while patronising, if only on an alternative slate, one of the other branches. Word would filter back to the 'Vatican' that the suspected proselyte was merely falling into venial sin.

Nonetheless, one had to cough up sooner or later. Big Paddy Dunne, subsequently a neighbour of ours, was manager of the Mother House. One particularly dreary winter, coming up to Christmas, he sent far from fair or speechless messages to some of us whose patronage had outpaced our payments, to the effect that he would appreciate our presence at the upstairs lounge (access by lift only) at a stated time. We ambled in, one at a time, feigning unconcern, each unaware that the others had also been summoned, all slightly puzzled by the sudden flight to the lounge. It began to dawn on us that those assembled were the heaviest into the deficit columns. An uneasy jocularity reigned. Finally the lift doors opened to reveal the towering physique of Paddy Dunne, his craggy face a study in solemnity. His eyes swept around the lounge, checking that all the condemned had turned up. He raised his arms above his shoulders and smiled. 'Reprieve to all. Happy Christmas!' And the party went on till closing time. This firm, so far as I know, would not have known what a PR man was.

The first time I darkened the door of the Embankment in Tallaght was at the invitation of Mick McCarthy, the owner. But I didn't know this.

It was while *Borstal Boy* was still on its very first run, in 1967. An artist called Brian Mulvaney had done a portrait of Brendan Behan to be hung in the bar of the Embankment. He rang me and asked if I would unveil the picture on a Sunday night. I'm sure there was some fundraising tie-in as well. Sunday was my only night off, and I had never heard of this Brian Mulvaney, so I declined the invitation. On the Saturday evening a telegram was delivered to my house, which read: 'Thanks, Niall. God bless you. Look forward to seeing you again on Sunday night. Love, Kathleen Behan.'

That settled that. There was no way I could leave Kathleen Behan in the lurch. I turned up, unveiled the picture, sang a few songs, said a few words, drank a few pints. Kathleen was there with Rory Furlong, her son from her first marriage, and a few more of the family.

'Jesus, you were great to come,' said Rory, as the party was in full swing.

'I'll tell you the truth. I only came because Kathleen asked me.'

'How do you mean? Sure, Kathleen knew fuck all about this until she walked in the door. We just picked her up as a surprise for her birthday.'

I produced the telegram. Rory laughed.

'Mick McCarthy sent that, you eejit. He told everyone you'd be doing the unveiling, so he had to get you, and he knows how.'

Mick McCarthy's neck was of a calloused toughness unmatched

by Lester Piggott's most intimate parts. A spell-binding story-teller, he held me in the little bar in the Embankment, even when on the dry, playing darts till three a.m., while he talked of his days as a shop steward in Belfast during the war, when he brought the building workers on a US army base out on strike, and lived to tell the tale.

McCarthy was at his best in impromptu appearances on his own stages. His introductions in the Embankment were worthy of the best warm-up men in the business, especially when the audience was mostly composed of Dubs. It is not an inaccuracy, though it may be unkind, to say that Mick McCarthy bears less resemblance to a tailor's dummy than to a pipe-smoking monkey in a suit. He would amble about the audience, stoking the foul-smelling pipe, looking like a herring smoker on his break. He knew most of his regular audience by their first names, and enquired after their relations. Eventually he would mount the stage, snapping the lighter and sucking the dudeen.

'Boys and girls, come here to me, listen. What did ye think of the chicken? Tough? The bloody cheek of you. Our chickens tough? I'll have you know they walked all the way from Kerry to be with us here tonight.'

More barracking would ensue, especially in the years when Kerry and Dublin met in the later stages of the Football Championship.

'What about the Sam Maguire Cup?'

'That's another thing. Mick O'Connell's grandmother kept her knitting in that cup for years.'

Or after losing a match: 'Well done, we like to see the weaker counties coming through. But if there is as much as one scratch on that cup when it comes back next year . . .'

Finally, to the introduction proper. The pipe would go into the jacket.

'Boys and girls, ye remember when I brought the great Mícheál MacLiammóir out here? They said it couldn't be done! We had the Pecker Dunne, the Dubliners, the Dublin City Ramblers, Box-Car Willie, The Furey brothers, The Clancys. Tonight you are the most privileged people in this country. Tonight we have a man of such talent that his name is a household word in London, Paris and

Amsterdam. There are queues four blocks long to see him on Broadway, the Russians stand up to their knees in the Moscow snow to catch a glimpse of him. The funniest man in the world. But he's a cranky whore as well — he would rear up on his own mother, so for Jasus' sake give us a bit of hush for the one and only . . .'

All these establishments, as well as the Tower Bar mentioned earlier, have now either gone out of business or changed hands. Maybe I shouldn't have gone on the wagon so early.

\* \* \* \*

When you don't allow yourself a drink, and find going to the theatre or cinema a bit like work, your entertainment options are pretty limited. Poker, Promiscuity and Prayer, considered as pastimes, all present problems.

There is, of course, golf. Like drink, sex and religion, golf is better practised than talked about. Granted, we spend a lot of time at golf, but no more than we do sleeping. We do not, however, subdivide our sleep into eighteen arbitrary stretches and bore the neighbours with accounts of how we traversed each one. Golf does have in common with the Three Ps mentioned above, that it is a gamble, is sometimes performed with multiple partners, and frequently involves the name of the Lord.

Golf is as dear to my heart as it is to my pocket. I have been shelling out so regularly for so long, to bandits using six irons for six shooters, that I should really turn up on the first tee in a Santa outfit. Golf is all things to all men (though, as Lady Associates will acidly point out, only some things to some women). It can be both substitute and therapy for sex, drink, worship, work, flagellation, aggression or timidity. It can also be used as an allegory by the poetic for Life, by the devout for This Valley of Tears, by the randy as a Khamasutra.

Golfers will believe anything. They are to marketing men what rubes are to snake-oil salesmen. Deep down they know the idea is to get them to spend, spend and spend again. But they no more stop buying than the faithful of yore who queued up at Mission stalls to buy Infants of Prague and Miraculous Medals. When Jack Nicklaus once won a big American tournament, his success was attributed to his use on the greens of an implement called the Jumbo, which was not unlike the lever of a pre-war car jack — although it was well-known, in the elegant American phrase, that the same man could hole putts with his pecker. Soon the world was awash with Jumbos. People bought them because they were infallible. But balls slid by the cup as mockingly as ever. The Jumbo today is a museum piece. One might find a stray one, forlorn and rusted, supporting a raspberry cane in a council allotment in Stoke-on-Trent, but I imagine most were melted down to make Calaway Big Berthas.

Before the Gulf War, we managed to persuade the Yanks that Ireland was *the* place for golf. They fell for this proposition in such large numbers that we began to turn everything not totally submerged in water or cowshit into golf courses, with the aid of EC grants. Everyone said golf would benefit the tourist industry. Oh, sure. But will it benefit golf, or more to the point, golfers? Golf is, after all, the cocaine of the correct, the rock-and-roll of the elderly. Must it be subsumed into the all-assimilating tourist industry? Greater love, it appears, hath no man than that he suffer the green swards of his native land to be over-run by American grandmothers photographing each other missing putts. Was it for this that the Wild Geese spread the grey wing on every tide? Most assuredly not. Real golf has nothing to do with tourism. It is a private fantasy indulged in by fanatics who do not wish to throw open their play-pens to boost the economy.

I see a parallel with making movies. People play golf because it is a passion. Likewise, I think of film-makers as people who make movies because they cannot bear to do anything else, like Ed Wood. He was bloody awful, but he loved the game. Pioneers of the film industry in Ireland edited prints together with their life's blood. But recently the country has become one huge location and part of the tourist industry. When you start making movies because the money-movers see them as a way of not paying their taxes, the end product means little. 'In and out like a fiddler's elbow' must be the motto. Pay bottom dollar, recruit trainees, cut meal breaks, make them pay their own transport, and then complain that production values are inferior to those in Malaysia.

A company whose PR man had revealed that the director was getting three million dollars and the lead actor five million, sent in a location manager to ask the denizens of a city slum for permission to borrow their street and keep them awake all night for free. They told him to get knotted.

That's us — no gratitude.

# TWENTY-TWO

Looking over much of what I have written, I realise that my harshest words are for those gone beyond caring. The dead cannot defend themselves, it is true, but who knows whether they would bother. They do have one huge advantage over the living, best summed up in a remark I heard at a wake in Neary's of Chatham Street. The maudlin stage had been reached, and the deceased's most banal remarks were being invested with a sagacity they never had. Then one man broke with tradition. 'God be good to him,' he said, 'but he was a desperate ignorant man.' 'Maybe so,' came the soft rejoinder, 'but he knows more than any of us now.'

I seem to have been especially unkind to one director, for instance. Yet to anybody who knew us both, it probably wouldn't seem so. He was so outrageously over the top in his views on everything, and so close to incoherence, especially in drink, that one's final reaction could only be one of affection.

My intention has never been to belittle anybody who has taken to the theatre as a way of living, as this very choice suggests an inherent instability. I will trot out Byron's words that 'If I laugh at any mortal thing, 'tis that I may not weep'.

So if anybody should ask if I have never met people notorious for cruelty, pederasty, banking, body odour, treachery, poetry, drunkenness, whoring, rugby, mockery, plagiarism, drunken driving, or simply for being a complete and utter ballocks, then I can only answer, 'Yes, of course I have, I do live in Ireland after all.'

I have also known people memorable for piety, sportsmanship, charity, thrift, scruples, unfailing cheerfulness, philanthropy, sobriety, tolerance, compassion, incorruptibility, and the ability to play the harpsichord, who are in equal measure either candidates for canonisation, or a royal pain in the arse. None of the above traits qualified anybody for inclusion in this chronicle, which is personal, whimsical, arbitrary, anecdotal, and sometimes true. I notice also that in trying to maintain a narrative flow, I have resisted attractive digressions, something I think I should rectify. I cannot impose a retrospective order on a series of unplanned moves in what we shall call a career — an odd word, meaning as a noun 'advancement through life', and as a verb, 'to move or swerve about madly'.

When I started doing my one-man stunt, I felt no great change of atmosphere in the profession. It was considered a temporary success, an aberration not to be worried about. When I strayed into the realms of cabaret and clubs, the barometer dropped a bit. After I had stooped to being a comic, a persistent frost appeared on several critical countenances. Noses tilted perceptibly upwards.

One distinguished disemboweller of all performers, other than kilted colleens with silver-buckled shoes, even called me to one side. 'A word in your shell-like,' he said, lifting another freebie from a passing tray of booze, 'Why do you do it? Telling dirty jokes, a man of your talent. You don't need to, you know.' This from a man who habitually either ignored or panned me in print.

In my 'swerving about madly' career, I found myself, one summer in the 1980s, in Iceland, where I had agreed to do a show, in English, about Brendan Behan. I cannot for the life of me remember how this came about. I flew from Heathrow, we picked up someone in Glasgow, and landed some two hours later in Reykjavik, which was like Dingle on a misty day with all the scenery removed.

I had lunch at the hotel with the Modern Jazz Quartet, consisting of Percy Heath, John Lewis, Connie Kaye and Milt Jackson. This was highly enjoyable, though somewhat marred by the intrusion of a minor managerial figure who enquired as to which of the gentlemen had ordered a prostitute. He left uninformed, though not unanswered. When the quartet found I was from Ireland, they spoke with great affection of the Cork Jazz Festival. My show was to be at five p.m., which I had at first objected to as being too early. 'Well', the organisers said, 'You can do it at two thirty a.m. In either case it will be broad daylight.' I had forgotten this, so I did my five o'clock matinee. As I left the table, Jackson said, 'Knock 'em dead man, you're goin' to be great. I heard all about you. Just go in there and knock 'em dead.' They invited me to their own show at nine p.m.

I performed to a polite and I think somewhat puzzled audience of about one hundred and fifty, at the Opera House (Royal Opera House even, if I mistake not), and I met the Quartet later, as they left the hotel.

'I heard you knocked 'em dead,' said Milt.

'It was OK,' I said.

'Oh come on, it was sensational, everybody says so. It's the talk of Keflavik.'

'This', I said, 'is Reykjavik.'

'Yeah, sure, like I say *everybody's* talking about you.'

It was no bad review, quite a good notice in fact from somebody who hadn't seen the show — on a par with another notice I got at the Kevin Moran testimonial dinner in the Burlington Hotel in Dublin. After I had done my stint there, I went to our table, at the head of which was one Jack Charlton. Slightly to one side was Paddy Cullen, the Dublin goalie of a former era. 'I never laughed so much,' said Cullen, whacking me on the back, 'I was in stitches. I never took my eyes off Jack Charlton. He didn't understand one bloody word you said. It was great.'

For many years I have had a London agent, to look for and after work in Britain. It is even more necessary to have an agent at home in Ireland, otherwise some summer's evening you may find yourself driving through some entrancing village such as Bunatoodera, of which you have only vaguely heard, to find a poster proudly announcing your appearance in Biddy's Bordello, along with the Sensational Scrotums' All Saxophone Band, a fortnight hence. You hurry in to book a front row seat while stocks last.

'Ah no, you just pays at the door on the night.'

'Is he a big draw, this fella?'

'Ah, big enough. But you'll get in on the night, no bother.'

Fuming, you ask for the boss, who inevitably is gone to the races, out playing golf, accompanying the diocesan pilgrimage to Lourdes, or all three together. You rear up on everybody in sight, remove the posters and threaten the law on everyone over the age of three in the town.

Two years later, you go for a piss in John T McGurk's Irish House in St Louis Missouri, to find yourself being sized up by a solemn-faced stud at the next trough. He doesn't look like a male hooker, but you never know. Then he speaks.

'You're Niall Toibin.'

'Yes.'

'You're welcome to St Louis.'

'Thank you.'

'But they wouldn't bid you the time of day in Bunatoodera, let me tell you. God, you let 'em down badly. Only for the *Shaska Shay* Senior Citizens' singalong, they were ballocksed completely. Poor Patty Killoran had a heart attack that same night. You're a very callous man to be treating the poor neglected people in out-of-the-way places like dirt.'

The effect of this abusive intelligence is unnerving. The Bunatoodera Mafia do not jest. The Illinois border ain't all that far. Breaking a non-existent contract in Bunatoodera is probably not yet a Federal offence, so you zip up your flies and hit the trail for Chicago.

Why do these impresarios of the remote regions advertise someone they haven't booked? Because if the publicity is limited to local targets, but not enough to attract a decent house, the proprietor can blame that duplicitous bastard Toibin, who never showed. 'Sure, isn't he noted for not turning up, the Cork whoor?' Who's going to verify the booking? Why should anyone disbelieve this decent man who is trying to brighten the long evenings? (Fade in slow fiddle music . . .)

Once when I was working in London I got a call from Connemara at the Cottesloe Theatre stage door, as obscure a spot to contact from west Galway as the An Óige Hostel on Nanga Parbat. A pleasantly spoken man, who sounded of late middle age, introduced himself.

(I'll call him Andrew Campbell.) He spoke at length of his admiration for my work, the dearth of entertainment of quality in his part of the west, his pleasure at finally having run me to ground after months of persistent searching (which excluded looking up my home number in the phone book). He had recently extended his fine cabaret lounge, and described its glories in detail. Would I not come to do an evening for them? 'Money, my dear fellow, is incidental. Just name it. I never quibble with artists.' I looked across the South Bank at a heat mist enveloping the Thames. Connemara called, with its crystal-clear streams, blue skies, and crisp, invigorating air. I named a day and a price. Andrew showered the blessings of all the saints of Connemara upon my benevolent cranium.

The date I'd chosen was two months away, of course, in early November. I set out in the fullness of time from Dublin, upon my mission of mercy, to lift the black dog from the shoulders of the rural people. Having left Carraroe behind me, I negotiated a few more twisted miles of road, shrouded in a mist as thick as that on the Thames in September, without the accompanying heat. A vague unease stirred in my bosom. This was Bunatoodera, arse over tip. Here, where I was booked, were no posters proclaiming my advent. There, where I had not been booked, there were plenty.

I finally located the premises, parked in the deserted forecourt in the dusk, and went inside. A personable young man was reading the *Connacht Tribune* behind the bar. He looked up, did a double take, then with an 'Ah, the hard and the wild!', he shot out his hand. 'Fancy seeing you here at this time of year. Jesus, the weather has been melodeon. You'll have something to warm you, your first time here.'

His evident pleasure at meeting me was deeply moving, but was just as evidently unexpected.

'What are you doing in this neck of the woods? Not that there's any woods for fifty miles.'

I decided to play it up the wing a bit. 'Oh, visiting,' I said. 'Do you happen to know a Mr Andrew Campbell hereabouts?'

'Jesus, why wouldn't I? Me own ould fella.'

'Is he about?'

'Jesus, not at all. Sure, he's in the nut house, getting dried out, this month or more.'

'Well,' I said, 'this is very awkward.'

'Don't tell me. He booked you to do a show tonight.'

Mr Campbell apparently used to get bitten by the impresario bug at certain stages of alcoholic transport. He issued invites to acts, usually by telephone, then completely forgot to tell anyone else.

'How much did you quote him?' he asked.

I told him. 'But we can forget about that,' I said, meaning, let's do a deal.

'No,' he said, 'we'll pay up. I'll get my brother to write you a cheque. There'll be a few in the lounge later on. You might do half an hour for them, as you're here.'

I settled for half the fee, did a short spot, declined the offer of a room, and headed for the Great Southern Hotel in Galway.

There is a story of a concert organised for a Holy Cause in the old Capitol Theatre, otherwise La Scala, in Prince's Street, beside the GPO in Dublin. The band engaged were all federation musicians, their union deputy a Londoner not all that long in Dublin. The event was a complete bummer. It became clear that somebody wasn't going to get paid. The Reverend Impresario decided to sing the blues and pluck the strings of sympathy. He outlined the likely celestial awards for forgoing the wages of the day, but he was dealing with a coldhearted Cockney, whom the Heads had warned to get their bleedin' fees, no messin'.

At the end of the priest's appeal to their better nature, if any, they sat there, defiant of divine retribution.

'I know you all have your own commitments, so I will honour mine,' said the priest, almost in tears. 'Even though', he added after a weighty pause, 'I have to pay the money out of my own pocket.'

'That's fuckin' sportin' of yer, Padre,' enthused the deputy. 'Three cheers for His Holiness.'

I've mentioned already that actors in a communal situation reminisce and celebrate flops more enthusiastically than hits. This is probably because the star and the spear-carrier are in the same boat, even if one is in steerage.

People in commerce and industry, not to mention Government outfits, who look upon the theatre as an unstructured, *ad hoc* agglomeration of free spirits, too lazy to work, too randy for fidelity, too undisciplined to conform to executive or administrative direction, know sweet Fanny Adams about the business. This is why the takeover of performing arts by accountants will fail, the sooner the better. It is impossible to quantify or evaluate a combination of performances in terms of productivity or precise financial return. How can anybody measure the commercial wealth of the chemistry between Des Keogh and Ros Linehan, for instance, or the lisping, square-chinned jeer of Eamonn Morrissey, or the sheer menace of Donal McCann's resentful glare.

I doubt if anybody capable of programming a computer has the faintest chance of handling the developing relationship, over an intense rehearsal period, between two gifted, selfish, vulnerable people. I have used the word vulnerable about actors more than once. We trade in delusions, sleight of mind, dreams, fantasies, make-believe. The primary delusion is convincing ourselves that what we are up to matters a damn. Having conned ourselves into accepting this proposition, we are qualified to hawk our hypnosis to others. Any more of this, and I will be breaking my own rule: once you analyse it, it will go away.

Actors, regardless of any of the foregoing, are great pragmatists, realists, buriers of hatchets, not always in each other. Where leader writers and purists scream at the idea of coalitions between opposites, no actor gives them a second thought. We form coalitions every time we get a job.

How often have we sworn never again to tread the boards with 'that lighting bitch', 'that megalomanic masseuse of her own ego', 'that thundering, self-opinionated old blatherskite', 'that slithery rattlesnake, poxed to the eyeballs with her own prestige', 'that two-faced, saccharin-spoken arse-bandit', and so on. But the prospects of employment after a long fast, or the lure of a part coveted for years, can effect miraculous reconciliations.

'Darling, how lovely to see you! How fabulous you look. Oh, you've got your hair done.'

'Ah, me ould Segocia. Great to see ya. How are the gee-gees going? Treating you well?'

Apart from the well-publicised affairs between members of the profession, straight or gay, intense non-sexual attachments of near-marital fidelity are formed within theatre companies or film units. Crossword buffs, for instance, crouch together in a semi-circle, in physical attitudes suggestive of kinky group sex, groaning, 'Blank, blank . . . n, y, blank N . . . "rocky gorge".' (The solution, incidentally, is 'canyon'.)

In a corner, women whose buttocks, breasts and pouting lips form part of the national landscape, huddle in smocks and legwarmers, clicking needles in unison to produce ganseys for burly sons and husbands. One head nods in isolation, trying to wish away a hangover.

There is a cross-over between groups, naturally, especially where roles require intensive and long rehearsal together. It is a cliché that an actor brings a part of his own personality to a role. It follows that two people probing a scene, over sustained and demanding rehearsal, develop a very close emotional relationship, in which the real life and the dramatic personalities overlap. This produces a receptivity to underlying subtleties, which forms a powerful and potentially dangerous bond. At the end of a run, this closeness may survive, or they may recoil from it so violently that yesterday's darling becomes the 'blistering bitch' of today, or, to give the sexes parity of esteem, the soulmate of Saturday becomes Monday's fourteen-carat prick.

Until, that is, the First Read-through of the next play, when those gathered together greet and congratulate each other as the Truly Talented, finally recognised and rewarded.

Since I quit the booze, I have avoided 'Wrap' parties or late-night hoolies, since it is at these that the special relationships show signs of disintegration, usually with a sudden explosion. I recall a seemingly innocuous reply to a casual question, causing near-nuclear fallout.

'What'll you have?' asked some PR prat from the production company of one of the team, seated beside his constant companion of many years' standing.

'Bacardi and coke,' he replied.

There was a silence, insofar as that is possible when the walls are buckling from the thud of heavy metal. An air of puzzlement in the lady's face preceded an icily elocuted query.

'Wot dew you mean, a Back-cardy end cook?'

He tossed a carefree head. 'I mean a Bacardi rum and coca-cola.'

'I didn't ask what it was, I asked why you ordered it. What's gone wrong with the vodka and tonic you always drink, all of a sudden? Why the change?'

'I just felt like a change.'

'Oh, you feel like a change, all right, in more ways than one. It's because that's what that English nympho you've been shaggin' all summer drinks. Far from Bacardi and coke you were reared, or her either. Lady fuckin' muck, her face has had more lifts than a hitchhiking whore.'

The quality of the invective even challenged the rock band. People began to earwig. Though not mentioned by name, the said English nympho at an adjoining table responded to her description, and charged at full tilt, handbag swinging.

Wrap parties only rarely entertain at that high standard, however. They do not often conform to the fevered imaginings of the paparazzi. Nevertheless, the fascination of filming, for those not directly involved in it, is a continuing mystery, seeing that we've had movies with us for over a century now — though there are increasing signs that the Irish peasantry, lay or uniformed, have had it up to the eyeballs with the disruption of their daily routine by arrogant film folk.

I saw a straw in the wind when filming in County Clare, and traffic had been halted before shooting a scene. As the standby was called, a middle-aged lady, upright and fearsome, wheeled her prehistoric High Nelly bike out of a shop door, the carrier laden with vegetables. She proceeded up the main street with commanding dignity.

'Could you hold it just a moment, madam,' cried an assistant, 'We're filming here.'

'And I am living here,' she responded, without breaking her stride.

The dogs bark, the caravan moves on.

To use a phrase from another 'them and us' situation, 'Gone are the days when our arse was over our shoulders from tugging our forelocks.' But a sizeable slice of the populace still drops everything to stand for hours, looking at people they cannot hear, endlessly re-enacting twenty-four-second segments, out of sequence, of a story they cannot follow. Still, I suppose, they might as well. They may no longer be able to enjoy such sights at the rate that film technology has been developing in recent times. I am so totally flummoxed by the whole thing that I suspect that shortly it will be possible to make a film without using actors, or even people, at all. The term 'virtual reality' has, I must confess, stolen up on me. It is tied in, in my mind, with the repugnant world of computers, bytes, software, and all the other hideous jargon that the ageing find bewildering.

Each generation has denounced the innovations of the next, from way back. The first time a farmer in Kerry saw a scythe in use, he stood awe-struck with his sickle in his hand. Another neighbour, witnessing the hay falling smoothly to the sweep of the blade, cutting twenty times as much as the sickle would, said, 'Whoever invented that thing was a clever man.'

'He was,' said the sickle man, 'and a lazy bastard.'

I am as aware as the next of the antipathy within me to improvements, progress, modernisation, change, whatever you want to call it. You are, after all, reading the thoughts of a man who let Elvis Presley pass by, somewhere out there on the horizon, only dimly aware of the cacophony; who listened consciously to a John Lennon lyric only after his assassination had made the songs topical again.

Still, I would plead that fear of the whole 'virtual reality' concept is not over-reaction. I was struck by the appalling vista it conjures up as I watched the film *Forrest Gump*, of which, out of sheer perversity, I loved every minute. When you can place Tom Hanks, in 1995, in front of cheering thousands at the Lincoln Memorial, while the long-dead Lyndon Johnson admires the bullet-holes in his arse, or JFK actually holds a jocose conversation with Hanks, and nobody can spot the join, then the words 'appalling vista' seem very apt.

When the good Lord Denning used that phrase in connection with the Birmingham Six case, this technique was not available. It certainly was not available at the time of the Birmingham bombings. But today it would be possible, on film, using these techniques, to place all six at the scene of the explosion, or indeed anywhere else. So far has this development of 'virtual reality' gone, that it should be child's play to put the Pope in any brothel of your choice, or to show Tony Blair engaged in bestiality with the Abominable Snowman.

The ultimate result, inevitably, must be that all photographic, electronic or recorded evidence will be inadmissible in court, since all of these things are so susceptible to tampering that it would be impossible to prove their veracity. Up to now, 'virtual reality' to me would have meant very good documentary-style acting. My own life has been largely involved with 'virtual reality' — with being placed in situations where the line between the actual and the apparent, while clear to me, is very blurred to the spectator.

One can become so accustomed to costume and make-up that they cease to exist. You can see through them to the reality, while others can only believe what they see. Filming a commercial for Air Canada, in which I played a friendly, jolly parish priest of a Shannonside village, I took a break during the morning and wandered into a pub in Mount Shannon. I ordered a Paddy and a bottle of stout, this being my tipple at that time, and opened the weekly paper, which carried a photo of the local Youth Hostel. It listed the countries from which the guests had come during the year, under the headline 'Mount Shannon Hostel Beckons the Globe'. I was chuckling at this splendid hyperbole, when I was rudely interrupted by an elderly man at the bar's end.

'So well you may laugh,' he snarled. 'I know who you are. You think you're very smart, passing yourself off as a priest, bringing the Church into ridicule, making a fool of the poor woman of the house here. Well, we can do without you and your filth, and your mockery of religion.'

'Ara, leave him alone,' said the bar lady, 'sure he's only making a film below on the lake, and can't he have his curer in peace, the same as you?'

Once I was playing a zoo-keeper in a road-safety film called *Zoo Logic*, shot, astonishingly enough, in the Zoological Gardens in the Phoenix Park. I wore a keeper's uniform, a false moustache, steel spectacle frames with no glass, and stood at the top of the steps up to the main entrance, looking at a line of schoolkids crossing the road. A zoom lens was recording my facial reactions from some eighty yards away. I became aware of a current of hostility directed from the bottom of the steps, in my direction. I looked and saw a woman with a stroller, in which were strapped twin boys.

'Are you', she screamed, 'going to stand there admiring yourself all bloody day? Can you not see I want a hand with the go-car?'

Heavily made up as I was, I went to her assistance, and hauled her two grandchildren backwards up the steps, to a tirade of abuse and comparisons.

'Not like Paddy Whalen's time. He was a lovely man. This fella really fancies himself, you know. Did you see him preening himself? Heh! In with the peacocks you should be.'

Contributions from external sources of this nature are not all that unusual. Somebody will always heckle at an exciting play, and in a cabaret situation, contributions from the public are even welcome sometimes. But the opposite procedure is rather unusual. Offhand I can only think of one. It was in the early seventies. Conor Cruise O'Brien's play, *Murderous Angels*, was produced at the Gaiety as a Festival offering. It was the story of the rise and death of Patrice Lumumba. It caused quite a stir critically, and, more interestingly perhaps, backstage as well. The cast was drawn from far and wide, with Nigerian actor Yemi Adjubade playing Moishe Tshombe, Norman Beaton as Lumumba, Andrew Keir as Dag Hammarsjold, and sundry English and Irish actors in other roles. I played the bishop of somewhere.

To further encourage the punters, we had Ginger Johnson and his all-steel West Indian Band. Johnson was quite remarkable in his appearance, for that time anyway, with a reddish tinge to his Afro hair and light brown freckles on his darker skin.

Someone in the Gaiety management felt that it would be prudent to close down the backstage bar in the Green Room. After all, you couldn't tell what these black chaps would be getting up to, or on.

It didn't bother Ginger or the band. Some of them were so stoned on pot, they never even noticed that the bar was closed. Nor did the management notice the marijuana, the smell of which was wafting right through the theatre. They were too busy congratulating themselves on the wisdom of their pre-emptive strike. There was no drunkenness among the band. How quiet it was in the Green Room.

Yemi was wonderful as Tshombe. During his offstage moments, he kept up a running battle with the accountant's office, who on foot of a communication from some invisible tax agent, was withholding tax arrears due to HM Inland Revenue by the above Mr Ajubade. In one scene, with the Rhodesian high commissioner, played by the legendary A J Brown, Tshombe used a large map to illustrate a point, the lines going something as follows: 'You are a reasonable man, Mr High Commissioner, but these bastards up here . . .' (and he indicates where 'here' is on the map).

One night, he came to the scene fresh from an argument about his taxes with Fred O'Donovan, the Boss man. To the great delight of the others on the stage, and the bafflement of the audience, he finished the scene thus: 'You are a reasonable man, Mr High Commissioner, but that fucker up there . . .' and he pointed out front, in the general direction of Fred's office.

*Mass Appeal*, a play by Bill Davis in which Geraldine Fitzgerald, that most gracious, talented and warm-hearted lady, directed myself and Barry Lynch, seemed to attract hecklers and outside interference willy-nilly.

Geraldine and her husband Stewart Scheftel, former schoolboy golf champion of Great Britain, though a New Yorker, had been friends to us for years, though I only worked with her for the first time on the ill-fated *Tristan*. We realised a wish to work together with *Mass Appeal*, the story of a bibulous parish priest at loggerheads with a young seminarian whom he has instructed in the art of sermon-composition. Barry Lynch played the seminarian.

We opened at the Olympia in the middle of an electricity strike. About six minutes into the play, the lights went out all over Dublin. Barry and I continued to rabbit on at each other. Noel Pearson, the producer, made his début in the dark to announce that the lights were out, but that emergency generators would be used as soon as they could be located in the dark. This all sorted itself out when the lights were restored after half an hour. Some of those who had been enjoying a candlelit gin and snog in the bar took a bit of persuading back into the auditorium. We went at it again from the curtain-up, to the delighted cries of 'action replay' from some. In the second Act, I had to deliver a sermon, preceded by a choir singing 'Praise be the Lord, the Almighty, the King of Creation', a fairly strident number which woke up a wino who slept on the step of the emergency exit in the Lane.

'Shut up, yez crowd of religious fanatics,' he roared, kicking at the door. The choir faded out, not at his behest, but he was mollified, until I commenced my sermon.

'Dearly beloved brothers and sisters in Christ,' I said, or words to similar effect.

'Shut up, ya bollicks, you're worse than the fuckin' choir. I wanna go to sleep.'

The situation seemed beyond retrieval. One more interruption came as I, having poured a glass of wine in a hungover state, thought better of it and poured it back into the bottle. Very neatly. Too bloody neatly. A deep Kerry voice in the front row said, 'Christ, haven't you the fine steady hand, and you on the batter all night!'

Later, on tour in Belfast, this time with Brendan Conroy, I delivered a pretty controversial line in an argument with the seminarian. I'd already advised him to suppress his scruples when answering some questions at an interview board. 'No, Father,' he says, 'You're asking me to lie.'

In exasperation at this pious little prig, Father Farley says, 'All right, Mark, if you want to be a hero, tell the truth.' Then swinging round to him from an upstage position, he adds, 'But if you want to be a priest, lie!'

An intake of breath nearly sucked the tabs off their rail, before a metallic female voice commented with the satisfaction of vindicated prejudice, 'This is very good, you know. They're all terrible liars.' I don't think she just meant priests, she meant 'them' as opposed to 'us'.

Dear old Vernon Hayden, straight man par excellence, and golfer extraordinary, came to see the play, as escort for Maureen Potter, with whom he was working. Vernon, not being a Catholic, had already decided he didn't understand the jokes, but made appropriate noises of agreement as Maureen enthused about the play.

'Well Vern,' I said, in a quiet moment, 'what do you think?' I meant, of the play's chance of a run, of course.

He shook his head in regretful sympathy. 'Not enough golf in it,' he said. There was one scene where Father Farley wards off another temptation to drink by practising his putting on the carpet as he awaits a phone call.

In fact, we ran for two months, transferred to the Gaiety, and toured Cork, Limerick and Belfast.

# TWENTY-THREE

In the early days of television in Ireland and Britain, actors had a very uneasy attitude towards advertising. It was held that, bad and all as it was to be vocally associated with selling soapflakes, to be seen brandishing snow-white knickers and nappies at the public on the screen was very death. Nobody would ever employ you as a straight actor after that.

The American attitude as always was more practical, more pragmatic, greedier. An actor in New York (and let me emphasise that he was only in New York to collect some residuals — naturally he lived in LA), showed me photos of his yacht, the marine equivalent of a white stretch limo, moored by his private beach. He cried salt tears into my beer as he voiced his admiration for my integrity. 'You are an artist. Jesus, what I wouldn't give to have that love (know what I mean?) for the theatre. But I guess I sold out, see. I'm just a prostitute, artistically. God, I envy you! Oh, here, let me show you my wife's Porsche.'

I sold out too. Artistic prostitute I may not be — more likely the last of the old-fashioned whores, but judicious meretriciousness has contributed to my coffers. The odd thing is that I have never felt personally associated with the products. I did eat the fish I claimed to catch, but I advertised Guinness for years after I had totally given up gargle of any brand or hue. I advertised a bank, and endured excruciating jokes about my cousin Martin, the bank manager, without giving the same outfit a ha'p'orth of custom.

Budweiser beer has become one of the world's best-known thirst-quenchers, with the slogan 'This Bud is for you' spoken in a matter-of-fact yet seductive baritone. In a special St Patrick's Day promotion for the US market, the Budweiser people once produced a very attractive version of their TV ad, with the body of the text in English, but they decided to run the slogan in Gaelic. *'Duit-se an Bud seo.'* I was hired to speak the ad, recorded in Dublin, with some American executives in attendance.

My expression obviously must have conveyed my unease, because one young executive asked if I had a problem. 'No,' I said, 'but you certainly have.'

'Sure, I don't speak Gaelic. Is that a problem?'

'Well, not to beat about the Anheuser-busch,' I said, 'it is, rather. *Bud* is the Gaelic for penis.'

'Oh. So the sentence means "this prick is for you".'

'Yes.'

Needless to say, it was changed to *'Duit-se an Budweiser seo'*, which of course caused any Irish speaker first to wonder, and then to understand, why we didn't say *Duit-se an Bud seo.*

I did a campaign for Bord Iascaigh Mhara, the Irish Sea Fisheries Board, back in the days before black and white TV was even called monochrome. In a yellow plastic sou'wester and wellies, I ambled along the quayside in Dunmore East, from barrel to barrel, languidly hoisting a hake, or prodding a pollock towards the camera lens, also extolling the heart-enhancing qualities of cod, kipper and crab. Paddy Bawn Brosnan, himself a fisherman as well as a publican, was drawing pints in his pub in Dingle one evening when he glanced up at the television as I pronounced the smarmy pay-off from the screen. 'You keep cookin' and I'll keep catchin.'

'Well, will you look at Toibin,' he said to the drinkers in general, to whom I was no stranger. 'And the whoor couldn't tell a mackerel from a cow.'

And many years after the closure of the Crannac factory, whose slogan dwelt on the handy sixty minutes it took to reach the city, and whose furniture I advertised, a man on an upgoing escalator in Los Angeles airport roared across at me on the downward ditto, 'By God Niall, you're more than an hour from Dublin now.'

After a reading of a play by a mutual acquaintance, Seán Mac Réamoinn complimented me, but added: 'The trouble is that the excellence of the performances may reinforce his notion that this assemblage of historically dubious trivia constitutes a play'.

That's how I feel about this chronicle. Does my haphazard round-up of rose-tinted, wine-washed or plain deluded memories constitute an entity? I don't really care, and if you've followed me this far, neither probably do you. I've said what I set out to say, by and large. Whatever by and large means. On the face of it it cannot mean anything, since no phrase in which a preposition and an adjective are linked by a conjunction can convey a concept. I've never found a proper definition. But seeking one is a good example of the kind of nit-picking curiosity that keeps boredom at bay, makes me play Scrabble, do crosswords of impenetrable complexity, indulge my obsession with words.

Hold it. We are now cruising on a magic carpet of waffle, away above our station. It is time to start the descent.

I began my tale in Cork. I might as well finish there too.

I was to entertain the guests of the Cork Chamber of Commerce in the City Hall, during Garret Fitzgerald's time as Taoiseach. He was the main speaker at their Annual Dinner. My train was delayed, so I arrived a bit worried about the time. I asked an attendant at the main door, 'Has the Taoiseach finished his Speech yet?'

'Oh, he has,' he said, 'but he's still speaking.'

Let that be a lesson to us all.

If you've enjoyed the show, please tell your friends. Thank you, and Good Evening.

# APPENDIX

Niall Toibin has played in the following:

**1947–53**
Civil Service, amateur drama.
Panto and semi-professional work with the Abbey Theatre and
Compántas Amharclainne na Gaeilge

**1953–67**
Radio Éireann Players (Repertory Company):
*Man Alive,* by James O'Toole, directed by Jim Fitzgerald. Olympia
Theatre, Dublin (1958)
*Spailpín a Rún,* by Seán O'Riada, directed by Frank Dermody. Damer Hall,
Dublin (1961)
*Tycoo*n, by Seán O'Driscoll, directed by Noel O'Briain. Damer Hall,
Dublin (1965)
*The Big Finish,* by Gerry Simpson, directed by Frank Bailey. Irish Life
Theatre, Dublin (1963)
*Design for a Headstone,* by Seamus Byrne, directed by Jim Fitzgerald.
Olympia Theatre, Dublin (1960)
Croke Park '1916' Pageants, directed by Martin Dempsey and Tomás
MacAnna (1966)

**1960s**
*Capallology, Golf, Fleadh,* three short films directed by Louis Marcus for
Gael-Linn, narrated by Niall Toibin

**1964**
*Daughter from Over the Water,* by M J Molloy, directed by Siobhán
McKenna. Gaiety Theatre, Dublin
*The Hostage,* by Brendan Behan, directed by Louis Lentin. Gaiety Theatre,
Dublin

**1967**
*Lovers,* by Brian Friel, directed by Hilton Edwards. Gate Theatre, Dublin
*Borstal Boy,* by Brendan Behan, directed by Tomás MacAnna. Abbey
Theatre, Dublin

**1968**
*Death and Resurrection of Mr Roche*, by Tom Kilroy, directed by Jim
Fitzgerald. Olympia Theatre, Dublin
*Borstal Boy*, directed by Tomás MacAnna. Grove Theatre, Belfast
*Famine*, by Tom Murphy, directed by Tomás MacAnna. Peacock Theatre,
Dublin
*Guns in the Heather*, directed by Bob Butler. Disney

**1969**
*Ryan's Daughter*, directed by David Lean. MGM. Dingle, County Kerry

**1970**
*Borstal Boy*, directed by Tomás MacAnna. Broadway (Best Play–Tony
Award). Lyceum Theatre, New York
*Flight of the Doves*, directed by Ralph Nelson
*Christy Browne.* ABC TV

**1971**
*Legal Aid.* Granada TV
*Patrick Pearse Motel*, by Hugh Leonard, directed by Barry Cassin. City
Theatre, Limerick
*Playboy of the Western World*, by J M Synge, directed by Barry Cassin. City
Theatre, Limerick
*The Hostage*, directed by Richard Eyre. Lyceum Theatre, Edinburgh
*Confusion* — first one-man show, directed by Donall Farmer. Gaiety
Theatre, Dublin
*Waiting for Godot*, by Samuel Beckett, directed by Peter O'Toole and Nat
Brenner. Nottingham Playhouse

**1972**
*Less of That* — one-man show, directed by Donall Farmer. Gaiety Theatre,
Dublin
*Lovers*, directed by Barry Cassin. St Paul, Minnesota; Opera House, Cork
*Juno and the Paycock* and *Confusion*, directed by Seán Kenny. Toronto,
Canada
*House of Blue Leaves*, by John Guare. Olympia Theatre, Dublin

**1973**
*Tartuffe*, directed by Maurice Jacguemot. Royal Dublin Society
*Up 'Em All.* Review. Olympia Theatre, Dublin
*Borstal Boy*, directed by Tomás MacAnna. Opera House, Cork
*If the Cap Fits*, directed by Brian MacLochlainn. RTE TV